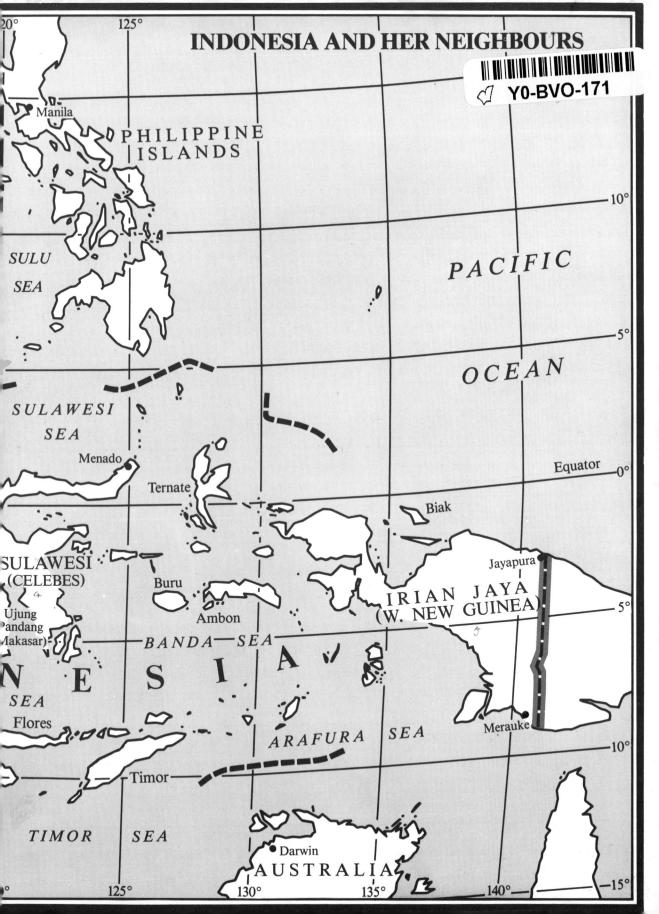

INDONESIA AND HER NEIGHBOURS

Y0-BVO-171

PHILIPPINE
ISLANDS

Manila

SULU
SEA

PACIFIC

OCEAN

SULAWESI
SEA

Menado

Ternate

Equator

Biak

SULAWESI
(CELEBES)

Buru

Jayapura

IRIAN JAYA
(W. NEW GUINEA)

Ujung
Pandang
(Makasar)

Ambon

BANDA — SEA

N E S I A

SEA

Flores

ARAFURA   SEA

Merauke

Timor

TIMOR   SEA

Darwin

AUSTRALIA

20°
125°
10°
5°
0°
5°
10°
125°
130°
135°
140°
15°

Emerging Indonesia

DONALD WILHELM

Emerging Indonesia

CASSELL
LONDON

To Renée,
who has shared the Indonesian experience

CASSELL LTD
35 Red Lion Square, London WC1R 4SG
and at Sydney, Auckland, Toronto, Johannesburg,
an affiliate of
Macmillan Publishing Co., Inc.,
New York

First published 1980

ISBN   0 304 30501 4

Typeset by Inforum Ltd, Portsmouth
Printed in the United States of America

Contents

Preface

When you look at the matter objectively, it is astonishing that the world's fifth most populous country (after mainland China, India, the Soviet Union, and the United States) should be so little known in the West. The country's population exceeds 140 million, and her horizontal geographical spread is greater than that of the U.S.A. Her 13,667 islands — ranging from tiny atolls to island giants of 100,000 square miles and more — make her the world's largest archipelago. She possesses rich and varied human and natural resources together with remarkable cultural diversity. The charm of her people blends with their tropical environment in never-to-be-forgotten fashion. She is Indonesia.

In a series of wide-ranging visits to Indonesia from 1972 onwards, I have been struck by her dynamic pace of development — coupled with a growing awareness that rapid change can bring its attendant dangers. Indonesia is a land of incredibly fascinating complexity, and I wish that Western academicians, correspondents, and commentators could show more awareness of this reality. Too often they pay fleeting visits to the country's capital city and one or two other places and then concoct a series of simplistic assertions which are broadcast to the world. Or they may stay for more extended periods, associate with an unrepresentative range of contacts, and continue to view things in terms of their Western presuppositions. Their superficial impressions can actually prejudice the cause of freedom and development.

So rich is the tapestry of Indonesia that almost any statement about her represents an oversimplification. But that does not mean that no accuracy can be achieved. One must learn to identify and cast aside one's own prior assumptions and to embrace the Indonesian experience as something both exhilarating and unique; and then one finds that a multitude of elements form themselves into a pattern — and one which I believe to be of potential significance for the whole of mankind.

In writing this book I have consulted with many leaders of government and also with many people who are in no way connected with the government establishment and who are not necessarily sympathetic to it. In the course of my investigations and consultations I have both requested and received complete academic freedom. My itinerary has been prescribed by nobody but myself, and I have freely visited wherever and whomever I have wished. One could readily compile an extended list of countries where such academic and investigative freedom would be totally impossible.

Special mention should be made of my meetings with six key ambassadors. In connection with the preparation of this book I have had a series of valuable discussions with the Australian, British, Canadian, French, United States, and West German ambassadors to Indonesia. They, together with their able and experienced staffs, constitute an authoritative group of first-hand observers of the Indonesian scene and situation. All of the ambassadors had served in important previous posts, and all of them were thus able to make informed comparisons. I have also had helpful discussions with a number of other Jakarta-based ambassadors from the East as well as the West.

All of the ambassadors have testified to the remarkable progress which Indonesia has made over the past decade and longer. Among other things, the inflation rate has been brought down from literally several hundred per cent to a level comparable with those in, for example, Britain or America. Moreover, during the past ten years Indonesia has achieved a sustained annual growth rate substantially higher than those of the same two Western countries. And she has concurrently made significant advances in the political and social field including human rights.

The ambassadors' assessments have not constituted a blanket endorsement. The ambassadors do not for a moment deny that major problems remain, and their and their staffs' comments on these problems are reflected in various chapters of this book. But the ambassadors have emphasized their view that much solid progress has been achieved, and they believe that Indonesia's accomplishments should become far better known in the world at large and particularly in the West. That indeed is one of the aims of the present volume.

This book highlights problems as well as progress, but it does so in a constructive spirit. It avoids a bland touristic treatment; instead, it argues for vigorous measures to safeguard Indonesia's unique and priceless cultural heritage — which discerning tourists and other visitors will want to help to preserve rather than to desecrate. One of the book's major themes concerns the crucial contribution which the rising generation can make to harmonizing economic growth and technological change with the country's cultural integrity and social stability. Some kind people have suggested that the present work provides the best-balanced available treatment of contemporary Indonesia and the broad spectrum of issues involved in her overall development; but as to that I shall happily leave it to each reader to judge for himself or herself.

I wish to record my indebtedness to the above-mentioned ambassadors and their staffs, and likewise to numerous officials of the international aid agencies whom I have met. I am grateful for insights supplied by indigenous and expatriate businessmen, bankers, the more thoughtful of the news correspondents, men of religion, members of the armed forces, university rectors, deans, and faculty members, and many others — not only in the capital city but in diverse parts of the vast country. Perhaps most of all I want to express appreciation for the thoughtful comments of students in various of the country's far-flung chain of universities; they have helped me to gain an understanding of the viewpoint of Indonesia's youth, upon whom her future so largely depends.

This book should interest a broad range of readers both in the West and elsewhere: statesmen and civil servants, ambassadors and officials of international organizations, university and other teachers and students, academic and public and corporate librarians, and members of the wider public who want a fresh cultural experience from an outstandingly exotic part of the East. The book explains why Indonesia has much to teach the world at large, and such a learning process can be highly pleasurable as well as rewarding. I hope that this volume will lead many readers to visit Indonesia if they have not already done so; and if they succumb to such a temptation, they are likely to return more than once!

Delving into Indonesia's culture is an immensely exciting experience, and I only hope that the reader will derive from this chronicle some of the exhilaration which has come to me in the writing of it. I am, as already intimated, indebted to a great many people — far too many to list individually here — for information, ideas, and insights which are incorporated in this book; and I trust they will understand how much I owe them. Likewise it goes without saying that any errors of fact or interpretation rest with me alone.

1

The Road to Independence

According to the best available evidence, one of the earliest races of mankind made its home in what is now Indonesia. It appears that these original inhabitants were subsequently absorbed by people of Malayan stock who over the course of many centuries arrived from the Asian mainland. Thus began a remarkable story of ethnic and cultural assimilation.

Well before the beginning of the Christian era, the people of the archipelago had domesticated the ox and the water buffalo. They cultivated irrigated rice, and they worked metals including gold, copper, iron, and bronze. They were good seamen and they understood the principles of long-distance navigation.

From the 1st century A.D. — and continuing over the ensuing thousand years and more — came the period of close interaction between the archipelago and India. Indonesians visited India and brought back fresh ideas, particularly in religion, government, and the arts. Emissaries of the Brahman priestly caste of Hindus came from India to advise the Indonesian kings, who were themselves converted to Hinduism; and Buddhist and Hindu missionaries established monasteries in what is now Indonesia and successfully spread their faith.

Malcolm Caldwell refers to what he calls 'a characteristic aspect of Indonesian history — the ability to effect a synthesis of different ingredients, accepting the new without discarding the old, absorbing and blending rather than substituting'.[1] One should likewise note that, although geographically the archipelago lies more or less as close to mainland China as to India, it was the Indonesian–Indian cultural relationship which predominated for so many centuries. That cultural kinship is still reflected in, for example, Indonesia's drama, literature, and exquisite textile design, as well as in elements of her complex blend of religions.

In terms of political evolution, many states rose and fell in various parts of the archipelago during the centuries preceding the impact of Western colonialism. Although most of these states commanded only localized jurisdiction, two great exceptions stand out. One, the Sumatra-based Srivijaya empire, lasted for some 600 years — from the 7th to the 13th centuries — and at its height it encompassed most of present-day Indonesia and indeed included some parts of the Asian mainland. The empire became a great maritime and trading power as well as a centre for Buddhist learning.

Soon afterward came the Java-based Majapahit empire, which was founded in 1292 and which again succeeded in uniting much of the archipelago, even if more briefly than had its predecessor. The empire represented a fusion of Buddhist and Hindu traditions, and among other things it brought great vitality to the arts. Gaja Mada, the empire's most renowned prime minister, was probably the greatest administrator of pre-colonial Indonesia; and it is fitting that Indonesia's oldest and largest university, located at Yogyakarta, should today bear his name.

The Majapahit empire as such lasted for less than a hundred years, although a kingdom of that name persisted until the 16th century. Well before that time, Indonesia was receiving the first impact of the two new forces that would profoundly affect her subsequent evolution. These forces — on the one hand Islam, and on the other hand the Europeans — were in striking contrast both to each other and to all that had gone before.

Arabs are thought to have visited what is now Indonesia as early as the 1st century A.D., and the first Muslims arrived soon after the birth of Islam in the 7th century. From then on, Arab traders brought their religious ideas as well as their goods to the archipelago, and the whole process was accelerated after the rise, early in the 15th century, of Malacca (on Malaya's southwest coast) as a major Islamic trading centre.

In due course various of the Indonesian kingdoms were converted to Islam, and indeed the faith spread all over the archipelago; the only major exception was Bali, which to this day has resisted Islam and cleaved to its Hindu tradition. But in fact the sweep of Islam across Indonesia took the form of an infusion and blending rather than a religious or cultural replacement. In one sense the country is today overwhelmingly Islamic, but in a deeper sense its culture represents a unique and fascinating combination of Islamic, Buddhist, Hindu, Christian, and even animistic elements.

In 1292 — the year of the founding of the Majapahit empire — Marco Polo, the Venetian traveller and author (c.1254-1324), became the first European to visit the archipelago. In 1497 and 1498, the Portuguese explorer Vasco da Gama circumnavigated Africa and discovered a sea route from Europe to

Marco Polo

11

A scene in old Batavia, now Jakarta

India. Other Portuguese and Spanish explorers followed after him, and in 1511 the Portuguese captured Malacca, built a fort there, and pre-empted much of the rich Indonesian trade.

By the end of the century, English and Dutch traders were challenging the Portuguese hold on the area's trade. In 1600 the English formed their East India Company as a private venture, and two years later the Dutch established a counterpart company. Gradually the latter company squeezed the former out of the archipelago. In 1641 the Dutch staged a great coup by capturing Malacca from the Portuguese. Asian merchants continued to trade with the archipelago, but increasingly the Europeans, and pre-eminently the Dutch, gained the ascendancy.

In 1677, the ruler of the Mataram kingdom in Java asked the Dutch for aid in fighting a rebel uprising. The Dutch obliged, and in return they received territories as well as trading rights. Other acquisitions, by force or otherwise, soon followed. Well before the end of the century the Dutch East India Company controlled most of Java as well as port towns on other of the islands, and the archipelago had become known as the Dutch East Indies or Netherlands Indies.

Meanwhile, however, the Company was increasingly plagued by maladministration and corruption as well as by methods of exploitation — including forced delivery of crops at set prices — which alienated and outraged the Indonesians. The Company went bankrupt, and in 1799 the Dutch government took over its assets including its lands in the archipelago.

Soon afterward Holland was overrun by Napoleon, and in a pre-emptive move the British took over the Dutch East Indies for some five years (1811-16). It was during this period that the illustrious Thomas (later Sir Thomas) Stamford Raffles (1781-1826) served as British chief administrator in the archipelago. He instituted numerous reforms which provided precedents for a somewhat more enlightened later colonial policy under the Dutch; but such a policy still lay a long way in the future.

Raffles arrived back in England in 1816; in the following year he was elected a Fellow of the Royal Society, published his book *The History of Java*, was knighted, and sailed to take up his appointment at a romantic place that is too little known by the world at large. This was Bengkulu (also spelled in diverse other ways) in southern Sumatra, where in 1714 the British had built a fortress called Fort York, later renamed Fort Marlborough. The British remained in the area until 1825, and even today the town has a decidedly English atmosphere.

Soon afterward Raffles established the colony of Singapore. He raised the British flag there on 6 February 1819, returned for a spell to Bengkulu, and in 1822 came back to Singapore to organize the administration there. As one source expresses it, 'He left the East for England in April 1824, secure in the knowledge that Singapore was a flourishing free-trade port'.[2]

Sir Stamford Raffles

When the Dutch resumed control of the archipelago late in 1816, they faced the dilemma of whether to continue with the freer arrangements established by Raffles or to return to their old system. They chose the latter, or a modified version of it which they now named the Cultivation System. Under the system so much land was devoted to producing export commodities — notably sugar and coffee — that food crops were neglected and serious famines occurred on Java in the 1840s. The peasants were in effect subjected to forced labour and Java became a vast Dutch government plantation.

In one sense the system was a resounding success, for exports from Indonesia soon rose sensationally, with exports of coffee quadrupling and those of sugar increasing tenfold. But the social costs were tremendous, and rising popular resentment helped to pave the way for the later independence movement. In 1870 the Dutch enacted laws back home which threw open the archipelago to private investment from both the Netherlands and elsewhere; this in turn led to further production increases coupled with abuses.

13

EMERGING INDONESIA

In justice to the Dutch it must be said that they had in the East Indies many able and conscientious administrators who tried to ameliorate conditions.[3] Around the turn of the century, under Holland's so-called Ethical Policy, expenditure for educational, welfare and other purposes in Indonesia rose dramatically and for a time actually exceeded revenues from the colony. But this was a belated response which did little to alter the fundamental inequities. Perhaps most serious of all, the Indonesians increasingly felt like bystanders in their own country; their participation in controlling their destinies remained minimal.

It would be a great mistake, however, to think of the Dutch experience in Indonesia simply as one of colonialism and imperialism. At a deeper level it symbolized the tensions engendered by the collision between Western science and technology and more traditional values. The traumatic effects of such collisions can today be seen in many countries including the so-called classless society of the Soviet Union. As Solzhenitsyn has bitterly remarked in that context, the Russian people 'have followed Western technology too long and too faithfully'.[4] Few countries in the world have escaped the social effects of Western science and technology, and almost by definition the more traditional societies have in some ways been hit the hardest.

A Dutch mission church on Samosir Island, Lake Toba, Sumatra

It is ironical that, especially under their so-called Ethical Policy, the Dutch sent increasing numbers of young Indonesians to study in the Netherlands, where they vividly and personally experienced this kind of cultural shock. In addition to acquiring professional expertise, many of them returned home with their heads full of Western ideas about freedom, individualism, liberalism, and Marxism. This served to hasten the movement toward independence from the Dutch, but it also had more far-reaching and long-lasting effects carrying over beyond independence and even to the present day.

In one sense the Indonesian independence movement had begun even centuries before its final success. For example, in 1629 Sultan Agung

Hanyokrokusumo, the head of the kingdom of Mataram, sent troops to attack Batavia (as Jakarta was called in Dutch days), but they were repulsed by the Dutch Governor General and his forces. In 1740 the Dutch suppressed a rebellion in Batavia itself. In 1825, Prince Diponegoro, the elder son of the Sultan of Yogyakarta, mounted a sustained onslaught — the great Javanese Revolt — against the Dutch which it took them five years to put down. In 1873 began what became a 30-year war to subjugate the northern Sumatran state of Aceh, whose piratical activities had proved a headache for the colonial powers. In 1906 and 1908 there were uprisings on Bali.

It was indeed not until shortly before World War I that virtually all of present-day Indonesia was firmly under Dutch rule. It should be added, however, that from the beginning it had been Dutch policy to leave control in most parts of the archipelago largely in the hands of pliant local rulers. On the whole the Dutch found this policy easier and more economical, and only in the closing days of their colonial tenure did they institute what could be regarded as unified rule.

In this eventual unification process lay another piece of historical irony, for clearly it helped to prepare the way for the independence movement. It was all very well to talk of the glories of ancient days when, as we have seen, the archipelago had twice been unified; but the Dutch achievement was far more relevant because so recent.

Likewise, as Ruslan Abdulgani has pointed out,[5] the Dutch language furnished for Indonesians a powerful liberating influence. In a land with scores of mutually unintelligible languages, Dutch at last provided a linguistic common denominator. Moreover, particularly in Java, it offered a welcome escape from a tradition in which class and status differences were rigidly reflected in widely different forms of address and usage. Later, of course, Bahasa Indonesia (an adaptation of the Malayan language) took over as the primary linguistic common denominator, with English supplanting Dutch as the secondary one.

Be that as it may, an institutionalized nationalist movement or movements began to take shape soon after the beginning of the 20th century. In 1908 a group of Javanese medical students formed what they called the High Endeavour Society, and in 1918 the Society began to undertake political activities. Meanwhile a nationalist political movement called the Islamic Union — itself the outgrowth of an earlier Javanese businessmen's association — had been established in 1912. Students likewise formed study clubs including one at what is today the justly-famous Bandung Institute of Technology or ITB. That study club was headed by a dynamic young man called Sukarno.

It was under his leadership that the Indonesian Nationalist Party (PNI) was created in 1927. But in the early 1930s the Dutch suppressed all of the nationalist groups and exiled their leaders, including Sukarno, to remote outer islands. At that time the Indonesian nationalist movement consisted of a relative handful of students and intellectuals, including those who had been trained in Holland; and it was easy for the Dutch to clamp down on them.

The leaders remained incarcerated until World War II, when the invading Japanese freed them. Already, in 1905, the Japanese had impressed Indonesians as well as other Asians by their dramatic defeat of a Western

The young Sukarno

power in the shape of Czarist Russia. Now, in 1942, as Dutch resistance rapidly crumbled in the face of the Japanese advance, Indonesians were again reminded that Western powers were not necessarily invincible. Understandably, the freed nationalist leaders at first welcomed the Japanese victory in Indonesia, and they resolved to take full advantage of it.

Among the nationalist leaders it was agreed that some of them, including Sukarno and Mohammad Hatta, would initially co-operate with the Japanese, while others would go underground. This plan worked well, for the above-ground leaders were able to win concessions from the Japanese while the underground ones helped to prepare for the expected armed independence struggle.

The Dutch had installed almost no Indonesians in responsible posts in the civil administration or in the military. Reversing this policy, the Japanese appointed hundreds of Indonesians to responsible civil service positions and in due course they even established Indonesian-officered armies. They created quasi-military youth organizations, and they catered to the nationalists by allowing them to use the Indonesian flag, the national anthem, and Bahasa Indonesia as the national language.

Sukarno and others were allowed to go about the country, ostensibly berating the West but actually fostering nationalist sentiments. Meanwhile the Indonesians were becoming progressively more disillusioned about their role in Japan's so-called Greater East Asia Co-Prosperity Sphere. They were repelled by their new rulers' arrogance and cruelty which, as they now realized, was by no means peculiar to white imperialists. Especially in the final year of Japan's occupation of Indonesia, guerrilla raids against the Japanese became increasingly common.

No doubt the Japanese could see the writing on the wall, for in March 1945 they appointed a joint committee, composed mostly of Indonesians, to discuss plans for independence. On 7 August the local Japanese authorities authorized the creation of an Indonesian Independence Preparatory Committee, with Sukarno as Chairman and Hatta as Vice-Chairman. A week later Japan surrendered to the Allies, and three days after that, on 17 August 1945, Sukarno and Hatta proclaimed Indonesia's independence.

Yet in spite of all these momentous events, the Indonesian independence drama had by no means reached its climax. Just as in the case of the American Declaration of Independence in 1776, Indonesia's formal independence declaration signalled the beginning rather than the end of the most crucial phase of the overt struggle.

Moreover, as experience in Africa as well as in Asia has so amply shown, it is one thing to secure political independence and it is quite another thing to achieve a viable state. It is to this struggle for effective Indonesian nationhood that we now turn.

Striving for Nationhood

At Bogor (formerly Buitenzorg), in the setting of one of the world's most famous botanical gardens, is situated the splendid palace built by the Dutch and occupied by a succession of their governors as well as by Raffles during his sojourn in Java. Under Sukarno, the historic building became the Presidential Palace; and, some twenty years after Indonesia's Declaration of Independence, the palace still remained under the oversight of the country's first President.[1] Sukarno's impact on Indonesia had been incalculable.

In spite of his later follies, it cannot be denied that Sukarno successfully led the Indonesian Revolution, and in this sense he was the father of his country. A leader of charismatic charm, he in many ways symbolized the spirit of humanity and tolerance. From the beginning he preached the doctrine of national unity and of racial, religious, and cultural brotherhood, and he pioneered in the quest for a national ideology. He must unquestionably be ranked as one of the greatest Asian leaders of the early post-World War II period.

Sukarno (as with many Indonesians, he used only one name) was born near Surabaya in East Java in 1901 and died in 1970 while living in reasonable comfort under house arrest in Jakarta. His father was a Javanese school teacher of Islamic faith, while his mother was a Balinese Hindu; and Sukarno recounts that, following their tradition-violating 'mixed' marriage, the couple had actually been fined by a magistrate's court. It is perhaps no wonder that Sukarno, with his customary self-confidence, was later to say this of himself:

> One of Sukarno's miracles is that he united his people. The color of our skin may differ, the shape of our noses and foreheads may differ: Irians are black, Sumatrans brown, Javanese are short, inhabitants of the Moluccas taller, people from Lampung have their own features, those from Pasundan have their own features, but no more are we islanders and strangers. Today we are Indonesians and we are one. Our country's motto is *Bhineka Tunggal Ika* — 'Unity in Diversity'.[2]

Notwithstanding his subsequent degree in civil engineering, Sukarno from first to last showed a strong mystical streak, which he frankly acknowledged. This is well illustrated, for example, by his portrayal of how he arrived at the concept of Marhaenism, or populist proletarianism. 'I was only 20', he says, 'when a powerful political revelation dawned on me. At

The presidential palace at Bogor

first it was but the germ of an idea gnawing away at my brain, but it was soon to become the platform on which our movement stood.'

He then describes how, when he was cycling one day among small farms near Bandung, his gaze became fixed on a poor and ragged peasant at work. In response to Sukarno's questions, the peasant explained that he owned his tiny plot, his house such as it was, and his primitive tools; but he nevertheless lived in squalid poverty.

That peasant, Sukarno thought to himself, symbolized millions like him. Asked his name, the peasant replied 'Marhaen' — a common enough name in Indonesia. 'At that moment', recounts Sukarno, 'the light of inspiration flooded my brain. I would use that name for all Indonesians with the same miserable lot. From then on I would call my people Marhaenists.

'The rest of the day I bicycled around working out my new concept. And that night I gave an indoctrination lecture on it to my youth group.'[3]

Sukarno's charisma and his mysticism, interacting as they did with the Indonesian cultural context, undoubtedly go far to explain why, by the time of the Declaration of Independence, he was acknowledged as Indonesia's foremost revolutionary leader. Closely associated with Sukarno was of course the remarkable Mohammad Hatta. A Sumatran, Hatta was born in 1902, later went to the University of Rotterdam, distinguished himself in economics there, and helped to organize the Indonesian nationalist student movement. Still later, as we have seen, Hatta was among the nationalist leaders freed by the Japanese. Hatta and Sukarno then collaborated closely together for many years until, after growing disagreement with Sukarno, Hatta, in 1956, resigned from the government but remained active as a highly respected elder statesman.

Sukarno recounts how, on the day before he and Hatta proclaimed independence, a group of young Indonesian militants kidnapped them. Apparently the young people were intent on stirring up an armed revolt against the still-formidable Japanese. Released after considerable argument, Sukarno and Hatta joined a meeting of the Independence Preparatory Committee which was at that very time discussing the wording of the forthcoming independence proclamation.

In consultation with his friends, Sukarno himself penned what he later called the 'terse unemotional statement with which we finally demanded our place in the sun after 350 years'. The statement, as signed by him and Hatta, 'On behalf of the Indonesian people', read in its entirety as follows:

> We the people of Indonesia hereby declare Indonesia's independence. Matters concerning the transfer of power and other matters will be executed in an orderly manner and in the shortest possible time.[4]

It was on that same day in 1945 — the 'Holy Seventeenth of August' — that Sukarno read Indonesia's Declaration of Independence to a crowd of a few hundred people. The Japanese military authorities had objected to the independence proclamation on the ground that it violated the terms of their surrender to the Allies; but within hours news of the proclamation had been transmitted far and wide by diverse means, including Indonesians working in the Japanese-controlled media. It was a *fait accompli*.

Immediately after the promulgation of the Constitution of 1945, Sukarno and Hatta were elected President and Vice-President, respectively, by the Preparatory Committee for Independence. The new Constitution stipulated, in Article 6, how the President and Vice-President were thenceforward to be elected; and the Constitution likewise provided for elections to the proposed People's Consultative Assembly (MPR), the supreme legislative body. Until elections to the Assembly could be organized, the President was to rely on an advisory committee appointed by himself. Sukarno was thus in effect given a blank check.

Meanwhile, the independence struggle was unfolding rather in the manner of a Greek tragedy. The Japanese surrender found the Allies in general, and the Dutch in particular, in a state of almost unbelievable ignorance about the climate of opinion inside Indonesia. To the Dutch, or at least to their government, Sukarno and Hatta were traitors and collaborators who would quickly be repudiated by their own people; yet to the Indonesians, these same men were the inspired leaders of the independence struggle.

Moreover, as Anthony J.S. Reid points out, the surrender 'caught the Allies totally unprepared to assume authority in Indonesia'.[5] The Allies had no adequate force ready to take over the country, and the situation was further complicated by the fact that the Indonesian theatre had just been transferred from MacArthur's Southwest Pacific Command to Mountbatten's Southeast Asia Command based in Ceylon.

To add still further to the confusion, there was no agreement among the Allies as to the fundamental objectives — apart from taking the Japanese surrender, rescuing the internees, and maintaining a minimum of law and order — of the impending Allied occupation. The Allied force was to be led by the British, and on 24 August 1945, they entered into a hastily-prepared agreement with the Dutch under which the Allied military mission would exercise *de facto* authority, but administration would be handled mainly by Dutch personnel, who would apply pre-war laws. But this begged the whole question whether the Dutch were to control an Indonesia which had already declared its independence.

One thing that gave the Dutch confidence was that they easily regained administrative control in most of the outer islands, where the population was generally much sparser than in Java and where the independence movement was on the whole not nearly so far advanced. But the Java picture was very different. The Dutch administrators, and the often trigger-happy Dutch troops accompanying them, found that their presence was bitterly resented, and disorders soon erupted in Jakarta, Bandung, and other places.

Sukarno and other Republican leaders tried to avoid confrontations with the Allies or with the Japanese who still controlled many areas, but they soon became powerless to determine events. Bloody excesses occurred on all sides, and the Republican leaders had particular difficulty in controlling their own youth. Sukarno, subsequently referring to 'our newly-liberated youngsters', said that some of them 'had turned into bandits and were causing great trouble. They delayed and derailed trains carrying innocent Dutch internees. They pillaged. They terrified. . . .'[6]

Surabaya was the principal Indonesian base of the Japanese Navy, and it was there that things reached a climax. Vice Admiral Shibata, the base commandant, was sympathetic to the Indonesian cause, and it was largely through him that large quantities of Japanese arms were turned over to the local Indonesian forces. Additional arms were seized from the Japanese, chiefly by Indonesian youth groups. Soon afterward, the Allies made the great mistake of sending an all-Dutch advance contingent to the city. Later the RAF dropped leaflets demanding the immediate surrender of all arms in Indonesian hands.

On 25 October 1945, Brigadier General A.W.S. Mallaby landed at Surabaya with a brigade of Indian troops. Soon afterward the Indonesians launched a violent attack against them, with massive casualties on both sides. In an effort to halt the carnage, the British flew Sukarno and other Republican leaders to Surabaya, where they persuaded the young Indonesian militants to accept a cease-fire agreement.

But renewed shooting broke out soon after the President had left Surabaya, and Brigadier Mallaby was shot and killed while trying to enforce the cease-fire. The British then evacuated some 6,000 Dutch detainees and brought in the 5th Indian Division. On the morning of 10 November — later to be known to all Indonesians as Heroes' Day — the Allied forces launched a devastating air, sea, and ground attack against the city.

Later the same day, as Sukarno recalls,

> we launched our counterattack. The fighting was fierce. If one of our men was machine-gunned, two came up to replace him. If two were killed, four rushed up to replace them. Only the frontline had weapons. When they were weary, they dropped their guns and retreated empty-handed. The next line then moved along and picked up the same weapons. . . .[7]

The British-led forces soon captured most of the city, but that was not the main point. Not only the British commanders, but also the world at large as it heard the news, were startled and amazed by the fanatical resistance of the Indonesians. The Dutch policy-makers, it was increasingly realized, had become hopelessly out of touch with Indonesian realities. In a valid sense the Battle of Surabaya marked a turning point in the Indonesian Revolution; but the struggle against the Dutch was nevertheless far from over.

Before the British left Indonesia at the end of November 1946, they helped to negotiate the Linggadjati Agreement, named after the Indonesian mountain resort where it was signed. Although the agreement provided for Dutch withdrawal from various of the Indonesian territories occupied by them, it conceded the principle — unacceptable to many Indonesians — of a federated United States of Indonesia in partnership with the Dutch.

The agreement was not ratified until the following March; and some four months later the Dutch launched their first so-called police action in Indonesia. Sumatra and most of Java — apart from Yogyakarta, which became the government's temporary capital — soon fell to the Dutch forces. Meanwhile the young nation was also having to face various armed internal revolts.

Following a groundswell of adverse world public opinion against the Dutch, a cease-fire was arranged. An American mediator was appointed and the result was the January 1948 Renville Agreement, named after the U.S. warship aboard which it was signed. Under the agreement the

The signing, on 17 January 1949, aboard the U.S.S. Renville, *of the so-called Renville Agreement*

Indonesians gave up some of their territory and again conceded the idea of a territorially-incomplete quasi-independent United States of Indonesia under the Dutch crown.

Soon afterward, in a renewal of trouble from internal sources, the Communists assumed leadership of an anti-government coalition which had to be forcibly suppressed by troops loyal to Sukarno and Hatta. But the government forces had little respite, for in December 1948 came the second Dutch so-called police action. Dutch forces quickly occupied Yogyakarta and other cities remaining to the government, and captured and temporarily interned Sukarno and Hatta; but a stalemate soon developed. As Sukarno expressed it,

> While the Netherlands held the cities, our soldiers took the highways leading to them, the towns surrounding them, the food coming into them. We had the villages, side roads, lakes, . . . the hills, the whole of what comprises Indonesia. Their cities were so cut off that several could

only be supplied by airlifts. Come darkness our guerrillas infiltrated the cities, attacked the enemy positions, blew up their trains and convoys, set fire to their provisions. The enemy had to battle for survival just to live through the night. A road they'd repair by day would be destroyed at night. The Dutch became confused. They didn't know where we'd strike. They hadn't men enough to blanket the entire terrain. All their forces were walled up within metropolises. At night their cities were under siege. By day their cities fell under a subtler form of destruction.[8]

The struggle against the Dutch also gave birth to the Indonesian conception of the dual role of the military. As the political scientist Ulf Sundhaussen points out, by the end of 1948 the government's defence strategy was based on a combination of guerrilla tactics and military socio-political applications. The military authorities 'assumed responsibility in practically every field of government activity, issuing detailed regulations governing, among other things, the people's health, welfare, housing, education, trade, finance and banking, agriculture, information, public safety, and the administration of the law'.[9] Later in this book we shall see how the dual role concept has been applied in latter-day Indonesia.

World opinion was now rapidly swinging against the Dutch. The UN Security Council called for a cease-fire and fresh negotiations, and the United States intimated that it might halt Marshall Aid to the Netherlands. Negotiations gradually got under way, the Indonesian government was forced to make major concessions, and eventually — on 27 December 1949 — the so-called Republic of the United States of Indonesia became a sovereign state, under a new constitution which was actually never implemented.

By the following May the decision had been taken to jettison the draft federal constitution and to replace it with a unitary one, thus for the second time creating a Republic of Indonesia. The new Republic came into being on 17 August 1950, with Jakarta as its capital, and later in that same year independent Indonesia became the 60th member of the United Nations.

The years from 1945 through 1950 had indeed been memorable for Indonesia and Indonesians, and throughout the entire period the country had of course relied upon Sukarno as its leader and chief source of inspiration and faith in the future. Indonesia's constitutional evolution during those years had likewise been eventful: a constitution had been promulgated in 1945 but never fully implemented; a second one had been adopted in 1949 but almost immediately proved abortive; and a third one was proclaimed in 1950 but, in the event, was to last only until 1959.

As Sukarno said of the achievement of independence, 'Thus ended our period of struggle. And thus began our struggle for survival. . . '.[10] This was no mere figure of speech, for Indonesia's experiment in self-determination and nation-building had barely started.

3

The Later Sukarno Phase

Sukarno, in his autobiography, recounts an incident which occurred in 1945, when Dutch forces controlled so much of his country. Red Cross planes, attempting to drop food and medical supplies on a Dutch refugee camp not far from Sukarno's home, overshot their mark and the relief goods landed close to his verandah. To the astonishment of his young followers, Sukarno ordered that the food and supplies should be delivered to the Dutch under a flag of truce. Insisting that the Dutch people were not Indonesia's enemies, he declared that 'if any human beings are hungry or in pain then we shall personally share our food and give our blood to ease their agonies. Politics is politics, but humanity is humanity.'[1]

In spite of Sukarno's many attractive and even noble qualities, it was under his leadership that his people endured the decline and virtual eclipse of constitutional democracy in Indonesia. As the parties, and the governments formed from them, showed themselves unable or unwilling to act constructively and decisively, things went from bad to worse. By the beginning of the 1960s, seasoned observers became convinced that Indonesia was irreversibly heading toward a Communist dictatorship. Only with the climactic events of 1965, and the ushering in of Indonesia's so-called New Order, was the seemingly remorseless trend reversed.

Yet it is essential to view this whole matter in proper international perspective. Especially in developing countries, constitutional democracy remains highly vulnerable even if it has been planted with tender and loving care. Earlier optimism about global democratic prospects has encountered rude jolts. As the French scholar Jean Blondel has pointed out,

> Before 1914, it was confidently expected that the political evolution of Western Europe and North America would be repeated in the rest of the world. Liberal representative institutions had slowly expanded eastward and southward from Britain and Scandinavia to Western and Central Europe during the nineteenth century. The rest of Europe, it was thought, would gradually develop in the same manner; indeed, Russia was already stirring in the first decade of the twentieth century. Party systems similar to those of Western Europe were expected to take root in the rest of the world.
>
> This was not to happen, however. . . .[2]

Particularly in the Third World, as Blondel suggests, parties often seem unable to solve problems or to 'keep a stable hold over the government and the population'. And in a pioneering analysis of 136 different countries throughout the world, he found that in 1976 no fewer than 81 of them — that is, well over half — were one-party or no-party states.[3] Clearly it is by no means only in Indonesia that political parties in the liberal democratic sense have failed to prove their continuing viability.

The plight of liberal democracy in Indonesia in the 1950s has been explored by a number of writers — perhaps most exhaustively by Herbert Feith in his definitive *The Decline of Constitutional Democracy in Indonesia*. Among the players on the political stage at that time were Muslim and other religious parties, secular social democratic parties, and the Communist Party or PKI as the second oldest Indonesian political party. Within a few years of Indonesia's achievement of independence in 1950, the number of her political parties had grown to more than 40[4] — all too reminiscent, for example, of the kind of party chaos which had arisen in Germany in the 1920s and which had presaged the rise of dictatorship there.

In addition to the parties, there were other principal actors on the Indonesian political stage. The military, particularly the Army, was and has remained one of them. Likewise there were formidable regional interests — sometimes represented by the Army, sometimes not — including those in the outer islands which deeply resented the extent to which power had been concentrated in Java in general and Jakarta in particular. Most important of all, during those years, was Sukarno himself. One further powerful force had been active in pre-independence days and was to become so again in the 1960s and 1970s — namely, the youth.

Sukarno showed remarkable consistency in his attitude toward Western-style democratic institutions. In his *Indonesia Accuses!*, his dramatic defence oration in the political trial of 1930 which led to his first imprisonment at the hands of the Dutch, Sukarno asked,

> But what about our present-day society? It is not healthy. It is not filled with possibilities for growth. It is sick, empty. Earlier when we spoke of the lot of Indonesians today, when we outlined imperialistic methods of bringing our society to ruin, you got some idea of present conditions. . . .
> It is crucial that we emphasize right here that what most gives rise to the national spirit of our people is *their consciousness of the misery of their lives at present.*

Clearly, added Sukarno, 'Discord which is really discord has not been our doing; genuine discord has been the work of imperialists themselves!'[5]

Closely connected with Sukarno's concept of imperialism was his Marxism — or rather the Marxist component of his eclecticism. As he wrote about himself in an article in 1941, 'What is this Sukarno? Is he a nationalist? A Moslem? A Marxist? Readers, Sukarno is — a mixture *of all these isms*'. And in the same article he called himself *'a convinced nationalist, a convinced Moslem, a convinced Marxist'*.[6]

In his own mind Sukarno readily linked Western parliamentary institutions with capitalism and imperialism. As he was to declare much later, 'We saw capitalism and Western democracy in action through the Dutch. We have no wish to maintain that system.'[7]

In any event, the practical working of the party system in Indonesia created much dissatisfaction. As John D. Legge remarks,

> By the mid-1950s there was growing feeling that party rivalry was not providing the country with the leadership it needed. This disillusioned judgment was not entirely fair. No post-revolutionary government could have been expected to satisfy popular expectations following nationalist victory. Dutch domination had been blamed for all the evils of the colonial era: its removal was expected to usher in a golden age. But in fact Indonesia's general economic situation, her dependence on foreign markets for a handful of staple exports and her need for foreign capital, remained substantially unchanged and indeed a shortage of technical and administrative skills affected her ability even to retain prewar levels of prosperity. These were fundamental facts. . . . Also of great importance was the existence of regional suspicion of any central government, a fact that made the normal operation of a party system within the framework of parliamentary institutions a hazardous matter at best. Nevertheless there were real grounds for disenchantment with the party system as such. The series of weak coalitions, inevitable in a multi-party situation, could not secure vigorous and stable government. . . .[8]

Vice President Hatta, centre, *with India's Prime Minister Nehru,* left, *and Vice President Radhakrishnan*

Increasingly Sukarno — 'the mouthpiece of the Indonesian people',[9] as he called himself — echoed and accentuated the growing dissatisfaction. In a speech in 1956 to an audience of young people, he had this to say:

> . . . There is a disease that is sometimes even worse than ethnic and

26

regional feeling! What is this disease, you ask? It is the disease of parties, brothers and sisters! Yes, I will be frank: the disease of parties.

In November 1945 — let us be quite frank — we made a most serious mistake. We suggested the establishment of parties, parties, parties. That was one of the mistakes of November 1945. Now it is taking its toll.

Just look at the situation. Quite apart from the disease of ethnic and regional loyalties, we are afflicted by the disease of parties which, alas, alas, make us forever work against one another.

And Sukarno then issued this rallying call: 'Let us act together now to bury all the parties!'[10]

In another speech two days later, he first gave expression to his vision of a new system. Insisting that he had no wish to become a dictator, he nevertheless declared that

the democracy I crave for Indonesia is not a liberal democracy such as exists for Western Europe. No! What I want for Indonesia is a guided democracy, a democracy with leadership. A guided democracy, a guided democracy, something which is guided but still democracy. . . .

Our situation with respect to the party system is one of complete disruption. It is not healthy; it must be transformed entirely. . . .

And referring again to the surfeit of parties in Indonesia, Sukarno asserted that nobody

can justify the existence of forty parties in our country. You cannot justify that, you cannot justify it, you cannot. . . .

If one wants to reduce the number of parties, which party is to be buried? One party will say: Why should I be buried? Why not you?

That is logical, it is logical. No one wants to have his own party buried while another party is left alone. You cannot do things that way. Therefore, I propose that we bury them all together, without favors to anyone. Let us bury them, bury them, bury them![11]

In his speech Sukarno intimated that he already had in mind what was to become known as his Concept for solving his country's chronic problem of government; and then early in 1957 he unveiled the Concept. 'In the history of the Republic of Indonesia, now more than eleven years old', he pointed out, 'we have never achieved stability in government.' Ever since the beginning of their independence movement, he continued, Indonesians

have been enthralled by democracy and have wanted to put democracy into practice. . . . However, the experiences of these eleven years have convinced me that the democracy we adopted, the democracy we have been using, is a democracy which is not in harmony with the soul of the Indonesia nation. . . . And since this democracy is an imported democracy, not an Indonesian one, not a democracy which is in harmony with our spirit, we have experienced all the excesses which result from effectuating an imported idea as well as all the excesses ensuing from implementation of a democracy which is not in harmony with our personality.

A major defect in Western-style parliamentary democracy, said Sukarno, lies in the idea of the opposition, 'and it is this idea of the opposition which has made us go through hardships for eleven years, because we have interpreted this idea of opposition in a way which does not accord with the Indonesian spirit'.[12]

As Sukarno was later to expound his position,

> Indonesian democracy, much misunderstood outside our shores, works on a consensus, not a show of hands. We could no longer afford this Western democracy with its majority voting, where 51 per cent wins and 49 per cent ends up with a grudge. As we discovered with our 40 political parties, the dissatisfied segment retaliates by sucking the lifeblood of the other. It's a good way for a baby nation to stunt its growth.[13]

'My Concept', said Sukarno in his February 1957 speech, 'consists of two points.' The first related to what might be called a coalition cabinet. He thought that the cabinet should contain representatives of all significant political groups, and with some plausibility he suggested that this would be more in keeping with the Indonesian spirit.

His second point concerned the idea of a representative National Council organized along functional lines. For example, such a council would include representatives of labour, agriculture, the intelligentsia, the entrepreneurs, Christian and Islamic religious groups, women, youth, the armed forces and the police, and so forth. 'And, God willing', said Sukarno, 'I myself will lead this National Council.'[14]

Thus Sukarno set forth his Concept to an Indonesian public which was initially largely incredulous — not least because he suggested that the ever-more-powerful Communist party should have representation in his proposed coalition cabinet. Meanwhile the country had been facing further serious threats to its unity and integrity. As Charles A. Fisher has pointed out in his monumental *South-East Asia*, 'the geographical character of the archipelago itself, with its 3,000 islands scattered over its vast distances of sea, presents the state-maker with an extremely difficult task, which indeed is without parallel elsewhere in the modern world. . .'.[15] Both for geographical and other reasons, Indonesia's body politic was being subjected to severe strains.

Open rebellion against Sukarno's regime, and against the rising power of the PKI, now broke out in Sumatra and Sulawesi, and in March 1957 Sukarno declared martial law. This in turn enhanced the power of the Army and accelerated its politicization. Already one could see the clear outlines of what was becoming a triangular balance of power between Sukarno, the PKI, and the Army.

Still another issue was meanwhile coming to the boil. In the negotiations which had led to Indonesia's independence from the Dutch, the question of Dutch-held West New Guinea (later to become known as Irian Jaya) had been deferred pending further discussion. Indonesia regarded West New Guinea as an integral part of her territory, but the Dutch refused to consider the matter seriously. Indonesia repeatedly tried to obtain from the United Nations General Assembly the necessary two-thirds majority in support of her claim; and after the third failure in 1957, most of the remaining Dutch in Indonesia were expelled and their extensive investments in the country were nationalized. These actions in turn paved the way to Indonesia's further economic deterioration.

As if all this were not enough, on 30 November 1957 Sukarno was the object of an assassination attempt which very nearly succeeded. When he was visiting a school in the centre of Jakarta, three hand grenades were thrown at him. Although Sukarno escaped unhurt, a number of children were killed and others seriously wounded.

Sukarno declaring a state of martial law, 15 March 1957

Indonesians, who value children so highly, were shocked by these murders, for which certain Muslim extremists were convicted. As C.L.M. Penders remarks, 'the miraculous escape of "the father of the nation" from death caused the charismatic prestige of Sukarno to rise even higher. Many of the common people began to believe that the President was not only politically indestructible but also especially protected by destiny to perform even greater deeds of glory.'[16] Two other unsuccessful attempts on Sukarno's life were to follow.

Early in 1958, the rebels in Sumatra and Sulawesi joined forces and also enlisted the collaboration of some distinguished anti-Communist leaders from Java; and on 15 February they declared the creation of the new Revolutionary Government of the Republic of Indonesia. Relations between Jakarta and Washington continued to deteriorate, not least because Sukarno accused the United States of covertly aiding the rebels. Sukarno later claimed that the then American ambassador, Howard Palfrey Jones, had been unable to deny this; and an American pilot, Allen Pope — widely regarded as a CIA agent — was actually captured by the Indonesians. He was sentenced to be executed, but Sukarno pardoned him following the intervention of Pope's wife, a former Pan American stewardess.[17]

Ambassador Jones, as he later recounted, found that some Washington officials believed that the rebels could overthrow the Sukarno regime or that Sumatra, with her rich resources, might secede from the rest of Indonesia. He persuaded Washington to discard any such thoughts, and it was through his intervention that America promised to send limited military aid to the Jakarta government. Initial consignments were quickly delivered by air.[18]

The Army moved with great vigour against the rebels, who within two months had been largely suppressed, although some resistance dragged on until 1961. This achievement enhanced the Army's morale and its sense of unity under the leadership of Nasution, and it likewise reinforced popular pride in Sukarno as the nation's Great Leader of the Revolution. Sukarno, with Army backing, could now move rapidly ahead along the lines of his earlier pronouncements.

In 1956, as we have seen, Sukarno had introduced his Guided Democracy notion, which was closely connected with his Concept. In February 1959, he suggested a return to the Constitution of 1945 as providing the best basis for his Guided Democracy, and soon afterward he asked the Constituent Assembly to approve the idea. When the Assembly failed to do so, Sukarno dissolved it and reinstated the 1945 Constitution by decree.

According to him, he took the action 'because of that failure of the Constituent Assembly, for the sake of the interests of the Country and People, and to safeguard the Revolution'.[19] In Legge's assessment, 'There can be little doubt that the decree was unconstitutional. . . . But when it came to the point there were few who were concerned to challenge the . . . decree on constitutional grounds. . . . Even his critics, wearied by the uncertainty and disagreements of the past two months, were disposed to feel a sense of relief that, for good or ill, the constitutional question was now disposed of, and the framework for Guided Democracy was now in being.'[20]

In the words of Fryer and Jackson, 'Indonesia's tragic experiment with Guided Democracy was now well launched'.[21] Although heralded by Sukarno as being based squarely upon traditional Indonesian values, Guided Democracy symbolized arbitrary rule. Sukarno operated the 1945 Constitution in a way that gave him seemingly unlimited power. Yet, in the event, his power was not unlimited. As Penders correctly analyses the 'new' situation,

> The vast majority of Indonesians had welcomed the debacle of liberal democracy and believed that Sukarno possessed the magic key which would finally open the door to the long promised era of prosperity and happiness. But neither Sukarno nor his system of guided democracy was able to solve the basic problems of political and ideological segmentation and economic deterioration. Sukarno was able to impose a pseudo-political stability on the country by forcing the political factions to kowtow to his ideas and by eliminating those who did not comply.
>
> Guided democracy, however, did not eradicate the inherent political and ideological divisiveness in the country; all the new system of government did was to streamline the problem by reducing it basically to a power contest between the Army and the Communists. Sukarno had by

no means become a complete dictator and his power depended on his success in manipulating this power struggle.[22]

Thus there still remained Indonesia's seemingly eternal political triangle — eternal, that is, as long as Sukarno continued as President. This was well illustrated by the ongoing saga of the West New Guinea or West Irian dispute, which was now reaching fever pitch. The PKI were in the forefront of the agitation to acquire West Irian; PKI agitators found the issue ideally suited to their purposes, and at times they outdid the oratory of the Great Leader himself. The Army, while publicly supporting a military campaign against the Dutch, was in fact more cautious. Army leaders realized the difficulties in mounting a major campaign, and they likewise did not wish to impair their ability to control the Communists if — as was soon to happen — that should prove necessary.

Particularly in view of the PKI role in the West Irian campaign, the United States showed itself unwilling to support the Indonesian case in the United Nations. On the other hand the Soviet Union provided the Sukarno regime with an estimated $1,000 million worth of arms on credit. In December 1961, Sukarno ordered total mobilization for the struggle against the Dutch over West Irian. A young officer named Soeharto — the future President — was put in charge of preparing combined operations against the Dutch. In initial probing attacks, Indonesian paratroops were dropped in various parts of West Irian and a Dutch frigate sank an Indonesian motor torpedo boat.

The United States, worried about the danger of large-scale warfare and about the accelerating leftward trend in Indonesia, now abandoned its neutralist attitude and played a mediating role in bringing the Dutch and the Indonesians to the conference table. In August 1962, agreement was reached that West Irian would be transferred to Indonesia as of 1 May 1963; a plebiscite was to be held not later than 1969 to ascertain if the people of West Irian agreed to the transfer, but this was to prove largely a formality.

At long last, then, what most Indonesians regarded as their legitimate territorial ambitions had thus been achieved. A later addition was East Timor, which had been under Portuguese colonial rule for some 400 years and which was to become an integral part of the Republic of Indonesia in July 1976 (though this incorporation was not initially recognized by the UN). The subject of East Timor receives further attention later in this book.

Sukarno hailed the West Irian settlement in his 17 August 1962 Independence Day address, which he called 'A Year of Triumph'. In the speech he further attacked Western capitalism and Western democratic institutions, and spoke in glowing terms of the virtues of his Guided Democracy.[23] In a real sense his speech marked the pinnacle of his career as the Great Leader; largely but by no means solely because of Sukarno's cumulative blunders, the delicate triangular balancing act could not be sustained much longer.

Even while the West Irian issue was being negotiated, Sukarno was moving toward another international crisis which would, if nothing else, temporarily divert attention from Indonesia's inflation-ridden and stagnant economy. In 1961, Tungku Abdul Rahman, the Malayan Prime Minister, had proposed the creation of Malaysia as a federation of Malaya, Singapore, and the North Borneo territories. Indonesia at first greeted the proposal with equanimity, but this soon changed to outright hostility. It seems that

An early Darul Islam leader

Sukarno, in his change of view, was among other things motivated by annoyance over aid which the rebels in Sumatra and Sulawesi had received from Malaya and Singapore, by envy of the solid economic progress which Malaya and Singapore were achieving, and by his conviction that they constituted neo-colonial appendages of British imperialism.

In what soon became known as the Confrontation, the PKI were again in the vanguard. The PKI, with Peking's backing, clamoured for all-out war against Malaya and Singapore as stooges of imperialism. Particularly after the formal inauguration of the Federation of Malaysia in September 1963 (Singapore was at first a constituent part of the Federation but was detached in 1965), Sukarno and the PKI accelerated the so-called 'Crush Malaysia Campaign'. As one contribution to the cause, PKI cadres organized mobs which burned the British Embassy in Jakarta and sacked or confiscated British-owned firms and estates.

The United Nations condemned Indonesia for confrontation with Malaysia. When Malaysia was formally accepted as a UN member in November 1964, Sukarno angrily cancelled Indonesia's UN membership. Among the community of nations, it was only Communist China which fully backed Sukarno's Confrontation adventure, and the Peking–Jakarta axis was steadily strengthened.

Much to the concern of the Indonesian Army, the PKI demanded the creation of a people's liberation force of armed workers and peasants, ostensibly to help in the Crush Malaysia Campaign. The Army, although it mounted token military operations against Malaysia, chose to bide its time and conserve its strength in anticipation of any possible domestic emergency. The Crush Malaysia Campaign developed into a military and diplomatic stalemate which was not to be resolved until Sukarno was relieved of supreme authority.

As J.A.C. Mackie points out in his definitive work *Konfrontasi*, 'Confrontation . . . suited Sukarno's personality and political requirements almost perfectly in the last flamboyant stage of "living dangerously". Once the ideological facade was shattered, however, the bankruptcy of his policies could no longer be hidden.'[24]

During the second decade of his twenty years in office, Sukarno had increasingly driven himself into an intellectual and political corner. By embracing Marxism as a major component of his thinking, and by trying to make it part of the Indonesian consensus, he paved the way to disaster. Much as the human body rejects substances which are physiologically alien to it, so the Indonesian people were to reject an alien Western import in the shape of Marxism. To these dramatic events we now turn.

The burning of the British Embassy in Jakarta

33

The Grand Conspiracy

The Indonesian Communist Party was the first such party in Southeast Asia. During the latter Sukarno period the party grew spectacularly until, by 1965, it could plausibly claim to have some three million members plus another seventeen million followers who belonged to its various 'front' organizations.[1] It had indeed become the largest Communist party anywhere in the non-Communist world. Then, just as the party seemed set to dominate the country, something went badly wrong.

It is symbolically significant that the seed which grew into the Indonesian Communist Party was planted not by an Indonesian but by a European who had brought his ideology from Europe. In 1914 the Dutch Communist H.J. Sneevliet founded, in Semarang in Central Java, the so-called Indies Social Democratic Association. Six years later, on 23 May 1920, the group changed its name to the Communist Party (or Association) of the Indies (in Indonesian the Perserikatan Kommunist di Hindia) or PKI; and when it subsequently became known as the Indonesian Communist Party (the Partai Komunis Indonesia) it still remained the PKI.[2]

In 1926, after a protracted period of organizational turmoil and confused planning, the PKI mounted its first attempt at overt revolution. As Arnold C. Brackman describes it,

> On November 13, 1926, at 12.30 a.m. 200 armed men seized the telephone-and-telegraph building in Batavia and severed communications. The capital of the Netherlands East Indies was isolated from the rest of the world. But at dawn, the Dutch Army easily retook it. The sabotage coincided with minor disturbances in Batavia's suburbs. That same night on Bantam, on the Western tip of Java, telephone lines were severed, railroad tracks demolished, and barricades erected on main roads. Several village heads and petty Indonesian officials in the colonial administration were murdered. Similar events occurred in West Java . . . and Central and East Java. . . . There, too, the Dutch encountered little difficulty in restoring order. By November 19, the 'revolution' on Java had evaporated. . . .

The revolt later surfaced again in West Sumatra but was quickly suppressed. As Brackman remarks, 'The hard fact was that the "broad masses" of Indonesia had failed to stir. The revolution had buckled, exposing the illusory nature of the PKI assessment of the political situation. . . .'[3]

As Ruth T. McVey points out, the Dutch took vigorous action to punish both the leaders of the revolt and their followers. Thirteen thousand people were arrested; and, of these,

> A few . . . were shot for having been involved in killings; 5,000 were placed in preventive detention, of which 4,500 were sentenced to prison after trial. This relieved the authorities of those persons whose participation in the revolt could be proved; however, many others whom they considered dangerous (including the great part of the PKI leadership) could not be convicted under the existing laws. Consequently, the government decided to use its powers of banishment on a massive scale, and ordered the removal of 1,308 persons, and such family members as desired to accompany them, to a spot on the upper reaches of the Digul River in New Guinea. None of the internees successfully escaped from the camp, and only a very few . . . survived physically and ideologically to take part in the movement after the fall of the Indies regime. . . .
>
> This action put an effective end to Communist activity in the Indies for the remaining period of Dutch rule. . . .[4]

The PKI did, however, continue to maintain a shadowy existence. After the Japanese invaded the country, PKI members took part in sporadic actions against them. Under the new conditions following Japan's surrender and Indonesia's Declaration of Independence, the PKI set about the task of rebuilding its strength. PKI cadres meanwhile gained further practical military experience through collaborating — for example, at Surabaya — with non-Communist Indonesian nationalists in the struggle against the Dutch.

In 1948 the PKI found itself involved in another armed revolt, this time against forces loyal to the new Republic. A prime reason for the revolt lay in relations with the military. Hatta, the then Indonesian vice-president under Sukarno, put forward a plan to rationalize the country's armed forces, and the PKI understandably feared that this might mean demobilization of guerrilla units which were under its control. The PKI leader Muso, who had lately arrived from Moscow after an absence from Indonesia of twelve years,

Muso, a leader in the 1948 Communist revolt

made fiery speeches exhorting the guerrilla groups to defy rationalization. Subsequent events again displayed the general confusion on the part of the PKI which had characterized the revolt of 1926.

On 18 September 1948, local Communist army commanders seized power in Madiun, a town in central Java. Although the PKI's national leaders had apparently been planning a rebellion, they were taken by surprise at this somewhat premature initiative. They nevertheless felt obliged to support it, and the result was, from their point of view, a disaster. As Bruce Grant has described it,

> Within three months, after guerrilla fighting in which the communists had little chance, the insurrection was at an end, broken by the now famous Siliwangi division (named after an ancient Sundanese king). . . . Almost the entire communist leadership had been liquidated — either dead like Muso, killed in a skirmish, or Amir Sjarifuddin, executed, or, like Sardjono, imprisoned. Perhaps more critical from the PKI's point of view was that the Madiun revolt was regarded by the Indonesian people as an act of treachery. The Republic was at that time undergoing a blockade on the eve of the second Dutch 'police action'; the communist 'stab in the back' is remembered to this day. The communists have twisted the history of Madiun, describing it as a 'provocation', but they have acknowledged that it was a disastrous mistake.[5]

The PKI initiatives of 1926 and 1948 provide an illuminating background to the events of the mid-1960s in which the PKI was again to be so intimately involved. Before we move on to these, however, it is important to point out the relationship between the present chapter of this book and those which follow. As my discussions with many thoughtful Indonesians have revealed, they are rightly less interested in condemning Communism than in determining how to improve upon it. Successive attempts have been made — and will no doubt continue to be made — to propagate the alien Marxist faith in the Indonesian environment. The study of previous such attempts can provide important pointers in the search for non-Marxist options more in harmony with Indonesia's cultural traditions. The object, then, is not to express anti-Communist sentiments but rather to seek guidelines for the future.

After the disaster of 1948, the PKI set about reconstructing itself. This process was greatly facilitated by the accession in 1951 of Dipa Nusantara Aidit as party Chairman. Aidit was born on 23 July 1923 in Sumatra, where his father was a forest worker. After early schooling in Sumatra, he was sent to high school in Batavia, where he later became a tailor's apprentice. In due course he joined the PKI, became a youth leader in it, and rapidly rose in the party hierarchy.[6]

Aidit, together with his young associates Lukman, Njoto, and Sudisman, energetically set about building a mass PKI following, and the party grew phenomenally. Between 1954 and 1959 the number of PKI followers increased nearly tenfold, and the PKI had hopes of topping all other parties in the general election scheduled for 1959. At this time Aidit and his colleagues were espousing the philosophy of the 'parliamentary road to socialism', as officially endorsed by Premier Khrushchev at the Twentieth Congress of the Communist Party of the Soviet Union in 1956.

But Sukarno, with the Army's support, postponed the general election and instead brought in Guided Democracy. Although it continued to press for a general election, the PKI, as Pauker notes, 'decided to make the best of a bad thing and began to cultivate President Sukarno in his new role as a dictator'.[7] If they could not ride the parliamentary road to power, reasoned the PKI leaders, then they could reach the same goal by holding on to Sukarno's coat-tails. In Pauker's characterization,

> the PKI leaders were trying an imaginative but dangerous gambit. For their own political purposes they were drawing on the unique popularity of Sukarno, who had used modern techniques of mass manipulation to bolster his charisma as the nation's leader, endowing himself with the aura surrounding traditional monarchs, whom most of the population considered to be possessed of divine, magical powers.
>
> As the leading nationalist agitator of his country for almost four decades and as principal national spokesman and leader for over 20 years, Sukarno had attained the summit of political power. The Provisional People's Consultative Assembly had proclaimed him, in May 1963, President for life, a decision which received enthusiastic Communist support. . . .
>
> The Communist leaders spared no efforts to establish in the public mind their closeness to the President. The statements of Aidit and his associates were replete with reverent quotations from Sukarno's pronouncements, which seemed to be recited as frequently as passages from the Communist classics.[8]

It appears that during 1963, however, Aidit was concurrently developing a rather more sinister strategy. By that time the PKI leadership was under increasing pressure from its younger cadres to adopt a more militant policy; but probably even more important was the influence of China. Aidit spent most of September 1963 in the People's Republic, where he came under the strong influence of the Maoist leadership.

D.N. Aidit, the PKI's chairman and a chief actor in the 1965 attempted coup

By the end of 1963, Aidit had jettisoned his previous careful neutrality as between China and the Soviet Union; instead, he had vigorously attacked the latter for, among other things, being too cosy with the U.S.A. and failing to give adequate support to national independence movements. He had also abandoned his previous tolerance of the Indonesian Army as an upholder of the national revolution; now the Army's leaders were branded as opponents of Sukarnoism and agents of imperialism.

Sukarno himself had meanwhile been cultivating ever-closer relations with China. During 1963, as he accentuated his anti-Malaysian policy of Confrontation, Indonesia and Maoist China in effect developed an alliance. Relations between the two countries were further solidified in 1964 as they joined forces in various international 'anti-imperialist' conferences. In November 1964, Sukarno went to China to confer with Chou En-lai;[9] and, in the opinion of Antonie C.A. Dake, that meeting 'set the stage for the conspiracy that within a year would start bringing doom to both the Indonesian President and the PKI'.[10]

Reference has been made in Chapter 3 to Aidit's demand for the arming of workers and peasants; and Pauker calls this 'Aidit's great strategic mistake'. Aidit first put forward his demand on 14 January 1965, and on the same day Sukarno rejected it. Undeterred, Aidit repeated it three days later at a public meeting, at which he called for the immediate arming of the workers and peasants as 'the pillars of the revolution'. As Pauker remarks, 'In thus trying to acquire a paramilitary capability, the PKI was challenging a cardinal principle of the Army. From the early days of the struggle for independence, when a multitude of armed groups had been established by spontaneous social action, the Army had been hostile to irregular military formations, some of which were affiliated with political parties.'[11]

On the following 17 August in his annual Independence Day address, Sukarno nevertheless broached the same idea, which he now presented as his own rather than Aidit's. He spoke sympathetically of the proposal and said that he would soon take a decision on it. A month later Sukarno, without informing his own Defence Minister, sent a secret mission to Peking to discuss among other things the matter of 100,000 small firearms which the Chinese government was to give Indonesia, ostensibly for use in the Confrontation with Malaysia.[12] Suspicions naturally arose in Indonesian military circles that these arms were actually intended for the use of workers and peasants in connection with a different sort of confrontation.

Aidit had meanwhile launched an appeal for class war in the countryside. Even by 1963 the PKI's Indonesian Farmers' Front claimed over seven million members; and pursuant to the newly-embraced Maoist revolutionary doctrine, the Front launched a so-called Unilateral Action Movement under which peasants were to take matters of land reform into their own hands. The Front's campaign did without doubt stimulate the implementation of land reform programmes; but by May 1965, even Aidit, evidently thinking that things were going too far, warned of the need for strict discipline in the peasant movement. In Pauker's assessment,

> If Aidit had already decided . . . to eliminate the anti-Communist leadership of the Army, he may have considered it undesirable to intensify further the revolutionary situation in the countryside, as these actions

increased the risk that the PKI's enemies might combine to crush the Party. In other words, if the September 30 Movement was already beginning to take shape in Aidit's mind as a preventive measure against future anti-Communist moves by the military, it made sense to keep the PKI's enemies from closing ranks prematurely.

But the decision to stop 'unilateral actions' came too late. The PKI was soon to suffer the consequences. In my opinion, by disrupting the harmony . . . of the Indonesian village community, the Farmers' Front unilateral actions set the stage for the gruesome massacre of hundreds of thousands of Communists in the aftermath of the September 30 Movement. . . .[13]

The PKI's 45th anniversary celebration in Jakarta

These two factors — the proposal for large-scale arming of workers and peasants, and the active and virulent campaign to foster class war in the villages — caused increasing disquiet among men of moderation, whether they were civilians or members of the armed forces. Aidit was soon to claim that a so-called Generals' Council was planning to launch a coup; but, viewed in another way, the Army would have been shirking its duty to the country if, in a situation of such extremity, it had not made some sort of contingency plans.

Sukarno's role during this period was to say the least ambiguous. He seemed, as Legge suggests, to be engaged in 'an increasingly desperate attempt . . . to maintain stability in an essentially unstable situation';[14] but in practice he was veering more and more sharply to the left. His long-cherished ideal of national unity was by now badly eroded, and his carefully-considered triangular balance of forces had become grotesquely contorted.

In addition there was the matter of Sukarno's health. It was well known that he had for some years been suffering from a chronic kidney condition, and his taste for high living no doubt did little to improve it. On the one hand he completely dominated the Indonesian political scene, and on the other hand he could not last forever. As Nugroho Notosusanto and Ismail Saleh pithily remark in their definitive study *The Coup Attempt of the 'September 30 Movement' in Indonesia*, 'It is quite natural that both sides began calculating their chances in the post-Sukarno era'.[15]

To complement its more visible activities throughout the country, the PKI had been busy infiltrating the armed forces. Aidit had in 1964 established in Jakarta a secret Special Bureau (Biro Chusus) which reported directly to him; the purpose of the Special Bureau was to 'manage' PKI-inclined members of the armed forces including those who would later be recruited for the projected coup. Aidit had likewise established counterpart Special Bureaus in the provinces for the purpose of managing assigned members of the armed forces there.

According to Wilfred T. Neill, the Communists 'had secretly set 1970 as the date for a complete takeover of Indonesia',[16] but several factors, most notably Sukarno's precarious health, had led them to accelerate their plans. In any event, something of a crisis was precipitated when, on 5 August 1965, Sukarno collapsed during a public engagement. It is possibly significant that on Sukarno's orders his secretariat immediately contacted Aidit, who was in China at the time, and called him back along with a team of Chinese doctors.

Although the President's condition soon improved, the Chinese doctors told Aidit that Sukarno's health remained delicate. They suggested that another attack could cause paralysis or death and that in any event a full recovery was unlikely.

Aidit quickly convened a series of meetings of his Politburo. He gave his colleagues an assessment of the President's health as gleaned from the Chinese doctors and from visits that he had made to Sukarno. He warned that the so-called Generals' Council stood ready to launch a coup which would be timed according to the condition of the President. And he testified to the readiness of a group of 'progressive' Army officers to pre-empt the threatened coup.

In the words of Notosusanto and Saleh, 'Aidit's influence in the Politburo was such that his views were accepted without much deliberation, and to him was entrusted the task of coordinating the project.'[17] The coup would be staged to appear as an internal Army affair but would be actually executed by the 'managed' PKI men in the officer corps.

Operational planning for the coup took place in a series of ten joint meetings of PKI Special Bureau chiefs and PKI sympathizers in the armed forces. The meetings occurred in August and September 1965, and the same authors give the exact places where the meetings were held and the names of most of those who attended. Detailed operational plans were formulated at the meetings, specific responsibilities were assigned, and logistical arrangements were agreed upon, including the provision of arms, vehicles, food supplies, and even cloth for making up special identification insignia for the troops.[18]

The actual implementation of the detailed plans began on the night of 30 September/1 October with a grisly series of murders. Six senior generals of the Indonesian Army were either shot down in their homes or kidnapped; and the living and the dead were taken by truck to the Halim Perdanakusuma Air Force Base (on the outskirts of Jakarta), which had become the headquarters of the conspirators. There, at the perimeter of the base, those who were still living were brutally put to death with the aid of young Communists including women cadres; and all the bodies were thrown down a well known as the Crocodile Hole.[19]

Another intended victim, Defence Minister and Chief of Staff of the Armed Forces General A.H. Nasution, escaped liquidation only by jumping over a wall at the back of his garden; but his five-year-old daughter was mortally wounded in the gunfire, and perhaps largely because of this personal tragedy, and the remorse which he felt in connection with it, he played very little part in the events which followed. Strangely enough the plotters had failed to include in their assassination list the key figure of Major General Soeharto, the Chief of the Army's Strategic Reserve Command. It was he who, through his coolness and resourcefulness, was to save the day.

General Nasution, a hero of the independence struggle and intended victim of the PKI

At about 5:30 on the morning of 1 October, General Soeharto received a message indicating that something was afoot; and after a quick shower he dressed and drove straight to his office at the headquarters of the Army Strategic Reserve Command adjoining the large Merdeka (Freedom) Square in the centre of Jakarta. There he received disquieting news: some of the rebel Army units had already captured the main Radio Republic Indonesia station and the Centre for Telecommunications, both of which also faced on to Merdeka Square. Additional rebel units were in position on the Square itself.

Undeterred, Soeharto sent emissaries who ordered the rebel commanders on Merdeka Square to come and see him. This they at first refused to do, but eventually they did come and Soeharto briefed them, and afterward their subordinates as well, on the false rumours that had been circulating. During the day, and after an ultimatum from Soeharto, most of the troops on the square surrendered.

Soeharto had meanwhile been checking on the attitudes of commanders in other parts of the country, and had summoned the assistance of both the elite Army Para-Commando group and the armoured 1st Cavalry Battalion of the Siliwangi Division, which, as already noted, had been instrumental in crushing the Communist uprising in 1948.[20] On the evening of the same day, with these forces at his disposal, Soeharto ordered the capture of the radio station and the Centre for Telecommunications. Faced with such impressive opposition, the rebels at those key locations surrendered without a single shot being fired.[21]

The rebels had been using the station to broadcast a number of announcements including a lengthy 'Decree No. 1' in which they referred to their 'cleaning-up operation' and to the formation of a so-called Revolutionary Council of Indonesia.[22] But as soon as the radio station had been captured, Soeharto employed it for the broadcasting of a statement signed by him in the name of 'The Temporary Army Leadership'. Referring to the rebels, the statement declared that it had become 'obvious that they are counter-revolutionaries committing a coup against the President . . . and having kidnapped several high-ranking Army Officers'. It asked the public to be 'calm, alert and watchful'.[23]

Later that same night the station broadcast a message signed by Sukarno in which he declared that he was in good health, that he continued as Head of State, that he was temporarily assuming the leadership of the armed forces, and that for day-to-day oversight of the Army he had appointed Major-General Pranoto Reksosamudro — well known as one of the 'progressive' officers with PKI sympathies. Meanwhile Soeharto, already aware that the rebel headquarters were at Halim Air Base, had turned his attention there. Having learned to his astonishment that Sukarno was actually at the rebel base, Soeharto sent a message to him advising him to leave since the base was to be attacked. Word soon came that the President had left the base and gone to the Presidential Palace at Bogor.

Armoured and other forces then proceeded under Soeharto's orders toward Halim Air Base and arrived there at about 3:00 on the morning of 2 October. By the early afternoon they had completely occupied the base and its environs with the loss of one soldier killed and several wounded.[24] The coup leaders, including Aidit and his associates as well as their ideological colleagues in the armed forces, had fled.

By that same afternoon, operations to suppress the attempted coup had likewise been completed throughout the capital city. In the provinces, however, operations took longer; and this was particularly so in Central Java. There the PKI leaders belatedly decided to discard the camouflage of non-involvement in the conspiracy, and they engaged in widespread armed resistance. By the end of November 1965, however, virtually all organized opposition had been crushed throughout the country. Aidit had been caught and summarily shot, and most of the other ringleaders had either been killed in engagements or captured and held for trial.

These military operations, however, were only a small part of the whirlwind which quickly swept over the country. On 3 October, the day after

Halim Air Base had been captured, Soeharto learned that the bodies of the murdered generals had been thrown into the Crocodile Hole. When the bodies were exhumed on 4 October, he broadcast from the spot, described the grisly scene, and clearly implied where he thought the responsibility lay. In Indonesia it is particularly offensive to dishonour dead bodies, and pictures of the victims, as carried by the media, spread a wave of revulsion throughout the country.[25]

These events, together with the campaign of hate which the PKI had for years carried on, helped to trigger off a mass slaughter which still defies complete explanation. Hundreds of thousands — some estimates say even a half million or more — of Communists, Communist sympathizers, and undoubtedly many uninvolved and innocent people as well, were killed in a frenzy of retribution. Some observers suggest that the Army encouraged or condoned the killings or at least did little to prevent them, but others point out that the Army could scarcely have contained the people's pent-up fury, particularly in the countryside.

Indonesia's justly-renowned tolerance had been strained beyond the breaking point. Peaceful Bali, for example, saw some of the most concentrated slaughter of all. In the words of the Dutch scholar Tas, 'What developed following the coup can scarcely be described as anything but a national revolt against Communism'.[26] According to Notosusanto and Saleh, 'an ideology which postulates atheism and an unavoidable struggle between groups within society should be considered a threat to the Indonesian way of life and acknowledged as such'.[27] Clearly the Indonesian people had signalled their distaste for the alien ideology which had been brought to their shores and nurtured there over a period of some fifty years.

A counter-Communist demonstration in Jakarta following the attempted coup

Leadership and Necessity

Sukarno's behaviour during and after the 1965 coup attempt became increasingly peculiar. It was as if the Marxist message — particularly as purveyed by the then Maoist Chinese regime and by Aidit as its protégé — had mesmerized him and destroyed his equilibrium. In his role as independent Indonesia's foremost founding father, Sukarno had for many years espoused national unity and the judicious balancing of all the various interests in the society. He had thought of himself as the mouthpiece of the nation as a whole, and countless millions of his followers had concurred in this view. But now it was as if he had been brainwashed.

According to Fryer and Jackson, 'the balance of evidence strongly suggests' that Sukarno 'knew that a preemptive strike . . . was being planned by the PKI, and did nothing to prevent it. . . . Sukarno's subsequent behaviour strongly suggests that he gave tacit approval to the removal of the generals. . . .'[1] My review of a wide range of scholarly materials suggests that this assessment is a fair one; and it has likewise been confirmed in informal discussions with many knowledgeable Indonesians, including those who still respect or even revere Sukarno's memory.

Certainly in the immediate aftermath of the attempted coup, when it became clear that Sukarno had been not a captive but rather a guest of the rebels at Halim Air Base, many people had plausibly concluded that there had been collusion between him and them. Their impression was reinforced when, on 5 October 1965, the funeral of the murdered generals took place. Although many other well-known personalities were present, Sukarno was conspicuous by his absence. At a cabinet meeting which he convened less than 24 hours after the funeral, Sukarno laughed and joked while making not a single adverse comment about the rebels.[2] This, when it became known, deeply offended many Indonesians; in addition, it scarcely supported any idea of the President's innocence.

Sukarno refused to ban the PKI or even to condemn it. At least in public,[3] he preferred to maintain the posture that the attempted coup had been a purely internal Army affair and had had little or nothing to do with the PKI; and in this he was joined by some members of the Western academic community. A good example was the so-called 'Cornell paper', which was prepared at Cornell University, was originally issued under the date of 10 January 1965, and for a time exerted considerable influence in Western academic circles. In the paper the authors argue that the coup attempt was perpetrated by an internal Army group who were not in collusion with the PKI or under its influence and that the PKI innocently became entangled in the affair.

Students marching to demand that Sukarno be brought to trial

But especially in the light of the voluminous evidence from the trials of some 200 alleged participants in the attempted coup, this position became increasingly difficult to sustain; as Mortimer suggests, 'The trials lent support to, and filled out, the Army's claim that the October 1 coup was masterminded by the PKI.'[4] Indeed in the introduction to a later issuance of the 'Cornell paper' (dated 1971 and including the original text), one of the authors, Benedict R. Anderson, manfully admits that 'The data on which our text is based, while clearly important, are partial in their scope and do not include the great mass of material contained in the transcripts of the political trials that have been held since early 1966.'[5]

Notosusanto and Saleh give a careful report on the organization and conduct of the trials and on the fascinating, and often disarmingly frank, testimony given by various of the principal defendants.[6] Some observers, including Mortimer, have not been completely happy about the trials; they contend, for example, that nobody can prove that they were completely devoid of coercion or persuasion and that in any event the Army had a vested interest in tarnishing the image of the PKI. In Legge's assessment, the transcripts from the trials 'can provide a quarry for future studies of the coup, but since the Tribunal was concerned to establish a particular case it cannot, in itself, yield a complete answer. Neither, however, can its massive accumulation of evidence be entirely brushed aside as representing an attempt to frame the PKI.'[7]

Legge elsewhere suggests, with commendable understatement, that 'The precise nature of the coup is likely to remain a matter for debate'.[8] According to Jones, 'The full story of this so-called coup has yet to be told; indeed, it may never be'.[9] The problem is in a sense comparable with that involving the murder of President John F. Kennedy on 22 November 1963 in Dallas, Texas. It is well known that, in order to investigate the matter in depth, a distinguished commission was established under the chairmanship of Chief Justice of the United States Supreme Court Earl Warren. The commission made a seemingly exhaustive investigation of the problem and presented a massive report. Yet the 1964 Warren Commission Report, if anything, raised more questions than it answered, and controversy on the whole matter has continued ever since.[10]

What is beyond controversy, however, is that in Indonesia the 1965 coup attempt created an emergency which required decisive action and that General Soeharto did act decisively. In pondering the question of the rise and role of the national leader, historians have often suggested that the times can call forth the man. Something like this seems to have happened in Indonesia in the mid-1960s; and Soeharto was to prove that, unlike able military men in various countries who have sometimes failed dismally in the realm of civil affairs, he could excel in both. This sort of adaptability derived in no small measure from the particular personal attributes of the man himself; but in addition, as we shall see, it stemmed from certain special characteristics of Indonesia's military tradition.

In Jones's assessment, 'The man whose prompt action frustrated the . . . coup possesses a quiet dignity and strength'.[11] It is interesting to speculate as to Soeharto's somewhat uncertain upbringing and whether it may have helped to engender such qualities in him. His background was nothing if not humble. He was born on 8 June 1921 in Kemusu Argamulja, a small hamlet set amidst paddy fields near Yogyakarta in Central Java. His father, a landless peasant, nevertheless served as a minor village official who regulated the flow of irrigation water to the fields.[12]

When Soeharto was only two years old, his father separated from his mother, although he never lost interest in his son. His grandmother, who as a midwife had helped to deliver the child, took him to live with her. When the boy was four years old, his mother married again, and he was taken back to his mother's house. At the age of eight he was enrolled in the local primary school, but a year later his own father took him away to Solo, in Central Java, where young Soeharto's aunt looked after him. But in the same year, 1930, his aunt and her husband took the boy with them when they moved to the town of Wonogiri, about 30 miles from Solo.

There Soeharto was enrolled in the third year of primary school, and his studies included learning to read the Koran. He also joined the Hisbulwathon, an Islamic youth movement in which nationalist ideas were inculcated as well. In order to attend intermediate school, Soeharto had to move again, to the home of another relative, and yet again to stay with a friend of his father's; there he came into contact with an Islamic religious teacher who was also a Javanese mystic. It has often been suggested that Soeharto himself has a strong streak of the mystic in him.

In due course he returned to the hamlet where he had been born, and from there he cycled daily to Yogyakarta to attend a middle school run by the Muhammadiyah, a cultural and social Islamic organization. Then in 1940 he was admitted to the NCO school of the Royal Netherlands Indies Army at Gombong, Central Java. There he received his basic training, became known as a model soldier, and was quickly promoted to the rank of sergeant.

In 1942, after the Japanese had overrun Indonesia, Soeharto joined the police force which they sponsored, and soon afterward he transferred to their so-called PETA Volunteer Army. Again he rose rapidly, and in 1944 the Japanese sent him to their officers' school at Bogor. In the following year, one PETA unit revolted against the Japanese; a number of that group were shot and others were interned.

After the Japanese surrender, Soeharto showed his flair for leadership in the course of the independence struggle, and Roeder has well chronicled his exploits during those years.[13] Soeharto had become known as a highly competent career officer with little interest in politics, and his climb up the ladder continued: by 1957 he was a full colonel, by 1960 a brigadier general, and by 1962 a major general. On 1 May 1963 he was made commander of the Army's Strategic Reserve Command.

In Roeder's characterization, Soeharto was 'brave, disciplined, cautious, reliable';[14] yet he remained little known outside of Indonesian military circles. At the same time the pressure of events was modifying his previous aloofness from politics; Sukarno's leftward lurch increasingly disturbed both Soeharto and other patriotic officers. Thus, when the grand conspiracy exploded in 1965 into overt action on 30 September/1 October, Soeharto was psychologically prepared to act and to exert his leadership ability.

It is fascinating to observe how, following the attempted coup, Soeharto applied the philosophy of the dual role of the military. Before he could do this, however, he had to set about relieving Sukarno of effective control. According to Brackman, 'For practical purposes Soeharto came into power on 1 October, the morning the Sukarno-PKI putsch misfired, and won immediate popular support'.[15] Be that as it may, Soeharto found it wise to move slowly and carefully in actually taking over the reins from the charismatic President/Supreme Commander of the Armed Forces of the Republic of Indonesia/Great Leader of the Revolution.

In the weeks following the abortive coup, a new force — or at least new since the achievement of independence — had appeared on the Indonesian political scene. This consisted of groups of highly articulate and vocal students. Especially influential were KAMI, the Indonesian University Students' Action Front, and later KAPPI, the Action Front of High School Students.[16] It would be quite misleading to say that these student organizations received no encouragement from the Army; and paradoxically, after the event of Soeharto's New Order, the students were to turn their indignation against some aspects of it as well.

The students made Sukarno one of their first targets, and they demanded that he be both dismissed and brought to trial. Many other citizens joined in these demands, and the case for trying Sukarno received further support from the mass of evidence which accumulated from the trials of others who had been indicted for involvement in the attempted coup. Fryer and Jackson seem justified in suggesting that 'there is little doubt that the Army had the evidence against Sukarno to obtain a conviction of complicity'[17] in the plot; but Soeharto and his advisors resisted any such move, and in this I believe they acted wisely. It could not be denied that Sukarno, more than anybody else, ranked as the father of independent Indonesia, and the continuing popular sympathy for him was to be dramatized when huge crowds turned out for his funeral in 1970. Everything considered, the authorities likewise acted sensibly when, in 1978, they ordered the construction of a rather elaborate mausoleum for Sukarno.

Sukarno and one of his wives: Dewi, from Japan

As for Sukarno's dismissal as a sequel to the abortive coup, this was accomplished with customary Javanese indirection. In 1966 the Soeharto team officially banned the PKI, the Confrontation with Malaysia was ended, and Indonesia rejoined the United Nations; and in the following year diplomatic relations with Maoist China were suspended. Sukarno was meanwhile being pressured into surrendering much of his formal power to Soeharto, and the way was paved for Soeharto to be named Acting President in 1967. By then he had already for many months been serving as effective chief executive and head of state, and in March 1968 the People's Consultative Assembly formally elected him as full President, for a term of five years.

From 1966 onward, as Sukarno's control was gradually whittled away,

Soeharto had applied with ever-increasing vigour the Indonesian philoso-phy of the dual role of the military. This conception had been born not long after the 1945 Declaration of Independence; and in Chapter 2 reference was made to the way in which, as early as the end of 1948, the young govern-ment's defence strategy was already based squarely on a combination of guerrilla tactics plus military socio-political applications covering a wide range of what are usually thought of as civil activities. The Army not only engaged in a wide variety of such activities; it also gradually evolved a body of doctrine concerning them.

Historically, as Sundhaussen points out,

> the particular type of defense strategy in Indonesia, and the degree of internal instability involving the Army in large-scale security operations, caused the military to develop an immediate interest in the social welfare of the masses. The direct support of the people was deemed imperative if guerrilla warfare against external enemies and counterinsurgency cam-paigns against internal rebels . . . [were] to be successful. . . .[18]

As Notosusanto has expressed it,

> Out of the ethos of being a freedom fighter first and a (professional) soldier second . . . [has] come the concept of the Dual Function, namely the function of freedom fighter later broadened into the function of socio-political force, and the function of (professional) soldier later broadened into the defense and security function or military function. The Indonesian Military's foremost interest is to increase national resili-ence and the way to do it is through national development or moderniza-tion. . . .[19]

Thus the Indonesian Army, through its historical experience and condition-ing, has become convinced that it must shoulder an on-going responsibility for the country's overall development. In Abdulgani's characterization, 'This "dual-function" concept stresses that the Army, because of its special

General Soeharto being sworn in as
Acting President, 12 March 1967

49

relationship with the people in gaining National Independence more than 30 years ago, has a continuing role in the development of a healthy State and society'.[20] Although the concept derived its legitimacy from those early years, its application received special impetus after the abortive coup and after what Abdulgani calls 'the failure of the civilians and politicians to rise to the occasion'. The Army, he suggests, then moved more and more into 'the centre of socio-economics and politics'.[21]

Early in his role as President, Soeharto emphasized that nation-building requires action in 'the ideological, political, economic and social fields and in that of defense and security'. He warned against the mistake of regarding the Army as 'a mere fire extinguisher'; instead, it 'should be able to carry out its task as an instrument of defense and security and be able also to play its role as a socio-political force'.[22]

The Army, he argued, should operate within a very broad context indeed: 'Our extensive motherland that is strategically located, its very big population, the advancement of technology and the development of the world in general. . .'. The Army, he declared, had never surrendered during the war of independence, and it would not surrender 'in facing the challenge of development'.[23]

General M.S.H. Panggabean, who in 1978 was to become Co-ordinating Minister for Defence and Political Affairs, had by 1970 called on the Army 'to participate in: (1) defining the country's policy; (2) promoting government administration; (3) implementing national programs'.[24] He declared that the Army did not wish 'to be a mere instrument of defence and security, nor to be a latent political instrument to be utilized only according to the wishes of whichever group is in power'.[25] At the same time he responded to various criticisms of the dual function concept, such as that it might lead to excessive Army domination or militarism or suppression of free speech or a monopolization of important government positions. He insisted that the Army would welcome constructive criticism and that it would 'continue to indulge in self-correction and strive for higher discipline to obliterate, or at least lessen, any excesses. . .'. On the other hand, he warned that the Army would not hesitate 'to take drastic steps' against anybody who tried to wreck the dual function philosophy.[26]

In general the Army tended to build from *ad hoc* developmental approaches to much more comprehensive ones. For example, a report issued in 1972 on 26 Army-assisted development projects in various parts of the country described such activities as airborne pest control and the scattering of seeds; the upgrading of roads, bridges, and irrigation systems; and the repair of schools, mosques, and churches.[27] Although these kinds of activities continued to be pursued, the Army in addition more and more seized the initiative in fostering comprehensive economic and social planning and the implementation of the five-year development plans. The Army habitually took the broad view.

In large measure the Army's comprehensive development emphasis was in constructive reaction to Sukarno's disastrous handling of the economy. By his own testimony he had little interest in economics, and my conversations with people who used to work with him confirm that he found economics boring and that he had a particular distaste for economists and accountants. According to Legge, Sukarno 'seemed to have no grasp of

The Sultan of Yogyakarta

Adam Malik, when Foreign Minister
during the latter days of Sukarno's regime

economic problems. . . . He was not effective as a practical administrator. He did much, indeed, to earn his reputation as an obstacle to ordered development. . . .[28]

During the Sukarno period an elaborate eight-year development plan was prepared, but Sukarno failed to carry through its implementation, and Sundhaussen is clearly justified in calling the episode 'largely ritualistic'.[29] Fryer and Jackson are not far wrong when they allude to Sukarno's 'economic ineptitude'[30] — something that a modern statesman can ill afford. Legge, going further, refers in sum to what he calls Sukarno's 'catastrophic failure to come to grips with economic problems'.[31]

The Soeharto regime brought a drastically different emphasis. Although in no sense a professional economist, Soeharto clearly saw the need to give economists a key role if his government was to fulfil its mission. As Roeder expressed it, 'There is rarely a speech of Soeharto's not connected with economic problems. . .'.[32] Soeharto brought in a highly knowledgeable team of economists including Widjojo Nitisastro, who became Chairman of the National Development Planning Agency (Bappenas) in 1967 and was in 1978 also made Co-ordinating Minister for Economic, Financial and Industrial Affairs. Soeharto and his colleagues have focused on the implementation as well as the planning side, with results which — as we shall see later in this book — have been nothing short of remarkable.

Particularly in the West, two kinds of misunderstanding have often prevailed in commentaries on the government of post-Sukarno Indonesia. In the first place, it has been assumed that Indonesian public affairs have been directed exclusively by military men and so-called technocrats. And in the second place, it has been taken for granted that, given such direction, mundane economic and technocratic values have inevitably received pride of place in determining the nation's destinies. The actual situation is far more complicated than these suppositions suggest, and it can be properly understood only in its historical and cultural context.

Virtually at the outset of his taking charge, Soeharto formed a sort of triumvirate composed of himself and two leading civilians both of whom had been active in the independence struggle and had gained reputations as men of patriotism and integrity. One of them was Hamengku Buwono IX, the Sultan of Yogyakarta, and the other was Adam Malik.

Jones calls the Sultan 'one of the most revered and influential leaders in Indonesia'.[33] Born in Yogyakarta in 1912 and descended from the thousand-year-old Javanese nobility, he had his university education in Holland. In mid-1966 Soeharto appointed him as First Minister for the Economic and Financial Sector, in which post he exerted much constructive influence. He served as Indonesia's Vice-President from 1973 until 1978, when he was succeeded by Adam Malik.

Born in 1917 in Pematang Siantar, North Sumatra, Malik early became a journalist and nationalist. During the independence struggle he followed a decidedly left-wing line, but his views were subsequently modified through his service as ambassador to the Soviet Union (1959-63) as well as to Poland. Upon his return, according to Jones, Malik told him 'If I had ever been inclined toward Communism, my service in the Soviet Union would have convinced me that this was not the path that Indonesia should follow'.[34] Among many other important posts, Malik served as Minister of Foreign Affairs and Chairman of the 26th General Assembly Session of the United Nations, where he attracted much attention as a skilled parliamentarian and champion of the cause of the emerging world.

Soeharto has in practice assembled a team which includes very able and dedicated military colleagues, technocrats of the stature of Nitisastro and his planning group, and others such as Malik who are neither military men nor technocrats. Indonesia, as we shall see, still has ample scope for administrative improvement, but I have been mightily impressed with the quality and energy and efficiency of many of her individual civil servants whether military or civilian. Moreover, some — albeit not yet nearly enough — of these men demonstrate a genuine interdisciplinary awareness of the social, cultural and ideological values which transcend economics.

After the eclipse of Sukarno and of what is now known as his Old Order, the New Order leadership faced a formidable triple problem: it was necessary to rescue the economy from the chaos into which it had fallen; it was necessary to modernize and develop the country in a way that would bring material benefits to many millions of ordinary people; it was at the same time necessary to preserve Indonesia's unique and precious cultural heritage. From his own boyhood days and from his work under the dual role philosophy, Soeharto had acquired first-hand knowledge of the rural mode of life— with its enduring values as well as its dearth of desirable amenities— of most of his fellow-citizens. He and some of his key advisors realized that not a few other emerging countries had, in their rush to modernize and Westernize, destroyed the very cultural and moral values which had knit the society together. They knew that the country must not stand still— and that at the same time it must not travel a one-way road toward cultural disintegration.

The Indonesian Tight-Rope

Without exception, all countries in this complex and interdependent world face thorny problems, and in Indonesia's case four such problems particularly stand out: how to cope with her population pressure; how to feed her people; how to provide them with jobs; and how to organize enough exports so that the country can pay her way in the world. In all of these matters, Indonesia has in recent years made substantial progress; she still has far to go, but with sufficient resourcefulness she can continue to score impressive gains.

Although Indonesia abounds in puzzling paradoxes, none is more long-standing than that relating to the extent of her resources. For many generations, what is now Indonesia has been regarded as a bottomless cornucopia; as one standard source expresses it, 'From the time of Columbus' search for the spice islands of the Indies in the 15th century until modern times, the archipelago has been considered an inexhaustible agricultural treasure-house. . .'.[1] In the opinion of Jackson and Fryer, 'The concept that what is now Indonesia possesses vast untapped, yet easily exploitable, resources has existed for centuries. It is a myth; but unfortunately, it is a myth that dies hard. . .'.[2] According to another source, which adopts a more intermediate position, 'having the world's fifth largest population, and endowed with extensive and varied natural resources, Indonesia has the potential to become a great and prosperous power'.[3]

One commonly hears it said that Indonesia's most valuable resource is her people, and to a degree nobody can deny this. But Indonesia, along with not a few other developing countries, possesses this particular kind of resource to the point of embarrassment. As a definitive World Bank report expresses it,

> Population pressures will continue to be a severe impediment to economic development in the Low Income countries of Asia. By the year 2000, the population of the six largest countries will have risen to 1.6 billion from the current level of slightly less than 1 billion. The demographic outlook is not uniformly bleak, however. Fertility rates have begun to decline in some countries — among them . . . Indonesia. . . .[4]

Indonesia is in fact endeavouring to cope with her population problem in two ways: on the one hand, through encouraging people to move, either spontaneously or under the official transmigration programme, from densely-populated Java and Bali (and adjacent Madura and Lombok) to the wide open spaces of the outer islands; and on the other hand, through fostering family planning. Transmigration, as we shall see in Chapter 10, is much more than a response to population pressure; it also carries profound implications for balanced national development and for national security.

In her response to population pressure, however, Indonesia must mainly continue to rely upon the reduction of human fertility; and here one finds a most remarkable success story. The country's family planning programme can indeed offer valuable lessons for other parts of the world — in terms not only of results achieved but also of the democratic *way* in which they have been achieved.

As early as 1802, Dutch officials considered Java overcrowded, but they were slow to do anything about it. Sukarno, as independent Indonesia's first President, wanted for his country as many children as possible and refused to take any action on birth control. When the Soeharto regime came to power, however, it took a very different position; realizing that population pressure could undo even the most energetic development efforts, it gave full backing to family planning.[5]

But the proper path was by no means clear. Family planning efforts had in a number of countries met with indifferent success, and some experts thought that it was hopeless to try to prevent Indonesia's population from outrunning available food and other resources. Various officials estimated that the population might reach between 250 and 280 million by the year 2000, while another more optimistic study indicated that the population was heading for some 330 million by the year 2500.[6]

To make matters worse, experts faced a seemingly circular situation offering no escape. Observation in a number of countries had suggested that people could be brought to value small families only *after* economic development had brought an adequate sense of personal and family security; but this happy state of affairs could be achieved only *after* population pressure had been reduced to manageable proportions. In addition, it was widely assumed that ordinary villagers were not sufficiently future-oriented to make long-term plans for their families' welfare.

In the event, this conventional wisdom has been shown up as inadequate, and Indonesia's family planning programme has become 'one of the most remarkable of all attempts to institute birth control on a mass scale'.[7] Fertility has been declining even faster than Indonesia's own population planners had anticipated. Although the country's population had by 1978 reached 141.6 million,[8] the rate of increase had by 1979 been brought down to less than 2 per cent.[9] Assuming no unforeseen interruptions, the government confidently hopes to reduce the population growth to one per cent by 1990, ten years ahead of the earlier target.

One of the most heartening aspects of the programme lies in the fact that the great majority of those accepting family planning come from the rural areas, earn their livelihood as farmers, and have less than a primary education; and it is indeed in the rural areas that the great breakthrough has occurred. The successful outcome derives very largely from the initiative taken by dedicated and imaginative officials in moving the programme out of the clinic — where in so many countries it has started and then foundered

— and into the village.

Expressed in another way, the success of the Indonesian programme resides very largely in the upwards of 40,000 village family planning clubs.[10] In densely-populated Java, for example, the village ladies meet monthly to receive contraceptive supplies and to compare notes on how they are getting along. In many villages the ladies, at their club meetings, prepare attractive small signs which, fastened to the fronts of their houses, proudly proclaim that the occupant is enrolled in the programme and which method she is using.

The authorities especially favour the IUD since, once installed, it fosters an excellent continuation rate; but the pill is increasingly taking over, while the condom or other methods are used by a minority of couples. Although Indonesia has depended mainly upon foreign aid for the millions of pills required, she has been rapidly expanding domestic output and expects to be self-sufficient within a few years. Production of other kinds of contraceptive supplies is also being undertaken.

A family planning clinic

The family planning clubs have increasingly branched out into other fields such as sewing, nutrition, hygiene, and child care; but this is only the beginning, for the village clubs are proving ideal vehicles for stimulating local interest in all kinds of development. Indonesia, then, is successfully integrating democratically-focused family planning with both local and national development programmes;[11] thus, as one of the leaders in fertility control efforts has expressed it, 'the people and their communities gradually assume greater responsibility for directing the future course of their lives, including their own program of fertility limitation'.[12]

Rampant population growth, according to Robert S. McNamara, ranks second only to the threat of thermonuclear war as 'the gravest issue the world faces over the decades immediately ahead'.[13] But clearly, in the world at large and in Indonesia in particular, the problem of population is intimately related to that of food. As one report succinctly puts it,

> Probably the major cause of poverty in Indonesia, particularly on Java, is too many people on too little land. Population density on Java is over 560 people per sq. km. Nearly half the farms in Indonesia are less than 0.5 of a hectare (one acre) with 73 percent one hectare or less. . . . It now appears that the sub-division of land has resulted in plots so small . . . that they are unviable bases even for production of basic subsistence needs, let alone additional income generation. . . .[14]

The paradoxical quality of Indonesia's resources extends pre-eminently into her agricultural sector. Rice is her staple food and the principal agricultural crop, and through intensive production methods she regularly achieves among the highest per-hectare or per-acre rice yields in tropical Asia.[15] Yet Indonesia is a chronic rice-deficit country which has in recent years been the largest single purchaser on the international rice market. Because of rising incomes as well as population growth, rice consumption has continued to outstrip production. Rice consumption increases have in recent years averaged around 4.5 per cent per annum as against production gains of less than four per cent.[16]

Indonesia has traditionally been regarded as part of the so-called Rice Bowl of Asia, and it is embarrassing for her to have to import a million tons or more — potentially much more — of rice each year. Such imports, needless to say, likewise constitute a heavy drain on foreign exchange. The government, in its attempts to deal with the rice problem, has been following three main lines: encouraging people to grow more and eat more non-rice foods; helping farmers still further to improve output from intensively-cultivated rice, and opening up more land for this purpose; and fostering the creation of more estates for the large-scale extensive production of rice.

Government spokesmen persuasively argue that the cultivation of more non-rice crops such as corn (maize), cassava, peanuts, and soybeans, can provide a more varied diet; and they also point out that the growing of such crops in rotation with rice can substantially reduce losses from the pests and diseases which often decimate fields of rice. Production of some of these non-rice crops has shown modest increases. Rice intensification efforts have likewise been under way for some years; indeed, it was in 1965 that the then government introduced the two continuing programmes known respectively as Bimas and Inmas.[17] The Bimas programme, as it has subsequently evolved, aims to improve and expand irrigation facilities for rice fields and to encourage wider use of high-yielding rice seeds, fertilizer, and insecticides. Bimas supports these activities with agricultural credits provided both in kind (seeds, fertilizer, and other inputs) and in cash.

The Inmas programme is similar to the Bimas one except that it normally does not include credit arrangements. In addition to these programmes the government has done much else — especially in terms of roads, bridges,

Jatiluhar Dam

dams, and other infrastructure as well as supporting research and education — in aid of agriculture in general and the rice-growing sector in particular. By no means least, the government has, both within the Bimas and Inmas programmes and outside of them, achieved a massive increase in the output, distribution and use of commercial fertilizer, which is produced largely from Indonesia's abundant natural gas. As a result of all such efforts, rice production has in recent years risen modestly — but, as already indicated, not enough to keep up with rising demand.

Personal observation indicates, and discussion with expatriate and other experts confirms, that the Indonesian farmer is knowledgeable, very hard-working, and nobody's fool. But, especially on fertile Java and Bali, he is faced with a formidable constraint: the limitation on land. Java and Bali are already suffering severe ecological damage, both from over-cropping and from over-cutting of firewood. Erosion and flooding are on the increase, and millions of tons of topsoil are being washed into the sea each year. Agricultural intensification programmes are desirable and necessary, but there is a limit to what hard-pressed Java and Bali can bear. Clearly the outer islands must share more of the burden; and government plans, as we shall see, call for putting the outer islands' vast resources to much better use.

In spite of Indonesia's chronically heavy rice deficits, she has shown her ability to achieve *a favourable overall agricultural trade balance*,[18] and in this performance the outer islands as well as Java and Bali are already heavily involved. Although some 14 million smallholders work the vast bulk of Indonesia's agricultural land, the country has nearly 2,000 large estates averaging some 1,200 hectares (3,000 acres) each; and many of these estates are located on Sumatra or other of the outer islands. Operated by the government or by private foreign or domestic interests (often organized as joint ventures with each other or with the government), the estates produce more than 40 per cent of total commercial as distinguished from subsistence crops.[19] It is likewise the estates which generate the lion's share of

Indonesia's agricultural exports, and they have a major role to play in providing employment as well as foreign exchange.

This leads to the third formidable problem, that of jobs. Both in Indonesia and in the world at large, rural and urban unemployment continues to cause plenty of headaches; and indeed it is essential to view the Indonesian job problem in its international context. As Colin Norman has written,

> Unemployment on an unprecedented scale has emerged as one of the most pressing political and social problems. . . . While governments in industrial countries have been grappling with a pernicious combination of inflation and unemployment, rates of joblessness throughout the Third World have reached extraordinary levels. Two ominous features of the global employment picture stand out: the job shortage will probably worsen before it improves, and it is unlikely that conventional economic remedies will offer sufficient relief.[20]

Even though, as already noted, Indonesia achieves among the highest average per-hectare or per-acre rice yields in tropical Asia, the yield per worker is among the lowest in the entire region. It is the phenomenon of underutilization of labour which explains this paradox. Particularly on Java and Bali, too many people are concentrated on too little arable land with too few alternative job opportunities. Such a situation depresses productivity and makes poverty inevitable.

According to one recent survey, which was based on Western concepts of employment, Indonesia's unemployment rate stood at the unbelievably low level of two per cent; in one sense such a figure is derisory, but in another sense it is all too true. In general, especially in rural areas, the people are so poor that in order to survive they must find work at all costs even if it is of the most menial and sporadic kind. Moreover, less than a third of Indonesia's labour force consists of 'paid' employees; virtually all the rest are unpaid family workers or 'own account' workers such as food-stall owners, street vendors or small subsistence farmers.

The number of Indonesian workers engaged in manufacturing has been steadily increasing, but here again a 'Western' interpretation of the figures can be thoroughly misleading. For only some 15 per cent of the recent increase in manufacturing workers has been in wage-earning jobs; instead, 'such figures indicate a poverty-induced move from agricultural employment to small self account manufacturing. For example, a woman who cannot find work hand harvesting rice because of improved agricultural techniques may become a rope maker or mat weaver at home in order to generate income'.[21]

According to a World Bank report, 'Gains in the productivity of small farmers, *even if equitably distributed*, will not suffice in dealing with the problems of absolute poverty in Low Income Asia'.[22] Many rural households do not have any land at all; and even if they do possess very small farms — such as those which predominate on Java and Bali — these commonly provide no adequate basis for rising above the poverty level.

In Indonesia, according to a census survey of 1976, some 44 per cent of the population were under fifteen years of age. Especially since the country has such a large proportion of young people, the total work force is growing very fast; from about 53 million in 1976 it is expected to rise to around 90 million by the year 2000. This dramatic rise in the available labour force suggests great production potentials, but it also presents a challenging problem: some 1½ million *new workers* must somehow be absorbed into the economy each year.[23] For any hope of success in this daunting enterprise, clearly fresh approaches will be required.

A fourth formidable problem is of course that of exports. For some years oil has, as it were, largely fuelled the development programme; throughout the latter part of the 1970s, oil was indeed providing around two-thirds of all of Indonesia's export earnings. But this situation has been changing, and non-oil exports are becoming ever more important in meeting the country's requirements for foreign exchange.

Commercial oil production started in Indonesia as early as 1883, and by the beginning of World War II the country had become a major oil exporter. The retreating Dutch destroyed most of the oil facilities to keep them from being used by the Japanese; but the latter vigorously rehabilitated and extended them. According to Sevinc Carlson, 'Indonesia's oil was vital to the Japanese war effort, and Japan's battleships, airplanes and tanks operated almost exclusively on it'.[24]

In the decades after World War II, Indonesia's oil industry gathered further momentum; and under Pertamina, the state gas and oil company, it scored remarkable increases in output and exports. But in the mid-1970s Pertamina encountered a liquidity crisis brought about by monumental mismanagement; an energetic and competent rescue operation was then mounted which put the company back on its feet albeit with a loss of several billion dollars in ill-conceived investments. Pertamina had also made other and wiser investments, however; for example, its initiative in the natural gas sector was by the latter 1970s yielding big dividends in the form of natural gas as a feedstock for the production of fertilizer and petrochemicals as well as LNG (liquefied natural gas) for export.

H.W. Arndt foresaw, even in 1978, that the Indonesian oil boom was over;

Arun liquefied natural gas plant, Aceh

and he referred to 'the oil boom in retrospect'.[25] It was true that initially only a very gradual decline in the country's total oil output was expected. It was likewise true that a spectacular new strike or strikes might alter the situation and that in any case the growing world oil shortage might drive per-barrel prices and revenues ever higher. In addition it was true that Indonesia's growing output and exports of LNG could help compensate for any sag in revenues from exports of oil as such.

But, in tune with Indonesia's rapid economic development, domestic consumption of oil was rising at around 14 per cent per annum,[26] and this was eating into the amount available for export. Moreover, as Carlson points out, the country faced a difficult dilemma: it had 'the choice either of producing as much oil as possible for increased revenues to finance its overall development and to pay its debts in the near term, or conserving the oil for the benefit of future generations'.[27] Many Indonesians wished to see a sensible compromise between these two options, and this could in due course lead to a deliberate reduction in the output of oil and possibly of natural gas as well.

Clearly there existed a strong case for meeting Indonesia's foreign exchange needs less from her non-renewable resources and more from her renewable ones. And, by the end of the 1970s, this was actually the way the

Rubber tapping

wind was blowing. Experts were predicting that, by say the early or mid-1980s, the value of the country's annual non-oil exports (including, however, certain non-renewable minerals) would outstrip that of oil and LNG.[28] When one looked at the history and potentialities of various of Indonesia's agricultural export commodities, the evidence certainly suggested that such a worthwhile goal could sensibly be adopted as national policy.

Forgetting for the moment the seamier sides of Dutch colonialism, it is true that in pre-World War II days Indonesia's abundant, fertile and rain-fed plains provided the backbone of a dynamic plantation economy. The country was famous for her rubber, palm oil, tobacco, tea, coffee, spices, and other commodities, which were eagerly sought after by countries in many parts of the world. Wartime destruction and neglect, plus postwar corruption and mismanagement in many cases, wrought havoc both with the great estates (most of which had meanwhile been taken over by the government) and with the smallholder farms producing commodities for export. But by the end of the 1970s the situation had fundamentally changed; management of the estates had greatly improved and so had market prospects in the world at large.

With a number of key commodities in the agriculture and forestry sector, the 1970s had brought stabilization of physical output at reasonable levels plus a dramatic upward trend in export revenues. For example, in the case of timber, in value terms the leading agriculture/forestry export commodity, revenue increases during the period averaged around 30 per cent per annum. With coffee, the second most valuable export in the sector, revenue increases averaged over 50 per cent per annum. With rubber, the third most valuable commodity, the figure was about 25 per cent; and with palm oil, the fourth most valuable, it was in the region of 35 per cent.[29] Much the same thing had happened with certain non-petroleum, non-agriculture/forestry export commodities such as tin.

It is perfectly true that the prices of basic commodities can go down as well as up, and this is well illustrated by coffee prices, which have shown wide variations while still maintaining a pronounced upward trend. It is likewise true that world prices for basic agricultural and other commodities have remained generally well below what developing producer countries consider fair levels, and this has of course led to recurring proposals to establish 'OPECs' for rubber, tin, and other commodities. It is also true that, because of Indonesia's growing population and rising levels of income, ever-larger quantities of basic commodities must be reserved to meet domestic demand.

But such constraints notwithstanding, the country remains a treasure-house of renewable agricultural resources; and as a World Bank report on

Unloading timber at Jakarta

Processing sugar cane

Indonesia expresses it, the scope 'for raising productivity of both traditional and non-traditional export crops, and thereby rural incomes, is enormous'.[30] As our planet becomes more and more densely populated, and as its total available non-renewable resources are steadily depleted, Indonesia's own renewable riches are bound to become progressively more valuable; and this principle carries relatively even more validity today than it did in the 15th century. In formulating its successive five-year development plans — that is, Repelita I, Repelita II, and Repelita III — the government has shown a gradually increasing awareness of the foregoing fundamental principle.

Even before Repelita I was promulgated, the New Order government had taken great strides in bringing under control the disastrous inflation of the later Sukarno period and in getting the stagnant economy moving again. The inflation rate was brought down from an estimated 639 per cent in 1966, when the new government took office, to 10 per cent in 1969. During those years the country's gross domestic product increased by around 6 per cent annually, exports by 14 per cent, and there was a substantial flow of investment and aid funds from abroad.[31]

Repelita I, which took effect on 1 April 1969, had as a central goal the expansion of agricultural output; for example, the plan called for an increase in rice production of some 52 per cent over the five years. The plan likewise emphasized expenditures for irrigation and transportation — both of course directly related to agriculture — together with industry, mining, electric power, communications, state enterprises, education, health, and family planning.

Results under Repelita I were generally impressive; the gross domestic product rose by an average of over 7 per cent per year, and for the first time in three decades there was a substantial increase in per capita income. Most major output targets were attained, except for those for fertilizer, cement, and notably rice, which, partly because of drought, experienced a serious shortfall. Oil production exceeded goals, some 700 new factories or plant extensions were completed, a persistent shortage of textiles was largely alleviated, and notable progress was made in upgrading roads, irrigation works, and transport and communications systems.[32] But job-creation tended to lag behind requirements.

Experience during the Repelita I period especially underlined the stubborn nature of two of the four problems mentioned at the beginning of this chapter: food and jobs. Repelita II, which took effect on 1 April 1974, again addressed these two pervasive problems together with others including those of income distribution, education, and regional growth.

This Second Plan continued the emphasis on agricultural and rural development; concurrently it focused on improving the living standards of ordinary peple, with special reference to food, clothing, housing, welfare benefits, and jobs. Regional and local development, education, health and family planning, and transmigration all received larger allocations of funds than under Repelita I.

Under Repelita II the economy continued to grow, albeit at the slightly lower rate of 6.7 per cent per annum,[33] and inflation continued to be contained. In spite of worsening global inflation, and in spite of huge losses arising from the Pertamina crisis, growing Indonesian oil production coupled with increasing world-wide oil prices permitted the government both to expand its development efforts and to augment its foreign exchange holdings. The industrial sector grew very rapidly indeed, but most of the funding was for capital-intensive projects. Partly because of drought and insect pests, production of food in general, and of rice in particular, fell substantially short of targets, and food imports had to be expanded. Employment rose too slowly to meet the need.[34]

On 15 November 1978, before the end of the Repelita II period, the

Packaging pharmaceuticals and, right, *paper-making*

government severed the tie between the Indonesian rupiah and the US dollar, devalued the rupiah by 33.6 per cent against the dollar,[35] and under a float allowed it to drift within managed limits. Although the devaluation initially added to inflationary pressures and brought considerable confusion to markets and to business planning, the government regarded it as an essential move for boosting non-oil exports and paving the way for the next five-year plan.

Repelita III, which took effect on 1 April 1979, sought to place still more stress on social equity than was the case under the two previous plans. But as President Soeharto pointed out, 'If we emphasize more equitable distribution while failing to achieve sufficient economic growth, in fact what we would more equitably distribute is poverty. I don't think equitably distributing poverty is a good development strategy.'[36] In practice the planners settled on a target average annual growth rate of 6.5 per cent for the Repelita III period, just slightly below the actual performance under Repelita II.

Under the Third Plan, the government emphasized monetary stability as well as economic growth and the equitable distribution of development gains. Again much attention was given to stimulating the agricultural sector, including intensifying rice-growing, diversifying into other crops, and opening up more agricultural areas in the outer islands. Although the government hoped to speed up growth in several sectors — notably industry, construction, and transportation and communication — it foresaw declining overall rates of increase in agriculture, in mining, and in petroleum exports.

The government had begun to concede the need for an employment-oriented development strategy, but the job problem remained far from being resolved — and the same applied to the problems of food and of exports. Meanwhile there were signs that fresh thinking was on the way, both inside the government establishment and outside — not least among the students. And the students' thoughts were focused not only on such economic dilemmas as the foregoing but also on broader questions having to do with human rights and the national ideology. It is to these matters that we now turn.

Opposite, *rice terraces, Gunung Kawi, Bali*

The Human Rights Dilemma

The only possible way to obtain a proper perspective on human rights in Indonesia — or indeed in any country — is to look at the matter in its international context. And here there is no better place to start than with the recent annual reports of the London-based Amnesty International group. For example, the 1978 report, which was published on the occasion of the 30th anniversary of the Universal Declaration of Human Rights, contains comments on the situation in numerous countries classified according to the Americas, Asia, Europe, and other regions.

The report, by its own testimony, gives 'a depressing picture of systematic violations of basic human rights *in most of the countries of the world*. People are imprisoned because of their opinions, prisoners are tortured and even executed.' The report also 'shows that there are new trends in repression. Dissidents are now confined in mental asylums in more countries in Eastern Europe. This is alarming as such a system of detention gives few opportunities for the prisoners to appeal, defend themselves or take any legal action. They suffer the strain of not knowing how long they will be held; they may even be subjected to drugs as "treatment". . . .'[1]

In Western Europe, says the report, 'there has been a tendency to meet terrorism with harsh anti-terrorist laws which in themselves may open the door to violation of human rights. Prisoners have been isolated in solitary confinement or in special "maximum security" cells. . . .' In some Latin American and African countries, the report adds, 'terrorist acts have been given authorization by governments. Kidnapping, torture and killing have been developed into a systematic method of wiping out opposition. Paramilitary groups or security forces have acted as death squads. . . .' In several Asian countries, according to the report, 'the rulers make use of emergency laws to "legalize" the preventive detention of political opponents: by this technique, governments detain people without trial for long periods. Other regimes make arrests and take years to prepare a trial, if they ever do so. . . .'[2]

In the words — perhaps written with unintended irony — of an American report on political prisoners throughout the world, 'Political imprisonment is a practice that appears to have grown rather than declined with the advance of civilization and the extension of national sovereignty to an increasing number of states. . . .'[3] And here one must guard against a serious moral and logical fallacy. One must never seek, as it were, safety in numbers; if, as Amnesty International claims, basic human rights are being systematically violated in most countries of the world, that in no way condones the violation of such rights in any individual country or countries. Instead, it indicates the magnitude of the moral challenge which confronts mankind.

In the annals of human rights, a landmark event occurred in 1215 A.D., when King John of England agreed to the following clause among others in the Magna Carta:

> No free man shall be taken or imprisoned or disseised [i.e., deprived of his lands] or in any way destroyed, nor will we go upon him nor put upon him, except by the lawful judgement of his peers or the law of the land.[4]

Considerably later, in 1776, came America's Declaration of Independence with its human rights provisions,[5] France's Declaration of the Rights of Man and of the Citizen followed in 1789,[6] and then came the Bill of Rights as ratified in 1791 as an addendum to the Constitution of the United States of America. In the Bill of Rights one of course finds a number of safeguards against Federal encroachment upon essential human rights. The Congress, for example, 'shall make no law respecting an establishment of religion, or prohibiting the free exercise thereof; or abridging the freedom of speech, or of the press; or the right of the people peaceably to assemble, and to petition the government for a redress of grievances'. And again, 'The right of the people to be secure in their persons, houses, papers, and effects, against unreasonable searches and seizures, shall not be violated. . .'. Likewise, 'Excessive bail shall not be required, nor excessive fines imposed, nor cruel and unusual punishments inflicted'.[7]

On the whole, and with occasional lapses, these safeguards have been maintained intact in America for some two centuries. It was Franklin D. Roosevelt who, more than any previous American president, emphasized the intimacy of the relationship between economic and political rights; for example, one finds this theme well underlined in his famous Four Freedoms declaration which in 1941 he set forth in the following words as part of a State of the Union Message to Congress:

> In the future days, which we seek to make secure, we look forward to a world founded upon four essential human freedoms.
>
> The first is freedom of speech and expression — everywhere in the world.
>
> The second is freedom of every person to worship God in his own way — everywhere in the world.
>
> The third is freedom from want — which, translated into world terms, means economic understandings which will secure to every nation a healthy peacetime life for its inhabitants — everywhere in the world.
>
> The fourth is freedom from fear — which, translated into world terms, means . . . that no nation will be in a position to commit any act of physical aggression against any neighbor — anywhere in the world.[8]

Perhaps the most remarkable document ever promulgated in its field was the Universal Declaration of Human Rights, as approved in 1948 by the United Nations General Assembly without a single dissenting vote. (For

The Toraja highlands, Sulawesi

Lake Toba, from Samosir Island

Dawn, Bali

Tending ducks

reasons which should become apparent in a moment, however, certain countries abstained.) Drafted to provide 'a common standard of achievement for all people and all nations', the Universal Declaration contains 30 fundamental articles of which the following excerpts are indicative:

> All human beings are born free and equal in dignity and rights. . . . Everyone has the right to life, liberty and security of person. All are equal before the law and are entitled without any discrimination to equal protection of the law. . . . No one shall be subjected to arbitrary interference with his privacy, home or correspondence, nor to attacks upon his honour or reputation. Everyone has the right to the protection of the law against such interference or attacks.

Such rights as the above were repugnant to various regimes, especially those in the Communist bloc, and even more does this hold true of the following additional rights as contained in the Universal Declaration:

> Everyone has the right to own property alone as well as in association with others. . . . No one shall be arbitrarily deprived of his property. . . . Everyone has the right to freedom of thought, conscience and religion. . . . Everyone has the right to freedom of opinion and expression; this right includes freedom to hold opinions without interference and to seek, receive and impart information and ideas through any media and regardless of frontiers. . . . Everyone has the right to take part in the government of his country, directly or through freely chosen representatives. . . . The will of the people shall be the basis of the authority of government; this will shall be expressed in periodic and genuine elections which shall be by universal and equal suffrage and shall be held by secret vote or by equivalent free voting procedures.[9]

Especially during the 1950s and 1960s, the European Convention on Human Rights and a number of other national and international conventions helped to complement the safeguards provided in the Universal Declaration; and an admirable collection of such measures has been put together by Ian Brownlie in his *Basic Documents on Human Rights*.[10] Unfortunately, however, many countries have largely ignored the provisions of the Universal Declaration and related documents; and among such countries, the worst post-World War II offenders— in terms of persistence, scale, and scope— have been first of all the Soviet Union and secondly the People's Republic of China.

Few balanced minds could fail to be moved by the searing account given by Alexander Solzhenitsyn in *The Gulag Archipelago*,[11] particularly in the second volume as published in 1975. It concerns one of the two great crimes committed in this century against humanity: first the Nazi extermination camps, and then the comprehensive Soviet system of destructive-labour camps for political victims. Solzhenitsyn's prefatory maps and extensive index give an indication of the scope of his work and of the magnitude of the soul-degrading system which he memorializes.

Again in 1976, Amnesty International published its influential report entitled *Prisoners of Conscience in the USSR: Their Treatment and Conditions*.[12] Particularly devastating were the report's revelations about the compulsory detention of political prisoners in Soviet psychiatric hospitals. Such disclosures have led to widespread condemnation by non-Communist psychiatrists, statesmen and others; and in certain cases — for example, that of the well-known dissident Vladimir Bukovsky — the protests have helped to bring about releases from the psychiatric hospitals. But this bizarre form of punishment has nevertheless continued, and the whole vast system of Soviet political detention has remained very much in being.

A good test of Soviet intentions was provided by the Helsinki and Belgrade conferences. The Helsinki Conference on European Security and Co-operation ran from July, 1973, to July, 1975 at Helsinki and then at Geneva; 35 states were represented including the Soviet Union and satellite members of the Warsaw Pact alliance, the NATO partners, and a number of neutral or non-aligned states.[13] The so-called Final Act, as issued by the conference, contained a number of important human rights provisions as illustrated by the following excerpts:

> The participating States will respect human rights and fundamental freedoms, including the freedom of thought, conscience, religion or belief, for all without distinction as to race, sex, language or religion.
>
> They will promote and encourage the effective exercise of civil, political, economic, social, cultural and other rights and freedoms all of which derive from the inherent dignity of the human person and are essential for his free and full development. . . .[14]

In the Final Act the conference clearly recognized, in the following as well as other passages, the essential universality of such rights:

> The participating States recognize the universal significance of human rights and fundamental freedoms, respect for which is an essential factor for the peace, justice and well-being necessary to ensure the development of friendly relations and cooperation among themselves as among all States.
>
> They will constantly respect these rights and freedoms in their mutual relations and will endeavor jointly and separately, including in cooperation with the United Nations, to promote universal and collective respect for them.
>
> They confirm the right of the individual to know and act upon his rights and duties in this field.
>
> In the field of human rights and fundamental freedoms, the participating States will act in conformity with the . . . Universal Declaration of Human Rights. . . .[15]

The Final Act likewise stated that the participating countries would hold a further meeting or meetings to permit 'a thorough exchange of views . . . on the implementation of the provisions of the Final Act' and other matters; and it was stipulated that the first such meeting would take place at Belgrade in 1977. Such a meeting did in fact occur there in that year, and it continued over into 1978. The results provided a rude awakening.

Taking an uncompromising line, the Russians refused to discuss the implementation of the Final Act's provisions either inside the Soviet Union or in their captive satellite countries in Eastern Europe. The Belgrade closing statement indeed made no mention of human rights.[16] As Robert Conquest has laconically put it, 'No attempt has been made' by the Russians 'to fulfil these obligations'.[17] Moreover, after Belgrade, the Soviet authorities

A paddy field at Sarangan, eastern Java

Ploughing

Picking tea

A fighting cock and his owner

Banana sellers

The local market

stepped up the persecution of their dissidents, and many harrowing reports of ill-treatment reached the outer world.[18]

Such reports were largely prepared by the unofficial groups which had been set up in various parts of the Soviet Union to monitor Soviet performance under the provisions of the Final Act. The reports were circulated inside the Soviet Union in typewritten *samizdat* form, and copies were also smuggled out of the country. Copies of the reports were actually sent to the Soviet Ministry of the Interior; and the monitoring groups pointed out to the authorities that such reports, far from being subversive, related to promises which the Soviet government had itself made at Helsinki.

Courageous members of the Soviet human rights movement had in fact founded a *samizdat* journal, entitled *A Chronicle of Current Events*, as early as 1968; and after Helsinki the journal became very much a vehicle for reports on performance in relation to the Final Act. In 1971, Amnesty International began publishing the reports in English,[19] and they make absorbing reading for anybody genuinely interested in human rights in any part of the world.

Parallel human rights movements have arisen in various of the Soviet satellite countries in Eastern Europe, and notable among such movements are those in Czechoslovakia and in Poland. In the former country the famous Charter 77 declaration of elemental rights,[20] together with follow-up documents, were issued in the face of furious reactions from the authorities; and various Polish initiatives led to the publication of a remarkable report entitled *Dissent in Poland*.[21] The visit of Pope John Paul II to his native Poland in 1979, and his fearless remarks on human rights, gave fresh hope to the people there as they sought to secure adherence to the spirit and the letter of the Universal Declaration and of the Final Act.

The year 1979 likewise saw the further growth of a human rights movement in that other Communist colossus, the People's Republic of China. China, even more than the Soviet Union, has in recent decades been such a closed society that gross violations of fundamental human rights may come to world attention only long after the event. For example, in 1978 it was reported that some 110,000 people had only recently been released after having been detained since the start of a so-called anti-rightist campaign *in 1957*. It was further reported that in Shanghai 'tens of thousands' of people had subsequently been 'cruelly tortured or persecuted' by radicals in their drive to control the city. In another incident, more than 1,000 former civil servants were reported to have been purged, imprisoned or tortured to extract confessions.[22]

Political Imprisonment in the People's Republic of China,[23] as prepared and published by Amnesty International, ranks as the most definitive single report on the post-World War II human rights situation in that country. The report nevertheless comments on the 'lack of detailed information on political imprisonment' in China, and it says that this 'is due to various factors, including the size and diversity of the country, the complexity of the issues involved in the handling of political offenders, the restriction of movement and the lack of free access to information. . .'.[24] Amnesty International also records that it had sent to the PRC several communications relating to 'prisoners of conscience, arrests and death penalties — including reported executions of political offenders', that it had emphasized its wish 'to discuss these cases and other matters of concern' with PRC representatives, and that in addition it had sent to the PRC a pre-publication typescript of its China report and had requested comments thereon; but in spite of all these overtures no reply was received.[25]

The report as published gives several estimates suggesting the magnitude of the human rights problem in the People's Republic. Chairman Mao, for example, is quoted as having said, at a Politbureau meeting in April 1956, that already 'two or three million counter-revolutionaries had been executed, imprisoned or placed under control. . .'. Another estimate attributed to Mao was that by 1954 the regime had actually executed some 800,000 people.[26]

It appears that in more recent years the pace of executions has been curtailed in favour of rigorous methods of thought-control. Political offenders have generally been tried in secret — with information about their fate often being withheld for years — or subjected to mass public trials where no practical defence is possible. Either kind of trial commonly leads to long-term imprisonment or to death. Political executions have tended to come back into favour in times of political tension, such as that associated with the continuing denunciation of alleged 'Gang of Four' followers in the late 1970s.[27]

In spite of Amnesty International's valuable contributions to our understanding of the human rights situation in the Soviet Union, China, and numerous other countries — including those ruled by right-wing as well as left-wing regimes — there are two key issues with which the organization has never satisfactorily grappled. One of these concerns the matter of human rights in the Third World context. Reference has already been made to Franklin D. Roosevelt's perception that freedom from want must rank as a cardinal human right. As the *International Encyclopedia of the Social Sciences* points out about human rights in developing countries,

> In most of the countries which have acceded to independence only recently the problems are aggravated. Many of the countries have implacable enemies: poverty, ignorance, disease and inertia. Western commentators have tended to underestimate the importance of illiteracy and ignorance, particularly in unsophisticated rural societies. . . .[28]

In addition, the political structures adopted by emerging countries clearly influence the human rights situation within them. As the Secretary-General of the International Commission of Jurists has observed, 'It is commonly assumed in the western world that the enjoyment of human rights and fundamental freedoms is to be found only in multi-party parliamentary democracies'. But this assumption, he adds, has been severely undermined. 'The experience of the last twenty-five years has shown that the western type of parliamentary democracy in its full sense has survived in very few third world countries, and then usually only in countries with a very small population. New forms of society have emerged. . . .'[29]

Clearly those who take a global view of human rights should pay much more attention to the subject in the context of emerging-countries. But Amnesty International, as it modestly explains,

> has a restricted mandate. It works for the release of prisoners of conscience and against torture and executions, but is not involved in work

A sailing craft at dusk

Polishing handmade silverware at Yogyakarta, Java

Batik making: applying wax to the pattern with a 'canting'

A puppeteer preparing for a Wayang *performance*

against unemployment, starvation or other social diseases. Our platform is the Universal Declaration of Human Rights. . . .[30]

Such a position is thoroughly understandable and perhaps — from an administrative point of view — necessary. But it easily gives rise, in the manner already intimated, to a certain myopia. And this shortcoming all too easily leads in turn to another — which, again, Amnesty International has never properly tackled. It has to do with the relationship between fundamental individual human rights on the one hand and national stability and security on the other.

According to Amnesty International, it refuses to accept a contradiction

> between the rights of peoples or nations on the one hand and the human rights of individuals on the other. Human rights have many times been violated in the name of so-called higher interests, such as the 'nation', the 'party', or the 'struggle'. But experience shows that these causes undermine themselves if they need the support of terror. Basic human rights must stand above all other political ambitions and should be respected under all circumstances and in all situations. . . .[31]

In one sense this position is thoroughly commendable; it harmonizes with the 'pure' principles of the Universal Declaration of Human Rights, and it avoids the 'safety in numbers' fallacy mentioned at the beginning of this chapter. But in another sense it is defective because it completely evades this question: what attitude should we adopt — especially in the context of an emerging country — toward those who wish to use and to exploit human rights for the purpose of denying those very rights to millions of their fellow-citizens?

In fact, the Universal Declaration itself deals with this problem. 'Nothing in this Declaration', says its final article, 'may be interpreted as implying for any State, group or person any right to engage in any activity or to perform any act aimed at the destruction of any of the rights and freedoms set forth herein.'[32] Thus the 'pure' principles of the Universal Declaration are properly qualified in the document itself.

As we saw in Chapter 4, Indonesia by 1965 possessed the world's largest Communist party outside the Communist bloc itself; and in 1965 that party, or people who were beholden to it, attempted a coup d'état which very nearly succeeded. In the reaction which followed, hundreds of thousands of people lost their lives, and many thousands more were imprisoned for indefinite periods.

Those who were detained were in effect political prisoners; and in terms of 'pure' human rights theory they should all have been immediately released — or at least all who were not proved guilty through prompt legal proceedings in independent and unbiased courts of law. Moreover, in terms of 'pure' theory the same principles would apply if ideologically the shoe were on the other foot — for example, in an analogous situation in the Soviet Union. There, too, in the event of a large-scale attempted coup against the established regime, all detainees who had actually or allegedly been involved in the attempt should immediately be released from detention or at least given the benefit of speedy and impartial trials.

Any outline of such scenarios clearly reveals their inherent limitations. In the Indonesian case, the government found itself face-to-face with the human rights dilemma. The government hesitated to release, or even to bring to trial, detainees who — so it was feared — might again present a threat to social stability and national security. The matter dragged on for years, to the ever-growing concern of human rights activists in many countries.

In 1977, Amnesty International published a report on Indonesia which completely ignored both the developing-country context and the stability and security factor. The report castigated the Indonesian government in such words as these:

> The situation of political prisoners in Indonesia is profoundly disturbing. With regard to numbers, time-scale, methods used by the government and the history of mass killings and massive arrests, political imprisonment in Indonesia is without parallel today. More than 55,000 political prisoners are distributed throughout the many islands of the Republic of Indonesia; and the correct figure is probably as many as 100,000.[33]

Yet in the following year an official US government report — and one prepared against the backdrop of the Carter administration's emphasis on human rights — gave the following strikingly different interpretation:

> The Government of Indonesia does not engage in consistent violations of human rights. There has been some controversy over its handling of prisoners arrested after the . . . 1965 Communist inspired coup attempt but most of these prisoners have either been tried or released. The remainder will be tried or released by the end of 1979. There have been occasional, ad hoc actions against student protestors and temporary closures of newspapers. These actions, however, do not follow a consistent pattern and almost all students or others arrested were released shortly after their original detention for questioning.
>
> The Government of Indonesia intends to bring to court any arrestees for whom evidence of law breaking exists. In any event, none of the GOI's actions constitute consistent or gross violations of human rights or are more serious in degree than many similar actions taken in response to temporary threats to public order elsewhere in the Third World. . . .[34]

Subsequently, in a report published in 1979, the US State Department commented as follows on Amnesty International's figures on the number of political prisoners held by the Indonesian government: 'Over the past year the Department of State has carefully reviewed all available information and has found no evidence to support these . . . estimates'.[35]

Clearly Indonesia's recent history well illustrates the nature of the human rights dilemma, and in the next chapter we shall consider the principles by which such a complex matter can be most fruitfully resolved.

'Going Straight'

It has been estimated that the Indonesian government held as many as 200,000 political prisoners immediately after the 1965 attempted coup, but by the following year the total number had been greatly reduced. Releases continued, and in 1974 the government announced that 30,000 prisoners remained;[1] such figures have, as we have seen, been the subject of controversy. It is also true that there have been relatively small numbers of fresh arrests each year. By the end of 1975, the programme of releases had become more systematized; but many thousands of detainees had by then been incarcerated for more than a decade, and several more years were to elapse before the 1965-related programme of releases had run its course.

Meanwhile, each and every prisoner represented an individual human life and a life that had been largely wasted during the long years of detention. The situation was by any reckoning full of pathos. On the other hand, the government had to consider crucial countervailing stability/security factors such as we examined in the previous chapter. The government, referring to millions rather than thousands of its citizens, used its own human rights argument; it contended that the Indonesian Communist Party had in 1965 been 'clearly guilty of violating the basic human rights and fundamental freedoms of the overwhelming majority of the Indonesian people'.[2]

To complicate matters, the internal Communist threat was not merely a thing of the past. For example, it is often forgotten that, as late as 1968, the Army had to launch a full-scale and successful offensive against PKI remnants in East Java. In the assessment of Harold Crouch,

> The vigilance of the army's intelligence and security apparatus and its capacity to mobilize overwhelming armed strength at the first sign of Communist regrouping enabled the government to prevent an open resurgence of the PKI. Nevertheless, the potential base of support for a resurgent, radical movement remained in the rural areas, towns, and cities of Java from which the PKI had drawn its support in the past. . . .[3]

Moreover, government officials have remained acutely aware that the country's evolving ideological and socioeconomic climate could largely determine whether the Communist remnant waxed or waned. In addition, as we shall see, a potential right-wing threat to Indonesia's stability and security

81

could by no means be entirely ruled out.

Significantly, the government has explicitly linked the idea of political detentions and releases with the idea of upholding not only the Constitution of 1945 but also the national ideology known as Pancasila (pronounced as 'Panchasila'). We shall be considering, in Chapter 11, that ideology's distinctive complexion; but for the moment it is sufficient to note that the ideology revolves around five themes or, in the words of an official pronouncement, five 'inseparable and mutually qualifying principles', as follows: belief in the one supreme God, just and civilized humanity, national unity, democracy wisely led by the wisdom of deliberations among representatives, and social justice for the whole Indonesian people.[4]

In, for example, a report on policy in dealing with those detained in connection with the 1965 coup attempt, the government could hardly have been more unambiguous in asserting such a linkage. In the words of the report, the coup attempt 'clearly constituted an armed insurrection aimed at the violent overthrow of the lawful Government and an act of treason against the very philosophical and constitutional bases of the Nation and State, i.e. the Pancasila and the 1945 Constitution'.[5] And this linkage was proclaimed in connection not only with detentions but also with releases.

The government has been in the habit of asking each detainee, at the time of his release, to sign a letter of affirmation pledging good behaviour. Upon his release, that is to say, each detainee is asked to promise that he will 'go straight'. And what, in this context, is the meaning of 'going straight'? The answer is clearly set forth in the text of the letter of affirmation; and understandably that text is riddled with ideological considerations.

In signing the letter, each individual among other things solemnly affirms that he will not engage in any action designed to spread 'Communist/Marxist/Leninist ideology or teaching' in any form or manifestation. He will do nothing that can provoke unrest or impair political stability or national security. He will not betray the people or the government of 'the Republic of Indonesia based on Pancasila (five principles) and the Constitution of 1945'. Finally, he — or she, since the detainees have included some women as well as men — agrees to accept the consequences of any or all actions in violation of the affirmation.[6]

The affirmation is based squarely and unabashedly on the assumption that some ideologies are better than others — not just in general but in terms of Indonesia's particular needs. It assumes that some ideologies harmonize better than others with Indonesian cultural traditions. And it bases that assumption not merely upon abstract analysis but also upon Indonesia's own practical experience over an extended period.

As we saw in Chapter 4, it was a Westerner who brought a Western ideological import — in the shape of Marxism — to Indonesia. For a period of over half a century — from 1914 to 1965 — dedicated Marxists worked unceasingly to make sure that the alien ideology would take root in Indonesia and would flourish there. Their efforts were punctuated by certain overt incidents including the insurrections of 1926, 1948, and 1965. Even after the 1965 debacle, the Communist remnants (including those who had fled abroad) by no means gave up hope or accepted the handwriting on the wall. They had blind faith that the alien plant was somehow bound to grow in the lush Indonesian tropical environment.

In my discussions in Indonesia with released 1965-related political detainees as well as with university students, I have found a keen awareness of the suffering and social disruption caused by Communist efforts to gain power in that country. Far from being ideologically indifferent, or aping the end-of-ideology viewpoint of some tired Western intellectuals, they clearly understand the importance of ideological factors in modern society. Moreover, they recognize that a negative ideological stance is simply not viable; man cannot believe in nothing, and he has to believe in something.

My discussions indicate that religion plays a remarkably important role in the lives of Indonesian released detainees as well as those of many students; and religious faith, as we have seen, constitutes one of the components of the ideology of Pancasila. But at the same time many of the released detainees, having earlier been Marxists themselves and having become disillusioned with the Marxist socioeconomic system, crave another, more attractive secular system and one that can harmonize with religion. Indonesian students, too, have been searching for the elements of a persuasive non-Marxist system.

In 1979, the University of Indonesia published the first Indonesian-language edition of my book entitled *Creative Alternatives to Communism: Guidelines for Tomorrow's World*.[7] The work, which had been translated at Gajah Mada University, was distributed throughout the Indonesian university system and also made available to released detainees and to the general public. The book's wide circulation in Indonesia (in both the Indonesian and English languages) highlighted a striking characteristic of the Indonesian people: their intense interest in ideological questions. Realizing the futility of both ideological apathy on the one hand and negative anti-Communism on the other, they search actively and energetically for fresh alternatives. A further illustration of this keen interest was provided when Indonesia's Ministry of Religion translated my book into Arabic, the University of Indonesia published the Arabic edition, and the product was sent to various countries in the Middle East as one of Indonesia's non-oil exports to that part of the world.

Reference has already been made to the government's linkage of ideological considerations with political detentions and releases, and this is well illustrated by the classification and release arrangements for detainees. As early as 1967 the detainees were classified into three main categories — A, B, and C.[8] Category A consisted of those who were deemed to have been 'clearly and directly involved as planners, leaders or executioners in the attempted coup, with sufficient evidence of their guilt so that their cases could be brought . . . for trial'.

Category B comprised 'those for whom strong indications exist that they played similar roles to those of A-category detainees, especially in the preparations for the attempted coup. Owing to an insufficient amount of evidence . . ., they could not . . . be brought to trail, but neither could they be set free precipitately without endangering national security and stability and their own safety.' Category C included those who were only indirectly involved in the attempted coup and who, 'after investigation established them as neither belonging to the A-category or the B-category, could hence be returned to society'. In practice, most of the Category C people had belonged not to the PKI itself but to various PKI-sponsored mass organiza-

83

tions. There was also a Category X, a temporary classification for detainees who were still being processed to determine whether they belonged in A or B or could be released.[9]

Although the release of political detainees was proceeding very rapidly in 1978 and 1979, questions continued to be raised about the conditions under which the remaining detainees were being held. Fortunately the Geneva-based International Committee of the Red Cross (ICRC), as founded in 1863,[10] has taken a very active interest in this matter. In Indonesia, as in so many other countries, the ICRC has worked impartially and yet in close liaison with the relevant government agencies.

I have met on a number of occasions with those involved in the ICRC investigations in Indonesia, and I have been much impressed with their dedication and their objectivity. They have gone on frequent, far-ranging tours of places of detention in the country, and they have particularly emphasized the idea of repeat visits which have permitted them to make 'then and now' comparisons. From non-ICRC sources I have been able to obtain sample copies of the ICRC's Indonesia reports, which serve to refute some of the wilder allegations about the government's handling of detainees. Typically the reports combine 'Positive Points' observed by the ICRC team with 'Negative Points' indicating needed improvements.

In one such report of an ICRC visit, for example, it was noted that 'the general atmosphere of the prison was much more relaxed' than at the time of the previous visit, and the detainees were happy about the closure of one block which had been in poor condition. The team noted with satisfaction that 'a wide range of Indonesian-language books had been provided in the prison library', and they offered to make an ICRC gift of further such books. They were glad to find that television had been made more available to the detainees, that family visits to detainees could now take place weekly, and that families could bring parcels each week. The team likewise 'appreciated the fact that the detainees had the opportunity not only to grow their own vegetables, but also to rear livestock and poultry'.

On the other hand, the team found that the prison doctor did not make frequent enough visits. They found that certain detainees were in need of medical treatment, and they recommended the immediate release of two detainees on health grounds. They likewise called for a more varied diet for detainees. They reported that 'the few relations between detainees and staff members which existed were formal and polite', but they wanted more informal detainee-staff discussions particularly with a view to assisting the 'approaching reintegration into society' of the detainees.[11]

Earlier there had been allegations that unnecessary restraints had been placed upon detainees after their release, and this matter was commented upon as follows by Amnesty International in its October 1978 supplement to its 1977 report on Indonesia:

> . . . It has become clear that prisoners released in December 1977 and in the course of 1978 have not been subjected to restrictions of house or town arrest as were detainees released in 1975 and 1976. This is a most welcome step. Amnesty International is also satisfied that the Indonesian Government has significantly scaled down its resettlement program and it is estimated that of the 10,000 prisoners released in December 1977, only a

few hundred were resettled. . . .[12]

Amnesty International contended, however, that there had been a few cases of forced resettlement in certain of the outer islands; and one may surmise that this might have taken place without the knowledge of the authorities in Jakarta, who would, it may be hoped, appreciate Amnesty International's bringing the matter to their attention.

When one recalls all the human suffering that has over the years stemmed from the 1965 attempted Communist coup, one might be tempted to assume that it is only left-wing groups which pose a potential threat to Indonesia's stability and security. But nothing could be farther from the truth, as my discussions with responsible Indonesians confirm. Interestingly, it is from Islamic public servants, scholars and students that one often hears the sharpest warnings about the danger of Islamic extremism; and devout Islamic students have told me with real vehemence that various fanatics use Islam as a smoke-screen to hide their political designs.

According to former American ambassador Howard Palfrey Jones, Sukarno once told him that there were two political elements that were seeking to destroy Indonesia's ideology of Pancasila: the fanatical Muslims and the Communists.[13] Jones adds that it was the Muslim fanatics who were responsible for most of the attempts on Sukarno's life; and Sukarno, in his autobiography, in effect confirms this.[14] The reference is of course to the militant Darul Islam movement, which was active especially in West Java,

Surrendered Fretilin guerrillas with, centre, *an Indonesian army colonel and,* left, *a Dutch television man*

North Sumatra, and southwest Sulawesi and which aimed at the creation of a theocratic Muslim state. Operating mainly in the 1950s and 1960s, the movement caused many casualties and much economic disruption before the Army suppressed it.[15]

More recently a so-called Jihad Command movement has attempted to

follow in the footsteps of Darul Islam. Acting on a much smaller scale than its predecessor, it has perpetrated various acts of sabotage and violence. In 1979, the then national leader of the Jihad Command was shot dead while resisting arrest. Again in 1979, a number of other Jihad Command leaders were convicted by the courts and sentenced to long terms of imprisonment. One of the charges against these defendants was that they had been seeking money and arms from Libya to support their scheme to overthrow the government.[16]

My discussions with diplomats from neighbouring Southeast Asian countries make clear that Libya has been aiding far-right Islamic insurgency movements in the Philippines and in Malaysia. The so-called Iranian Revolution of 1978-79 has likewise furnished certain Islamic fundamentalists in Indonesia with grist for their mills; in Iran, they have argued, the Shah's powerful army collapsed in the face of a determined drive for the creation of an Islamic state — so why not stage a repeat in Indonesia? It is well worth studying the reasons for the turmoil that came to Iran; but for the moment it is sufficient to note that the vast majority of Indonesians have no desire whatever to repeat the Iranian experiment.

Although exact figures are hard to come by, it appears that in the last few years the number of right-wing political detainees in Indonesia has fluctuated around the level of several hundred at any one time. With these detainees, just as with the left-wing ones, it is essential that they receive help in reintegrating themselves into society. In 1979, Admiral Sudomo, as Commander-in-Chief of the Operational Command for the Restoration of Security and Order and Vice Commander-in-Chief of the Armed Forces of Indonesia — and therefore very much in the centre of planning for national stability and security — emphasized the importance of adequate employment opportunities for released detainees.[17] Unemployment among them, he indicated, might well tempt them to resort to acts contrary to law.

The statement throws further light on the problem of motivating former Marxists — or former right-wing militants — to 'go straight' in the Indonesian context. Moreover, a close interrelationship clearly exists among the four factors — population, food, jobs, and exports — which we examined in Chapter 6. In addition, released detainees must be able to seek and to find adequate answers to their underlying ideological questions such as: 'If not Communism, then what?' 'If not direct militant Islamic action, then what?'

Another issue with important ideological as well as human rights implications concerns East Timor – known to Indonesians as Timor Timur or simply as Tim Tim. At the end of 1979 I paid a visit to Tim Tim, and it was a real revelation. I urge as many readers as possible to visit there, and it will be a revelation to them too. Although a great tragedy had previously overtaken East Timor, by the end of the 1970s the healing process in that former Portuguese colony had progressed to a remarkable degree.

By the beginning of 1980, a general election in Portugal had led to a centre-right government there. If such a government had succeeded Portugal's Caetano regime after the latter was overturned by a coup in 1974, the subsequent carnage in East Timor would very probably have been averted. In the event, a leftist government initially took control in Portugal, and the repercussions were soon felt in Angola, Mozambique, and other Portuguese possessions including East Timor. Out from Lisbon went leftist administrators who sought to combine decolonization with the installation of Marxist or quasi-Marxist regimes as part of the so-called liberation process. In East Timor they fostered the formation of the leftist/nationalist Fretilin (Frente Revolucionaria da Timor-Leste Independente) organization, whose leadership included former Timorese students who had picked up Marxist ideas in Portugal. The leftist administrators moreover supplied Fretilin with arms which had mostly been derived from NATO sources.

A bloody struggle erupted between Fretilin and the other more moderate groups contending for power. Fretilin tried to intimidate the population and unfortunately resorted to tactics including the shooting or hacking to death of many prisoners of war, whose trussed-up bodies were later discovered in mass graves by the Indonesian Red Cross.[18] One of those so butchered was a brother of the present Vice Governor.

It is important to realize that this internecine carnage had begun many months *before* Indonesian forces invaded Tim Tim in December 1975. After about a month of heavy fighting, the Indonesians and their Timorese allies had gained control of Dili and other key population centres, and they fanned out from there. As sporadic guerrilla actions continued, a pro-Indonesian provisional government was formed, and on 17 July 1976 the Indonesian parliament approved a petition to have Tim Tim incorporated into Indonesia as her twenty-seventh province.

The war had disrupted agriculture, created large numbers of refugees, and caused vast human suffering. Preoccupied as they were with anti-guerrilla operations, the Indonesian authorities belatedly gave approval for massive relief measures to be launched by the CRS (Catholic Relief Services) and the ICRC (International Committee of the Red Cross) in co-operation with the Indonesian Red Cross; and only toward the end of 1979 was the combined relief programme finally in full swing. The self-styled Fretilin 'President' had meanwhile been killed in an anti-guerrilla sweep, more and more of the guerrillas had surrendered leaving only a few remaining in the hills, and virtually the entire province had become safe for routine civilian travel.

The Indonesian government has accorded special development priority to Tim Tim, and one sees fresh development projects on every hand. Surrendered Fretilin members and their families have been very rapidly re-assimilated into the society. With connecting airliner flights from Jakarta to Dili six days per week, with excellent radiotelephone and telex services, and with superb television reception via satellite, the capital of Indonesia's youngest province is very much in touch with that of the nation. The Jakarta authorities should take vigorous action to streamline procedures so that more and more tourists, businessmen, diplomats and others can visit spectacularly beautiful Tim Tim, see with their own eyes, and draw their own conclusions.

In retrospect it has become clear that both the Australian and United States governments gave tacit approval to Indonesia's invasion of Tim Tim. All three governments feared the creation of an 'Asian Cuba' which could have served as a base for outside Communist powers and could have brought danger to the whole area. It is impossible to understand the East Timor issue of the 1970s without considering its ideological and strategic context.

Thus we are brought back again to such fundamental ideological questions as those mentioned above: 'If not Communism, then what?' 'If not direct militant Islamic action, then what?' The second question we shall discuss in the next chapter in terms of certain fundamental mistakes made in Iran. The first question can receive attention now in terms of a brief consideration of some of the ideological facts of life worldwide. To a remarkable extent, in my experience, both educated and nominally uneducated Indonesians keep in touch, through the media and otherwise, with the world outside. They show continuing curiosity about events and tendencies in other countries — the USSR, the PRC, India, Iran, or wherever — and they remain on the lookout for lessons that might be drawn from such countries. With great animation they discuss errors that other countries have fallen into as well as successes which they have achieved and which might have application in the Indonesian context. Especially to young Indonesians, cultural integrity never implies cultural isolation.

As we found in the preceding chapter, the major Communist countries have made a shambles of such human rights as those enshrined in the Universal Declaration. On the one hand this defective performance represents a profoundly disturbing practical or empirical phenomenon; but on the other hand — and of the utmost importance — it stands as a symptom of the inadequacy of Marxist doctrine. Western scholars, even after they have been repeatedly alerted to the pragmatic shortcomings of Marxist practice, have typically been much too slow in waking up to the vulnerabilities of the underlying Marxist theory itself.

A brilliant thinker, Marx was nevertheless a child of his time. Writing as he did mainly in 19th-century England where the initial Industrial Revolution chiefly took place, Marx was aware of the dramatic advances in science and technology that were under way there; and he chose to interpret them in a particular way. As he saw it, technological development leads to production units of ever-increasing size, technological imperatives bring together ever larger masses of workers and require ever larger amounts of capital per unit of labour, and finally only the community at large is capable of providing the organizational framework for modern production.

A key concept for Marx was that of the productive forces, which he defined as including working people, means of production, and raw materials.[19] According to him, an inevitable state of strain arises between the productive forces and the 'capitalist integument' which provides the institutional framework for production; and only a comprehensive socialist solution can resolve the strain. But in actual practice in today's Communist world, wholesale socialization has by no means eliminated the tension between the productive forces and the social organization. To the contrary, the state of strain refuses to go away. In the Communist world, a crisis in political and socioeconomic doctrine is at hand.

In short, contemporary Marxism fails to resolve the dilemma of the relations between human rights, the powerful productive forces released by modern science and technology, and the social organization. Resolving this dilemma will require responses which are radically new, even revolutionary; and, as we shall see later in this book, these responses will come from sources other than Marxism.

Meanwhile, a transformation has for several decades been under way in non-Marxist economic practice. This process of change has long since taken place even in that supposed bastion of capitalism, the United States of America. Even there, as Paul A. Samuelson has described it,

> the scene was drastically changed: almost unconsciously ours had become a mixed economy with both private and public initiative and control. The clock of history, sometimes, evolves so slowly that its moving hands are never *seen* to move. After the New Deal, American economic life was permanently changed. We had converged with Western Europe to the mixed economy.[20]

The transformation has indeed spread to virtually all of the non-Communist world. The international mixed economy has arrived, and the so-called socialist countries are themselves increasingly enmeshed in it.

This leads us straight to the global doctrine of the class struggle, which is so central to Marxist theory. As Marx and Engels expressed it in *The Communist Manifesto*, 'The history of all hitherto existing society . . . is the history of class struggles'.[21] Marx linked the class struggle concept with that of the above-mentioned productive forces; as he saw it, when — typically through technological change in the means of production — the productive forces become out of alignment with the social structure, the class struggle automatically ensues. It is the class struggle which powers social change.

But upon analysis the famous class struggle concept turns out to be *not a primary but a merely subsidiary or derivative concept*. It is subsidiary to the mode of evolution of the productive forces. Marx and his followers have indeed failed to grasp this cardinal principle. They have likewise failed to understand how — for example, at Indonesia's renowned Bandung Institute of Technology — those forces can be constructively re-shaped through scientific and engineering research and development.

The increasing vulnerability of Marxist doctrine has not gone unnoticed even inside the Soviet Union. In an historic development in the early 1970s, Andrei Sakharov,[22] Alexander Solzhenitsyn,[23] and other leading Soviet intellectuals publicly castigated the Marxist ideology as such. Solzhenitsyn likewise condemned the ideology as an alien import superimposed upon traditional Russian culture.

Sakharov provided a scathing indictment of Marxism as applied in the Soviet Union. He referred to the continuing claim that the Soviet political and economic system furnishes 'the prototype for all other countries: the most just, humane, and progressive system. . . . The more obvious the complete failure to live up to most of the promises in that dogma, the more insistently it is maintained. . . .'[24] And among other things he pointed to the destructive consequences of the State-Party monopoly in the sphere of culture and ideology. 'The complete unification of ideology at all times and places . . . demands that people become hypocrites, timeservers, mediocre, and stupidly self-deceiving. . . .'[25]

These are critiques of a marathon experiment — already lasting for more than 60 years and punctuated by vast human suffering — in what is correctly called the first major Marxist state. Perhaps it is not surprising that, in spite of its enormous arable land area in comparison with its population, the Soviet Union has still not solved its food problem and must go on importing foodgrains from the United States and other countries. And perhaps it is not surprising that, after more than six solid decades of concerted effort including much persecution, the godless Soviet regime has failed to extinguish the religious faith of the Russian people.

Reference was made in the last chapter to the final article of the Universal Declaration of Human Rights, which denies anybody the right 'to engage in any activity or to perform any act aimed at the destruction of any of the rights and freedoms set forth herein'. Many non-Marxist countries face the problem of Marxists who would exploit freedom in order to destroy freedom. In the Soviet Union and other Marxist states, by contrast, one finds future-conscious men and women who bravely call for the replacement of an ideology which they regard as an enemy of spiritual values and of human rights. Both in presently-Marxist countries and in others as well, we may hope that the power of fresh and good ideas will in due course prevail. Clearly it is the youth who will largely determine the outcome.

The Youth Challenge

Indonesia owes a great debt of gratitude to her students, past and present. Students of the so-called Generation of '45 helped Indonesia to win her independence. Students of what is styled the Generation of '66 aided in the defeat of the Communists and the coming into being of the New Order. Students of the 1970s and 1980s have been or will be preparing to play their role in Indonesia's national development.

Equally the indebtedness runs the other way. It is the New Order government which has been responsible for the massive expansion since 1966 of Indonesia's educational facilities at all levels. It is that same government which has planned and executed the bold and largely successful programmes of general national development symbolized by Repelita I and II. And if the government's development efforts require a substantial change of direction in the 1980s, then the students can be expected to help bring this about.

As already indicated in Chapter 6, Indonesia is a remarkably 'young' country; that is to say, a very large proportion of her population — much more than in Western countries — comprises young people, and these members of the youth sector in turn need much schooling and many jobs. It is widely recognized that the pre-school years, and the early years of schooling, are vitally important in moulding children's character; and according to Slamet Santosa,[1] one of Indonesia's best-known educational philosophers, the country's youngsters in general spend far too much time learning by rote and receive not nearly enough help in developing their creative thinking. High school and university instruction must perforce build upon the foundations that have previously been laid.

In spite of the importance of pre-school, elementary, and secondary education in the Indonesian context, our main focus here is on higher education (including teachers' and technical colleges) and on the university-level students in particular. As we saw in Chapter 1, Sukarno had been such a student — at the Dutch-founded Bandung Technical College, now the renowned Bandung Institute of Technology. It is significant that in the early 1920s, when Sukarno was studying there for his degree in civil engineering and architecture, that institution had already become a centre of student activism;[2] and up to the present day it has never lost its reputation for political as well as technological activity. For some six decades, that is to say, ITB (as it is now affectionately known in Indonesian)

Volleyball

has symbolized the interaction between Indonesia's student elite and her political system. The role of ITB has underlined the importance both of technology to politics and of students as agents of change.

To an extent then unprecedented in Indonesia, the student elite made its presence felt in the mid-1960s. As Stephen A. Douglas has expressed it, 'students, branding themselves the "Generation of 1966", seized upon every available avenue of political expression, including the streets in a literal sense, and forged for themselves a decisive role in the politics of that period'.[3] On 5 October 1965, almost immediately after the attempted coup, what Douglas calls 'the first spark of explosion' occurred when the Islamic Students' Association (HMI) staged a rally to demand that Sukarno should ban the PKI. HMI and other students likewise demolished the headquarters of the PKI and the home of D.N. Aidit, its secretary.[4]

It was later in that same month that KAMI, the Indonesian University Students' Action Front already mentioned in Chapter 5, was established with Army encouragement for the purpose of opposing leftist student and other organizations. Tension steadily mounted between left-wing students and their KAMI counterparts, and on 28 February 1966 a serious confrontation occurred. After Sukarno and Subandrio, his Foreign Minister, had delivered inflammatory addresses to a crowd of some 15,000 leftist students, many of the latter 'descended upon the University of Indonesia campus with the obvious aim of demolishing the headquarters of KAMI. They were turned back by a contingent of troops from the Jakarta military garrison. . . .' The incident was decisive because the then-powerful leftists realised that they could not match the strength of the moderate students plus the Army.[5]

As one high-ranking officer in a cabinet position was to tell me much later, 'Without the students you can do nothing; with the students and the Army you can do anything'.[6] From the abortive Communist coup onward, the nature of student-army relations has constituted a crucial determinant of Indonesia's stability and security. Some people say, only half-jokingly, that in Indonesia there are but two political parties — the students and the Army. Indonesians have a charmingly whimsical sense of humour, but the message is clear: it is the student elite who will largely determine the shape of their country's future.

On 10 January 1966, even before the above-mentioned decisive incident, KAMI leaders had at a mass student rally put forward their famous Three Demands of the People: dissolution of the PKI, formation of a new cabinet minus Sukarno, and reduction of prices.[7] This formulation suggested that the students were by no means interested only in power and influence, but also in programmatic considerations as such. My more recent discussions with many Indonesian university students certainly bear this out. A further illustration was provided by KAMI's organizing, especially in 1966, seminars convened for the purpose of promoting serious discussion of problems of national development. Military men as well as journalists and academic people were invited to the seminars, which thus also facilitated still closer liaison between the students and the Army.

Meanwhile, however, Sukarno was trying to reassert his authority. Knowing that they would support him, he moved toward releasing many of the PKI adherents who had been detained following the attempted coup; and on 21 February 1966 he announced a cabinet reshuffle which included the dismissal of General Nasution and other staunch opponents of the PKI.[8] The students reacted in various ways. On 23 February, in central Jakarta, 'KAMI students went to the State Secretariat behind the president's palace, broke into the building, smashed windows, and threw furniture into the street'. Sukarno's palace guard opened fire and wounded some of the students. On the following day, as Sukarno attempted to convene his reshuffled cabinet at the Presidential Palace and students tried to prevent the ministers from arriving, the palace guard again opened fire, killing a university medical student and a girl high school student.[9] But the students, completely undeterred, hounded Sukarno until he was effectively ejected from office. They felt that they were acting in the national interest.

It has been my privilege to meet with many students in Bandung, Jakarta, Yogyakarta, Medan, and other Indonesian academic centres. I have met with government-aligned 'establishment' students, with Islamic students, with Christian students, with so-called independent students; and in my suggestive and stimulating discussions with the students two characteristics have become especially apparent. One is that the overwhelming majority of the students are by Western standards moderate in outlook. The second is that they are deeply interested in public affairs. Notably absent is the political apathy which one has in recent years encountered on so many Western campuses; and the Indonesian students' concern reflects an awareness that in their country politics can so directly and immediately affect both their own and the nation's futures.

Indonesia's 20th-century tradition of overt student political involvement by no means ended in 1966. 'Beginning in 1967', as Harold Crouch points out, 'students and a section of the press increasingly took up the issue of "corruption", which they thought threatened the achievement of the New Order's stated goals.' Early in 1970 — almost exactly four years after the student acts that had so largely paved the way to Sukarno's final downfall — the students mounted large demonstrations against sudden increases in the domestic prices of oil products. The same year brought further student activism directed against alleged corruption in high places.[10] According to Crouch,

> In their approach to the 'corruption' issue, the government and its critics were talking about different matters. . . . In the long run, the government argued, when economic development leads to higher living standards, civil servants will receive adequate incomes and no longer need to be corrupt. On the other hand, the government's critics argued that . . ., if high-level corruption were permitted to continue unhindered, the nation would never reach the level of economic development that would permit low-level officials to live on their salaries.[11]

In the assessment of R. William Liddle, 'Student dissatisfaction with government policies and personnel has been a regular feature of New Order politics'.[12] This is well illustrated by what he calls the 'next cycle of protests, which began in October 1973 and ended in violence in January 1974. . .'.[13] Students at a number of Indonesia's academic centres issued a string of petitions and statements concerning alleged corruption, alleged failure of the development programme to do justice to the rural sector, favouritism allegedly shown to certain Chinese businessmen and foreign investors including the Japanese, and other issues. Tension steadily mounted, and on 14 January 1974 the situation erupted on the occasion of Japanese Prime Minister Tanaka's arrival in Jakarta on an official visit. 'Student demonstrators opposing Japan's role in the Indonesian economy were joined by the Jakarta poor, mobs roamed the streets, and incidents of burning and looting occurred in widely separated sections of the city during the next two days. . . .'[14]

Further demonstrations and violence were to occur in late 1977 and early 1978 in the run-up to President Soeharto's re-election, on 23 March 1978, for a further five-year term. It was in January 1978 that students at Bandung Institute of Technology published their so-called *White Book of the 1978 Students' Struggle*; it was banned in Indonesia but duly published in English in the United States.[15] Contrary to widespread popular assumptions about it, the book (actually it was a small pamphlet) by no means confined itself to criticizing certain government leaders as such; the student authors also dealt with development strategy. According to them, 'a development strategy oriented solely towards increasing GNP is a *stunted* strategy'.[16] With much use of italics they claimed that the 'widening abyss between the rich and the poor is a grave danger. *It invites the resurgence of communism in our country!*' Among other things the students demanded equal justice for all, an end to corruption, and the wiping out of what they called the 'consumer-oriented way of life'.[17]

The government reacted by arresting a number of student leaders and temporarily closing down various newspapers. Most of the newspapers soon resumed publication and within a few months nearly all of the students had been released — some pending trial on such charges as insulting the head of state. Previously-detained students with whom I have talked have agreed that they were well treated in prison; some have indeed complained that they were *too* well treated in that they received various privileges denied to their fellow prisoners who were not accredited members of the student elite.

It is perhaps understandable that government officials should be annoyed by such student activities as the foregoing; yet those who complain about today's students are in many cases themselves veterans of the Generation of '45 or '66 with their own proud records of student militancy. I have often joked with them about this generation-gap paradox; and usually they have generously and genially agreed upon the wisdom of paying close attention to what today's students are actually striving for. Later in this chapter we shall consider the question of how best to respond to student demands; but first it is pertinent to ponder a cautionary tale provided by events in Iran.

Although analogies are never exact, it is not surprising that thoughtful Indonesian leaders have been much preoccupied with the dramatic developments in another largely Islamic country culminating in the so-called Iranian Revolution of 1978-79. It is often forgotten that Shah Mohammed Reza Pahlavi had long been recognized as a very devout Muslim and that the Ayatollah Khomeini could scarcely claim superiority in this respect. It is likewise frequently overlooked that as early as the mid-1950s — when I first became well acquainted with that country — Iran was already experiencing student demonstrations and violent riots arising from the interaction of the security forces and the student elite. Moreover, it was no accident that, as the turmoil in Iran deepened toward the end of 1978 and in the beginning of 1979, the riot scenes, as witnessed by millions of television viewers in the West — and in Indonesia — so often showed Iranian campuses as their locale. Just as in earlier decades, it was the students who largely spearheaded the demonstrations and figured in the ensuing violence.

It is true that in Iran there was considerable corruption, which reached even to certain of the Shah's close relatives. It is likewise true that some political prisoners received torture that was thoroughly cruel, inhumane, and unjustified no matter the nature of their offences; in reporting on Iran in 1978, however, Amnesty International indicated that such torture appeared to be on the decrease.[18] Although the prevalence of corruption and the use of torture may be regarded as symbolizing two important kinds of policy defects under the Shah's regime, in my judgement two other kinds of defects contributed much more to bringing on the revolution.

One of these fundamental policy mistakes concerned economic growth. The Shah's father, Reza Shah, had done much to transform Iran into a modern state, and his son was determined to follow in his father's footsteps. He had a profound conviction that only through rapid economic growth could modern amenities be put within the reach of the people at large, and he worked day and night in his zeal to achieve such growth. In successive years Iran did in fact attain some of the highest growth rates in the world; and then, in the early 1970s came the quadrupling of world oil prices which seemed to the Shah to offer a great windfall opportunity. As Robert Graham points out, Iran's then current Five-Year Plan (1973-78) was thus accelerated in an effort still further to step up the developmental pace.[19]

Under such pressure, existing logistical and other bottlenecks worsened and fresh ones appeared; but that was not the main point. The Shah and his economic advisors had tragically failed to take into proper consideration *the cultural side-effects* of rapid economic growth. The cultural problem, already serious before the acceleration, became even worse after it. Big Western-style capital-intensive projects had been largely favoured, and increasingly the ordinary Iranian felt like a bystander in his own country — all the more so as he saw the technocrats and *nouveau-riche* entrepreneurs arrogantly rushing about in their expensive cars. Western films and the uncritical emulation of Western ways, particularly by the young, proved deeply disturbing to Iranians who cherished the values of their own traditional culture.

The fourth major policy mistake was if anything more serious than the third one. The Shah was thoroughly devoted to modern education, and with a truly religious fervour he wanted to bring it to all of his people. He rapidly expanded elementary education, he organized a pioneering Literacy Corps under which soldiers went to teach in the villages, and he lavished countless millions of dollars on building up the high schools, technical schools and colleges, and universities. His particular pride was the universities, and he expanded the existing campuses and spared no expense in building and equipping beautiful new ones on the most modern lines — including Pahlavi University, named after his family and situated in the exquisite city of Shiraz. Moreover, the Shah sent more students for training abroad than did any other Middle Eastern leader.

Tragically, however, the Shah and his advisers lost touch with the students. If the pace of economic growth accelerated, so did that of student demonstrations and riots; and Pahlavi University was among the favourite settings for such turmoil. University curricula, while designed to bring the youth as rapidly as possible into the modern age, seemed out of joint with Iranian traditions. The appearance and behaviour of some of the girl students deeply offended religious sensibilities. Many of the students who went abroad received superb Western training in medicine or engineering or whatever; but often they would return home with a supercargo in the shape of Marxist ideas — sometimes strangely blended with their religious tradition, in other cases supplanting it. In many instances they did not return at all but instead became professional militants who mounted propaganda from abroad against the 'reactionary' Shah and his government.

The sequel abounds in irony. Western observers showed remarkably little awareness of the nature, extent, and intensity of the real reaction that was in the making. Thus Graham, whose book was published in 1978, says of those in Iran 'who wish change, the majority merely want observance of the Constitution — not an end to the Shah. . .'.[20] It is true that Graham in passing mentions Khomeini, and it is true that in such passages as the following Graham recognizes, in a rather roundabout way, the importance of the religious factor: '. . . Revolutionary change could not be brought about without the backing of the religious community. . . . Religious dissent, of all forms of protest, has consistently proved the hardest to handle. . . .'[21] But nowhere in his book does one find any real indication of the handwriting that was on the wall.

The point emerges even more clearly from Fred Halliday's widely-circulated book on Iran, as published in 1979. According to his assessment, 'religious leaders such as Ayatollah Khomeini and his sympathizers in Iran offer an ill-defined, ambiguous, alternative to the Shah'.[22] He does concede, however, that 'the currents of opposition that phrase their hostility to the Shah in religious terms still have considerable powers of attraction. . .'.[23]

But if such Western observers were surprised and perhaps dismayed by the actual outcome, this applied even more forcibly to Iran's student elite. For all of the country's durable and pervasive culture, her student elite had — just as in the case of Indonesia — developed into a very cosmopolitan group. There is every reason to believe that many or most of the students — and the educated people generally — were both startled and appalled to see their country initially taken over by a far-right religious clique who were for that matter by no means representative of Iran's Islamic clergy as a whole.[24] The idea of a rigidly traditionalist Islamic state, of somewhat gruesome so-called people's courts, and of reversion to a starkly inward-looking cultural stance no doubt filled many of the students with horror. Yet it was the students themselves who had been largely responsible for bringing all this about. Meanwhile, of course, the Marxists waited in the wings.

Clearly Indonesia's student elite, just as much as her government leaders, can draw valuable lessons from Iran; and as one reflective Iranian said to me in Jakarta, 'We hope that Indonesia will learn from our mistakes'. According to Crouch, 'If past experience is a guide, militant Islam in the regions outside Java may represent a greater short-term threat to the government than Communist-led revolutionary movements based in Java'.[25] In my experience the vast majority of Indonesia's students wish for their country to follow a moderate middle way which avoids the extremes of either the right or the left. This indeed requires the students to help their government to avoid mistakes such as occurred in Iran.

In my extensive discussions with a diversity of Indonesian students, I have found five major problems which especially concern them. In the first place, they nearly always mention alleged corruption, especially in high places; they want it to be eliminated wherever it exists, and they want it to be *seen* to be eliminated. Secondly, they are concerned about what they regard as unbalanced development, in terms both of capital-intensive as against labour-intensive projects and of the urban as against the rural sector. Thirdly, they worry about jobs, not only in personal terms but also because of the vast number of new jobs required for Indonesia's youth in general.

Fourthly — and fundamental to the students' thinking — they are concerned about the cultural side-effects of economic growth. Finally, they feel deep frustration about what they regard as a lack of adequate mechanisms and channels for communicating with the government. The students want a sense of participation in *shaping* policies for national development as well as in carrying them out. This fifth point the students indeed regard as the most important of all, for they feel that action on all the others depends upon it. Just as members of the Generations of '45 and '66 assumed crucial roles in shaping the destinies of the nation, so today's students desire to do likewise. In effect they are saying that they want to avoid the tragedy of Iran, where the student elite became cut off and alienated from the government and head of state.

In my work with students in a number of countries, I have employed a particular approach which has met with an excellent response — in Indonesia as well as elsewhere. You would do well, I suggest to the students, to identify your own career planning with the needs of the national development programme. By equipping yourselves to play your own full roles in national development, you can help both yourselves and your country. Thus you can make your lives more interesting and more rewarding too. This approach can be applied among young people of diverse age groups; for example, those enrolled in Indonesia's vigorous Scout movement can be mobilized to help make appropriate technology available in the villages. Students in the higher educational sector can equally well be mobilized.

It was in this spirit that I met with the Rector of one of Indonesia's leading universities and put a proposal to him. What would he think, I asked him, if several of his students — perhaps one in economics, one in engineering, and one in sociology — came to him and said that they were forming a small interdisciplinary group to discuss problems of regional and national development. The Rector told me that he would have no objection to such an idea. But what would he think, I persisted, if the interdisciplinary group grew into a modest development centre and the students began to issue brief papers setting forth their constructive developmental ideas. 'That would be all right', replied the Rector, 'so long as the students did not take to the streets.' He even went so far as to say that he would be happy to have such interdisciplinary development centres on all of the country's campuses.

Indonesia's academic establishment has made major contributions to the national welfare. Its faculty members have served as government officials and advisers, it has trained many students who have moved into highly responsible positions, and it has conducted research of great value to the nation. Nevertheless, in Indonesia, as Soedjatmoko has remarked, 'there is a general consensus that higher education should adjust itself more effectively to the development problems of the country. . .'.[26] To put the matter more bluntly, Indonesia's higher education establishment has simply not been pulling its weight in terms of national development.

Let one hasten to add, however, that this problem is by no means unique to Indonesia. Indeed, such shortfalls tend to be the rule rather than the exception — in so-called developed as well as in developing countries. The problem is in fact very largely structural in nature. Mainly in obedience to Western precedents, universities nearly everywhere have been chopped up into faculties or their equivalent, departments within them, and narrow specialities within departments. Increasingly scholars, as the saying goes, know more and more about less and less. Such structural compartmentalization has meant that effective academic interdisciplinary programmes — encompassing the natural sciences and engineering as well as a broad spread of social sciences and cultural subjects — have been few and far between. Thus has academia's powerful potential support to comprehensive national development been severely impaired.

When a country faces a problem of student militancy such as described earlier in this chapter, some academic and government authorities are sure

University students

to call for taking a tough, no-nonsense line with the students. Firm discipline, they are likely to say, must have priority if the campuses are not to become a political arena and if scholarly pursuits are not to be neglected. Other authorities, taking a somewhat different line, will say that we must establish an on-going dialogue with the students and demonstrate a willingness of negotiate with them on any or all of their grievances. In my experience, *both* of these approaches, or any combination of them, are inadequate and unsatisfactory. Members of the student elite do not take kindly to negative restrictions placed upon them, and typically they find ongoing academic dialogues both dull and pointless.

In order to deal effectively with perceptive students and to win their support, a different strategy is in my judgement required. One must leapfrog over the subject of imposing restrictions and restraints, and over the subject of dialogues on current grievances, and reach the higher plane of student mobilization for tackling the country's big regional and national problems. Every campus must develop its interdisciplinary centre where students can focus their energies — both for career training and for practical patriotic service.

It is *on this higher plane* that government and academic leaders should then engage in continuous fruitful interaction with the students. It is in this way that the leaders can call forth in today's students the same spirit which animated those of the Generations of '45 and '66. And the interaction between the national leaders of today and those of tomorrow can bring mutual enlightenment.

10

Transmigration
and Transformation

During the Second World War, Vannevar Bush, the eminent American engineer, wrote a report with the memorable title *Science, the Endless Frontier*.[1] In the present chapter we consider two aspects of Indonesia's far-ranging frontiers — that suggested by the vast reaches of her outer islands, and that symbolized by technology developed and applied in response to social needs. We shall find that these two aspects are, in important and suggestive ways, intimately related to each other.

Indonesia's official transmigration programmes date from as early as 1905, when the Dutch established a resettlement colony in southern Sumatra.[2] Transmigration, in this official sense, may be viewed as the planned and guided movement of population from densely-populated Java (and neighbouring Madura, Bali, and Lombok) to the more sparsely-populated outer islands.[3] In the decades leading up to World War II, the Dutch made further sporadic attempts to sponsor such migration, but these were on a small scale and on the whole unsuccessful. The war put a stop to all such efforts; but after the retreat of the Japanese and Indonesia's Declaration of Independence, the Sukarno regime tried to launch its own transmigration programmes. The results were generally meagre.

On paper the New Order government gave transmigration an important place in its First Five-Year Development plan, as inaugurated in 1969; but again the results were disappointing.[4] The same was very much the case under the Second Five-Year Plan, which took effect in 1974; 250,000 families were supposed to be moved under official sponsorship during the plan period, but in practice only about a third of the target figure was attained.[5] The Third Five-Year Plan, effective from 1979, adopted a much more ambitious target, calling for the moving of 500,000 families or approximately 2,500,000 people.[6] The World Bank had earlier pledged in principle to give massive support to the transmigration programme, and in 1979 it reaffirmed this pledge to the tune of one billion dollars.[7]

After more than seven decades of experience with transmigration programmes in Indonesia, a number of valuable lessons have been learned by thoughtful observers — lessons which can greatly assist in bringing more success to future efforts. For example, it has become clear that the ecological plight of Java can no longer be safely neglected. According to M.J. Gauchon, 'Soil erosion in Java is one of the world's most outstanding ecological problems and offers the most frightening prospects for the coming decades. . .'. In his assessment, the 'main cause of erosion is the intense and rapidly increasing population pressure on the land', and the physical results of this erosion include declining soil fertility and productivity, increasing magnitude and frequency of floods, and the silting up of rivers, irrigation canals, reservoirs and lowlands.[8] Nowadays one finds general agreement that the main cure for Java's population pressure must lie with family planning, as discussed in Chapter 6; yet it is likewise agreed that vigorous transmigration programmes can to some degree help to ameliorate the problem.

Opinion in Indonesia has likewise moved toward a recognition that transmigration programmes must be viewed in their larger regional and national context. As one report aptly puts it, 'the concept of transmigration projects as isolated undertakings is no longer in keeping with the objectives of national development strategy'.[9] Moreover, experience over the years has finally brought a far broader awareness of the kinds of economic activities which can best be carried on by the migrants.

Earlier there was a natural tendency to assume that cultivators of irrigated rice in Java would, once transmigrated, again be cultivating irrigated rice; but now this is seen as a gross oversimplification. For one thing, while Java possesses some of the richest soils in the world, the outer islands generally lack such soils, and growing conditions on the outer islands are on the whole considerably less favourable than on Java.[10] On the other hand, as Alan M. Strout points out, the outer island soils, or at least those which have been exploited to date, 'may not be greatly below a world-wide average with respect to inherent productivity'.[11] With ecologically-sound cultural practices together with modest amounts of fertilizer, there seems no reason why the outer islands should not produce vast quantities of produce both for domestic consumption and for export.

Conditions in the outer islands in general encourage more agricultural diversification than has been prevalent on Java. Apart from irrigated rice, upland rice,[12] soy beans, mung beans, peanuts, corn, and sorghum are among the field crops that can thrive in many parts of the outer islands.[13] Plantations likewise offer tremendous scope for the future for producing such valuable crops as rubber, palm oil and palm kernel oil, and coconut in the outer islands. For example, in North Sumatra I drove for what seemed like hours within the borders of a single huge plantation; and I toured the plantation's own rubber factory and its factory for producing both palm oil and the associated palm kernel oil with their variety of uses for margarine, soap, cooking oil, cosmetics, special lubricating oils, and other purposes.[14] Transmigration projects can provide the labour needed on such plantations; individual migrants can likewise grow plantation crops on a smallholder basis; and the two concepts can be combined with so-called nucleus estates which provide job opportunities for migrants and also process the crops grown on nearby migrant smallholdings.

Even with irrigated rice — that mainstay of Java's traditional agriculture — thinking has been changing fast with respect to the outer islands. In off-the-record discussions, two ministers have told me flatly that Indonesia can never overcome her perennial rice deficits through traditional intensive rice farming alone and that she must turn to extensive outer-island rice estates as

An oil palm nursery

a supplement. They believe that, without doing too much violence to the need for labour-intensive techniques in Indonesia's agriculture as a whole, she can for this purpose borrow from the mechanized techniques employed by a major rice exporter in the shape of the United States.

Notwithstanding the importance of the agricultural sector to successful transmigration and outer-island development, experience over the decades has shown that too much reliance must not be placed upon that sector alone. Thinking has now moved much more toward the concept of growth centres which may take any of a variety of forms. The government can, for example, link transmigration project planning with that for new manufacturing or timber-extraction or mining projects in the outer islands. Moreover, the government can give its blessing to spontaneous, unsponsored migration in connection with such projects; once the word gets around, as experience has shown, thousands of enterprising people will leave Java to take advantage of the new jobs thus provided.[15] In many cases private enterprises initiate such non-agricultural as well as agricultural job-creating projects, and commonly such enterprises take the form of joint ventures including approved foreign investors. We shall consider this further in Chapter 13.

In sum, transmigration in the officially-sponsored sense moves people from Java and the adjacent overcrowded 'inner islands'; it relieves the severe ecological pressure on those islands; it carries major job-creation potentials; and it contributes to the expansion of both agricultural and non-agricultural production for domestic consumption and for export. Officially-sponsored transmigration likewise stimulates the creation of private enterprises in the outer islands; such enterprises can, as it were, magnetically attract many thousands of so-called spontaneous migrants; and this can in turn generate still more benefits of the kinds just mentioned.

In addition, transmigration — whether officially sponsored or unsponsored — has a crucial connection with Indonesia's national defence and security. Some observers have tended to minimize the importance of this aspect of transmigration, but I believe that they are quite wrong. In an increasingly crowded world — with mainland China's population, for example, about to top the one billion mark — Indonesia's vast and potentially rich 'empty' spaces offer natural temptations. Colonization and the building of roads, airports, harbours, and other infrastructure serve, as it were, to stake Indonesia's claim to every part of her own immense domain. A personal presence is required at strategic points throughout that domain, and economic growth centres can serve this further purpose. Moreover, as Martono points out, transmigration can contribute to national defence and security by reducing the possibility of social unrest and upheaval in Indonesia's most densely populated inner-island areas.[16]

Many people have no clear conception of the number of major steps involved in establishing transmigration projects in virgin territory in the outer islands. Before such projects can be activated, a daunting list of pre-implementation activities must be completed. Typically they include the following: site identification; aerial photography; land capability surveys, including soils, water supplies, and suitability of the site from the point of view of health; socioeconomic surveys both of the selected sites and of the areas of origin of the intending migrants; transmigrant recruitment planning; agricultural planning; physical project planning; transmigration logistics planning; land acquisition (often an extended process in itself); social services planning; agricultural services planning; organization and management planning; overall financial/economic analysis; budget planning; staff selection and training; and appointment of staff to specific sites.[17] As experience has shown, such systematic steps must be taken if the projects are to stand any reasonable chance of success when it comes to their actual implementation.

In view of all of these complexities, it is not surprising that attention should focus on the administrative aspect of what has now become a truly massive national programme of transmigration. As my discussions with government ministers and World Bank officials amply confirm, it is this factor which has gained recognition as the most important of all — at both the pre-implementation and implementation stages. And it is here that one finds the biggest bottlenecks.

The Ministry of Manpower and Transmigration, as it has come to be styled, bears primary responsibility for the overall government-sponsored transmigration programme, and to help expedite the programme a Junior Minister of Transmigration was appointed in 1978. Since transmigration involves so many different factors, a number of ministries are necessarily involved; and the government has established two inter-ministerial co-ordinating committees — one at the minister level and the other at the director-general level. These have greatly assisted in bringing teamwork into the effort. The relevant ministries likewise rely upon technical and financial assistance from a number of the aid missions operating in Indonesia, and most notably from the World Bank.

All of this is encouraging, but it is by no means enough to assure that Indonesia can attain her ambitious — yet, in terms of the need, still inadequate — transmigration targets under her Third Five-Year Development Plan. When one reflects upon Indonesia's vast geographical spread and her status as the world's largest archipelago, the magnitude of the logistical task — let alone the many other aspects of the transmigration programme — soon becomes apparent. The deployment of ships, planes, men, heavy engineering equipment, and much else calls for a high order of mobilization. The armed forces are already heavily involved in the programme, particularly on the logistical side, but they can become still more active and effective under a highly-geared joint chiefs of staff approach. Here is a perfect opportunity for the armed services to apply and extend their uniquely Indonesian conception of the dual function as already discussed in Chapter 5.

In addition, the transmigration programme can provide a splendid proving ground for what could become another uniquely Indonesian contribution — this time in the area of technological innovation and adaptation to Indonesia's own particular needs. Experience in many countries has shown that technological change can be socially disruptive, and perhaps nowhere is this more true than on Java. Strout, for example, has warned that fully applying the technology of the Green Revolution might well mean 'that social stability would further decrease, that agricultural densities could not be maintained at current levels, and that the shift of agricultural population to urban areas . . . might shortly become unmanageable'.[18]

A pioneer thinker on the subject of socially-acceptable technologies was E.F. Schumacher (1911-77); in various writings, particularly in his book *Small Is Beautiful*,[19] he set forth his philosophy, and he was also instrumental in giving it institutional expression. His work has already had a substantial impact, especially in developing countries including Indonesia — where, however, it is still not nearly well enough known among the planners.

Although Schumacher's style at times seems somewhat more epigrammatic than rigorous, it is nevertheless highly suggestive. He contends, for example, that

> one of the most fateful errors of our age is the belief that the problem of production has been solved. This illusion . . . is mainly due to our inability to recognize that the modern industrial system, with all of its intellectual sophistication, consumes the very basis on which it has been erected. To use the language of the economist, it lives on irreplaceable capital which it cheerfully treats as income. . . .[20]

And he notes three categories of such capital: fossil fuels, the 'tolerance margins of nature', and 'the very substance of industrial man'.

As Schumacher sees it, the modern world, which has been largely moulded by technology,

> tumbles from crisis to crisis; on all sides there are prophecies of disaster and, indeed, visible signs of breakdown.
>
> If that which has been shaped by technology, and continues to be so shaped, looks sick, it might be wise to have a look at technology itself. If technology is felt to be becoming more and more inhuman, we might do well to consider whether it is possible to have something better — a

technology with a human face.

Strange to say, technology, although of course the product of man, tends to develop by its own laws and principles, and these are very different from those of human nature or of living nature in general. . . . The system of nature, of which man is a part, tends to be self-balancing, self-adjusting, self-cleansing. Not so with technology, or perhaps I should say: not so with man dominated by technology and specialization. Technology recognizes no self-limiting principle— in terms, for instance, of size, speed, or violence. It therefore does not possess the virtues of being self-balancing, self-adjusting, and self-cleansing. In the subtle system of nature, technology, and in particular the super-technology of the modern world, acts like a foreign body, and there are now numerous signs of rejection.[21]

Not surprisingly, continues Schumacher, the modern world, shaped by its technology,

finds itself involved in three crises simultaneously. First, human nature revolts against inhuman technological, organizational, and political patterns, which it experiences as suffocating and debilitating; second, the living environment which supports human life aches and groans and gives signs of partial breakdown; and third, . . . the inroads being made into the world's non-renewable resources . . . are such that serious bottlenecks and virtual exhaustion loom ahead in the quite foreseeable future.

On the human side, modern technology has indeed

deprived man of the kind of work that he enjoys most, creative, useful work with hands and brains, and given him plenty of work of a fragmented kind, most of which he does not enjoy at all. It has multiplied the number of people who are exceedingly busy doing kinds of work which, if it is productive at all, is so only in an indirect or 'roundabout' way, and much of which would not be necessary at all if technology were rather less modern. . . .

Taking stock, we can say that we possess a vast accumulation of new knowledge, splendid scientific techniques to increase it further, and immense experience in its application. All this is truth of a kind. This truthful knowledge, as such, does *not* commit us to a technology of giantism, supersonic speed, violence, and the destruction of human work-enjoyment. The use we have made of our knowledge is only one of its possible uses and, as is now becoming ever more apparent, often an unwise and destructive use.[22]

Schumacher is particularly concerned about the 'dual economies' of the developing countries, with their sharply-contrasting modern and non-modern sectors. If, he says, 'the non-modern sector is not made the object of special development efforts, it will continue to disintegrate; this disintegration will continue to manifest itself in mass unemployment and mass migration into the metropolitan areas; and this will poison economic life in the modern sector as well'.[23]

Both the rural and urban poor 'can be helped to help themselves, but only by making available to them a technology that recognizes the economic

105

boundaries and limitations of poverty — an intermediate technology'. Particularly in what he refers to as the world's two million villages, it is essential to employ intermediate technology to provide improved low-cost farm equipment and low-cost workplaces for village production activities.

'In the excitement over the unfolding of his scientific and technical powers', Schumacher concludes, 'modern man has built a system of production that ravishes nature and a type of society that mutilates man.'[24] He was determined to take practical steps to change this situation, not least through the efforts of the London-based Intermediate Technology Development Group Ltd., or ITDG, which had earlier (in 1965) been established under his chairmanship.[25] Among the Group's main aims are these: 'to compile inventories of existing technologies which can be used within the concept of low-cost, labour-intensive production; to identify gaps in the range of existing technologies; to research into and develop by invention or modification new or more appropriate processes; to test and demonstrate in the field the results of its investigations; and to publish and make known the results of its work as widely as possible, so as to facilitate the transfer and use of appropriate technology'. The Group can correctly be called the world's leading focal point of ideas and information and publications in the rapidly-growing international realm of intermediate technology.

The Group has turned its attention to a remarkable range of alternative-technology projects, of which the following represent a fair sample: wheeled hand-hoes and cultivators, ox ploughs, animal toolbars, maize planters, rice seeders, knapsack sprayers, well-borers, piston pumps, chain pumps, bellows pumps, animal-drawn pumps, groundnut threshers, groundnut decorticators, maize shellers, chaff cutters, rice and grain threshers, rice hullers, palm-nut crackers, palm-oil presses, coffee pulpers, coffee shellers, coffee graders, grain grinding mills, cassava grinders, sugar-cane crushers, post-hole diggers, fence-post drivers, stump pullers, impregnated wood bearings, brick moulds, block-making machines, oil-drum forges, ferroconcrete boats, sail windmills, hydraulic rams, water storage tanks, wooden bridge spans, spinning/weaving machines, village-made corrugated roofing, methane generators.[26] These practical projects have to do with the lives and well-being of millions of the world's people.

In 1977, Schumacher visited Indonesia to attend a conference sponsored by the Indonesian Institute of Sciences (LIPI), and there he presented a paper prepared by him and his friend and colleague George McRobie,[27] who was to assume the chairmanship of ITDG after Schumacher's death later in that same year. Among other things the paper referred to the growing international network of organizations working specifically on intermediate technology, with many of them located in the developing countries themselves. The countries include the following, with others no doubt in process of joining the list: Argentina, Bangladesh, Botswana, Colombia, Ghana, India, Indonesia, Kenya, Nigeria, Pakistan, Philippines, Sri Lanka, Tanzania, Thailand, Uganda, and Zambia. Among the industrialized countries, a number of organizations exist which are more or less parallel to the ITDG, including the Brace Research Institute in Canada; the Tool Foundation in the Netherlands; and, in the United States, the Technology and Development Institute (linked to the East-West Center in Hawaii), Volunteers in Asia, and Volunteers in Technical Assistance.[28]

As the paper pointed out, 'The task of persuading senior administrators, treasuries and cabinets that intermediate technologies are feasible and often preferable is not easy, if only because of departmental pressures and practices and the educational backgrounds of the decision-makers'.[29] In the case of Indonesia, the intermediate technology movement had gained supporters in the Ministry for Research and Technology, several other of the ministries, the Indonesian Institute of Sciences, the Development Technology Centre at ITB, the Dian Desa Appropriate Technology Group at Yogyakarta, the Village Technology Unit (BUTSI), and a few other places. But the movement's gathering momentum had left the country's economic planners largely unmoved, and they had yet to make the indicated changes in the Third Five-Year Development Plan. At stake were literally millions of jobs.

Intermediate technology has a close conceptual linkage with the so-called Basic Needs Model, which has latterly attracted considerable attention in international development circles. The model is based squarely upon the recognition that, in all too many countries in recent years, even rapid economic growth has failed to meet the minimal legitimate needs of ordinary people — especially rural people — for food, clothing, shelter, health and education. As Soedjatmoko points out, 'The Basic Needs Model, with its emphasis on development from the bottom up, community participation and initiative, autonomy and village self-reliance, puts a premium on the development of the organizational-and-management capacity of rural communities, as well as on the development of cooperatives and other

Fishermen mending their nets

forms of organization, often derived from traditional institutions . . . with the right to run them under their own leaders'.[30]

One must guard against a narrowly simplistic interpretation of the Basic Needs Model; if, for example, one confines one's attention to the foregoing five elemental needs and at the same time neglects roads, basic sanitation, irrigation works and other infrastructure, then the whole exercise may be self-defeating. Moreover, as Soedjatmoko suggests, the model, in the present state of its articulation, is not yet a substitute for a development strategy. The Basic Needs Model expresses a particular emphasis, and a particular approach to the development process, presenting specific points of intervention. It becomes meaningful only when it is firmly set within a framework of . . . regional . . . and national development policies which are capable of coming to grips with the structural impediments to such change in emphasis, and to social development in general.[31]

He clearly recognizes that many present-day technologies are 'still too expensive to reach the poorest among the rural . . . as well as urban population. New, cheaper technologies will have to be developed which are replicable on a large scale. . . .'[32] This last theme has been further eludicated by Hans Singer in his *Appropriate Technology and Basic Needs*. As Singer sees it,

It is now becoming increasingly clear that conventional development strategies which emphasize the growth of gross national product *per se*, without at the same time inquiring into the pattern of growth which determines its fruits, do not, in most developing countries, alleviate mass poverty and unemployment. What has happened in many cases is that through conventional growth strategies the fruits of growth have been concentrated in the hands of a small privileged minority. . . .[33]

If past development patterns have not yielded the desired results, Singer continues, then they must be changed. And in this process the job factor must clearly be borne very much in mind.

. . . Both unemployment and underemployment prevent the majority of the population in developing countries from having access to minimum personal consumption needs such as adequate food and shelter, and to minimum social services such as water, education, sanitation, medical facilities and transport. Thus the technology required for a basic-needs strategy in a developing country must concentrate more than in the past on meeting the requirements of the small farmer, small-scale rural industry and the informal sector producer. Such a strategy calls for, and is supported by, a special kind of appropriate technology: a technology which differs from that developed in the industrialized countries. . . . This is so because under a basic-needs strategy technology must bear the double burden of adapting existing or imported new technology to the general situation of the developing country *and* of underpinning the redistribution of incomes which goes with a basic-needs strategy. For this reason it might be called a 'doubly appropriate' technology. . . .[34]

From the foregoing it is clear that the pressure of events in many parts of the world — and Indonesia is not immune to it — is calling forth suggestive new thinking on development strategies. To prevent any possible misunderstanding, it must be emphasized that I am in this book *not* contending that economic growth is irrelevant, that economic planning is irrelevant, or that capital-intensive projects are irrelevant. All have their place. But, as we shall see, that same pressure of events brings with it an ever-growing awareness that Indonesia urgently requires fresh developmental policies and programmes.

The National Philosophy

In a speech of 30 September 1960 before the UN General Assembly, Sukarno alluded to the American Declaration of Independence, as drafted by Jefferson, and the Communist Manifesto, as written by Marx and Engels.[1] Although, said Sukarno, Indonesians had drawn inspiration from both documents and had tried to synthesize them, 'we are not guided only by that. We follow neither the liberal conception nor the communist conception. Why should we? Out of our own experience and out of our own history there has evolved something else, something much more applicable, something much more fitting.'

Sukarno was of course referring to Pancasila (as it is now spelled), the Indonesian ideology already mentioned in Chapter 8. 'In speaking to you of Pantjasila', he declared to the world assemblage, 'I am expressing the essence of two thousand years of our civilization.'[2]

Steeped as he was in Javanese mysticism, and true as usual to his flamboyant nature, Sukarno was no doubt indulging in a degree of hyperbole. Yet clearly some of the elements of Pancasila can be traced back for centuries even if not millennia. Be that as it may, it was Sukarno himself who chiefly formulated the Pancasila philosophy as such, and he did so even before the principal phase of the independence struggle had begun. On 1 June 1945, well before Indonesia's Declaration of Independence on 17 August,[3] Sukarno delivered his famous address entitled 'The Birth of "Pantjasila": The Five Principles of the Indonesian State'. Anticipating the independence declaration, he said,

> Do not imagine that with the existence of the state of Free Indonesia, our struggle is at an end. Never! I even say: Within that free Indonesia our struggle must continue. The struggle, however, must be of a different nature from what we have been carrying on so far. Then we shall continue our struggle as a united people to bring realization to our ideals contained in Pantjasila. And, particularly in this time of war, have faith. . . . If the people of Indonesia are not united, and not determined to live or die for freedom, the freedom of Indonesia will never be the possession of the Indonesian people, never until the end of time!. . .[4]

Sukarno clearly saw the need for ideological first principles to provide the rationale and unifying basis for the freedom struggle, and these same principles were likewise to find their way into the preamble to the Constitution of 1945, the one in force today.[5] As Ruslan Abdulgani has expressed it, 'During five long years from 1945 to 1950 the new concept of freedom, based on the Pancasila, had to be defended . . . against the Japanese, the British and the returning Dutch colonial army, as well as against the communist rebellion in Madiun in 1948. The unifying force of Sukarno during these revolutionary years was instrumental for the national survival. . . .'[6]

In taking over from Sukarno in the mid-1960s, the New Order government, far from repudiating the Pancasila philosophy, warmly embraced it. Moreover, although the phraseology has changed somewhat over time, and although the sequence has been modified (for example, the reference to God has been moved from the final to the initial position), Sukarno's original five principles remain in formal terms the officially-accepted ones today: belief in the one and only God; just and civilized humanitarianism; Indonesian unity; democracy guided by wisdom through deliberation/representation; and social justice for the whole of the Indonesian people.[7] New Order spokesmen, from President Soeharto down, have repeatedly — even incessantly — reasserted the role of Pancasila as distilling the national ideology and providing a code of individual and national conduct.

But in one fundamental respect, which has too often been overlooked, the New Order has drastically diverged from the Old Order in its interpretation of Pancasila — namely, in the way it views the economic system. It is this contrast in interpretation which very largely accounts for the sharply differing styles of the two regimes. Sukarno, by his own testimony, had been much influenced by Marx, and he tended uncritically to accept Marx's indictment of so-called capitalism. For example, we find Sukarno, in his speech of 1 June 1945, commenting as follows on the American model:

> In America there is a people's representative body, and are not the capitalists throughout the Western Continent in control? And this whilst there are people's representative bodies! . . . What is called democracy there is merely a political democracy; there is no social justice and no economic democracy at all. . . .[8]

By the same token, asked Sukarno, 'Do we want a free Indonesia where capitalists bear sway [sic], or where the entire people prosper, where every man has enough to eat, enough to wear, live in prosperity, feel cherished by the homeland that gives him sufficient keep? . . .'[9] Such logic led him to opt for socialism, and he never lost that particular emphasis. As Ruslan Abdulgani has shown in his authoritative book *Pantjasila: The Prime Mover of the Indonesian Revolution*, the Sukarno regime from start to finish clearly identified Pancasila with socialism.[10] As is well known, the later Sukarno years were characterized by economic stagnation and roaring inflation, and the uncritically-held socialist concepts of Sukarno and his economic advisors may well have contributed to this. Ironically, the Old Order's gross economic mismanagement tended to jeopardize the survival of the very Pancasila principles which Sukarno had formulated and for which he had become justly famous.

After the economic catastrophe which characterized the closing years of the Sukarno regime, it is not surprising that the New Order adopted a different economic philosophy. With wide popular backing at home and encouragement from friendly countries abroad, the new government embraced the principle of the mixed economy. As we shall see in Chapter 13, however, this did not mean that the government welcomed any or all foreign investment; to the contrary, the government allowed such investment only in certain restricted categories and even then only under certain carefully-drawn conditions. Moreover, instead of denationalizing the very large socialized sector inherited from Sukarno, the New Order government did quite the reverse; just as the new government identified itself with the philosophy of Sukarno's Pancasila, so too it retained intact most of the relatively very large public sector which had likewise been created by Sukarno.

As for the Pancasila philosophy as a whole, opinions on it have naturally varied widely. Students provide a good touchstone; and among the many Indonesian students with whom I have talked, most seem to think that Pancasila provides a useful set of first principles. Some students, on the other hand, regard Pancasila as so vague as to be almost meaningless, if not actually hypocritical. Vagueness, however, does have its uses; scholars generally agree, for example, that the Constitution of the United States would never have survived for so long if it had been couched in highly specific terms. It is no accident, moreover, that major Western political parties — unlike small, special-interest ones — habitually present their platforms in terms of broad principles designed to appeal to a wide cross-section of the people in the country concerned.

One of the more caustic critiques of Pancasila has come from Brian May in his *The Indonesian Tragedy*. According to him,

> What was meant to provide a broad philosophic base for a nation threatened with disintegration at its birth has now been reduced from a set of principles that had some meaning to a shibboleth that has none. Almost any political action that a group may wish to take is justified by appeal to *Pancasila*, which Sukarno endowed with a mystical sanctity that has been exploited no less by his successors. . . . Where what is said to be a national philosophy has degenerated into a refuge for those afraid of their own ideas, there can be little chance of rational thought superseding the prevailing mysticism. Indonesians will make no progress until they can openly discuss what needs to be done without reference to a formula which is so vague that it is devoid of practical meaning.[11]

In making such comments, May clearly reflects the end-of-ideology bias which was, especially during the 1960s and 1970s, so characteristic of the West. It is a pity that he did not take the opportunity to read my analysis, entitled *Creative Alternatives to Communism* and already referred to in Chapter 8 above, which was first published in 1977, the year before May's book. Among other things my book focuses on the superficiality and transitory nature of the end-of-ideology syndrome.[12] It is symptomatic that, although May professes a deep concern about cultural factors in Indonesia, the extensive index to his book contains not a single entry under the heading 'ideology'.

That having been said, however, the fact remains that many students and others with whom I have talked in Indonesia strongly believe that much more must be done to systematize the Pancasila philosophy and to spell out its implications for the modern world. To the New Order's credit, it has taken several steps in this direction. In 1978, for example, the government published *The Guide to the Living and the Practice of Pancasila and the Broad Outlines of the State Policy*. This document refers, for instance, to the need for harnessing Indonesia's spiritual and mental and cultural capital, along with her other resources, in aid of national development. On the economic side, it contends that the state must control all natural resources and all branches of 'strategic industries which affect the life of most people', and that Indonesia must avoid what is termed the 'system of *"free-fight liberalism"* which gives rise to exploitation of other human beings and nations. . .'.[13]

On the other hand, according to the document, Indonesia must shun 'monopoly which is detrimental to society' and the 'system of *"etatism"*, in which the State with its economic apparatus is dominant', and which 'forces out and destroys the potential and creative ability of economic units outside the State sector'.[14] It is likewise refreshing to find the document insisting that development efforts 'must always be oriented towards . . . providing . . . greater job opportunities using applied technology' and with special reference to 'labor-intensive technology which is easily maintained. . .'.[15] In commenting on manpower, the document again refers to the need for job-creation measures, and in the section on transmigration it calls for emphasizing unofficial as well as officially-sponsored migration to the outer islands. It likewise demands that 'development efforts should be made to involve the younger generation in the process of state and national life and in the implementation of national development'.[16]

The President in 1978 appointed a seven-man Pancasila Commission chaired by Ruslan Abdulgani. A gracious old Dutch colonial building was allocated for the commission's headquarters, and I have visited it on various occasions. In one room the commission members sit around a huge horseshoe-shaped table, and there they deliberate on the meaning and implications of Pancasila. They also invite witnesses, including students, to come and give the commission the benefit of their ideas. They advise the President and other government leaders on matters connected with Pancasila, and they prepare materials for courses on the subject which are presented to military officers, civil servants, university students, and others. The approach followed by the commission is well illustrated by a course syllabus prepared especially for civil servants and dealing with what is called 'substantiating and implementing' Pancasila.[17]

The Foreword to the syllabus immediately highlights the contrast between the Indonesian outlook on such matters and that of the overly-secular West. 'Substantiation', says the syllabus, 'is a spiritual process, which before it is substantiated, requires a recognition and understanding of what is going to be substantiated. Furthermore, after it has been instilled in the heart, its implementation will be felt as something which comes out from self-consciousness, as something which becomes part and at the same time a purpose of life. It will therefore not be felt as something which is forced from outside. . . .'[18] One can readily visualize the sense of incomprehension and incredulity which such statements would engender in a correspondent like May, with his Western-oriented secular mentality in spite of his extended exposure to the East.

From a study of the history of Pancasila, says the syllabus, 'we gain a very

Eighth-century stupa, one of 72 —each containing a buddha
— at Borobudur, eastern Java

valuable lesson, namely that so far we have not yet substantiated and also not yet implemented Pancasila properly'.[19] Relating Pancasila to national development, the syllabus cautions that 'in the implementation of development . . . we cannot just copy or imitate the ways followed by other nations, without adjusting them to the view of life and the needs of our own nation. . .'.[20] Indeed, says the syllabus, 'We feel very grateful that our predecessors, the founders of this Republic, could formulate clearly the true philosophy of life of our nation, which we later called Pancasila. . . .' That philosophy was largely 'dug up from Indonesia's own soil'; but it had to go through 'a long process, matured by the history of our own nation's struggle, by looking to the experiences of other nations, inspired by the big ideas of the world, and by remaining rooted to the identity and the big ideas of our own nation'.[21]

Various groups, says the syllabus, have tried 'to distort Pancasila and to make it a shield to infiltrate other concepts and ideologies which were exactly contrary to the values of Pancasila. . .'.[22] Indonesia must guard against both Western Marxism and various other undesirable aspects of Western culture. The process of physical development

> should also bring along and very much needs social reforms. These . . .
> reforms have a dynamic force in them as they involve the pattern of
> values, attitudes, and behavior. In other words, development calls for
> *renovation*. For us who are building a society based on our own identity,
> renovation does not mean 'westernization' or a 'western-like' attitude.
> Renovation for us is no other than the effort of the nation to develop its
> own identity, by discarding the bad and strengthening the good, by
> making adjustments to the demands and needs of a modern society. But it
> should . . . be clear to us that this modern society *should also remain an
> Indonesian society*, which must grow stronger and develop on the basis of
> its own identity. A society which develops on the basis of another identity
> may be able to bring progress, but this progress will *make us feel like
> strangers in our own society*. . . .
>
> In a period of progress as at present, where relations between nations
> are so close, building up a modern society means that we must open up
> ourselves. A nation which closes itself to the outside world will be left
> behind by the progress of time, by the progress of other nations. In the
> effort to lay down the bases of a modern society we absorb not only
> capital, technology, scientific knowledge and skill from outside, but
> together with these *also social and political values originating from other
> cultures*. This inflow of the values of other cultures will grow even more in
> intensity in line with the freedom we . . . have consciously opened up
> again. The important thing for us is that we should be able *to select the
> values from outside*, so that we only absorb those values which are good
> and are in line with our own identity. We should be able to reject values
> which are not in line with, and even more those which may harm, our
> own identity. . . .[23]

Thus, with some eloquence, the syllabus summarizes Indonesia's official position on international cultural transfers and national cultural integrity. 'In the end', concludes the Pancasila syllabus, 'the philosophy of life of a nation is a matter of choice, a matter of a nation's decision on what is considered a good way of living together.'[24] One finds this Indonesian attitude decidedly refreshing; it is indeed reminiscent of 18th-century rationalism and of the spirit — so far removed from recent cynical Western postures — which animated America's Declaration of Independence.

Ever since the beginning of Sukarno's regime, Indonesia's leadership has placed much emphasis on the principles of Pancasila; but, as Abdulgani has expressed it, 'voices have also been heard advocating an Islamic State or a Socialist/Communist State'.[25] With regard to the latter potential danger, it is interesting to note the following assessment, from a Marxist-oriented book on Indonesia, on the future prospects of the PKI:

> There is no doubt . . . that the roots of the PKI are too tenaciously embedded in Indonesian history and society ever to yield. . . . PKI members know better than anyone the great obstacles and difficulties, setbacks and disappointments, which lie ahead. But without underestimating these, the Party is rightly confident of the final outcome of the struggle. . . .[26]

We have already seen, in earlier chapters of this book, how the PKI, as the first Communist party in Southeast Asia, has interacted with the Indonesian cultural environment. From the discussion thus far it should be evident that protecting the country from the alien Marxist creed requires a number of different kinds of responses. For example, Indonesia needs a viable non-Marxist ideology attuned to the cultural context; and both Old Order and New Order leaders have hoped that Pancasila would constitute such or would evolve into such. She needs adequate security arrangements for protection against both internal and external threats. She needs vigorous economic and social development which reaches out to all of her people and which harmonizes with her cultural traditions.

Comparable responses are needed to deal with the problem posed by the other kind of voices to which Abdulgani refers; and here one can well reflect upon Harold Crouch's assessment, as quoted in Chapter 9, to the effect that militant Islam may, in Indonesia in the short term, pose a greater threat than Communism. My own view is that the two dangers must be viewed as parallel and concurrent; and in addition, we may see strange interactions between the two kinds of militancy. As experience in Iran has shown, Islamic Marxism, although symbolic of only part of the larger problem, can never be entirely ruled out.

More than any other single country, Saudi Arabia can of course claim to serve as the seat of the historic Islamic faith; and it is therefore particularly instructive to find the following statement in an official publication of the Saudi Arabian government: 'Islam is one of the three great monotheistic religions of the world and has strong links to the other two, Judaism and Christianity. Moslems recognize and revere the prophets of the Old Testament and Jesus Christ.' According to the same official statement, 'The religion of Islam has distinguished itself among other religions by its relative tolerance and acceptance of other religions. . . . It preaches equality among men, tolerance of other religions, submission to the will of God. . . .'[27]

Most, albeit not all, of the students with whom I have talked in Saudi Arabia have shown an awareness of the close interrelationship of the great faiths; and in Indonesia, as my discussions with students and others testify,

115

ของประชุมหมู่
เท่านั้น ในสิมากา
ประ ยิ่งว่าไป ทาง
แบบเกาะ อีกว่า
เย็นเดียวกัน

*Tribal meeting house of
Simalungun bataks, at Pematang
Purba, near Lake Toba, northern
Sumatra*

วัด ๑๓๑๖๔
๓. หรือ เปรียวดังิน
เ จาก์ ด้าน ในจาก.

Kehen temple, Kota Bangli, Bali

Masjid Raya, Medan, Sumatra

*Palawa village Toraja houses
near Rantepao, Sulawesi*

one finds a highly-developed sense of religious toleration and interdependence. But toleration operates in a different context in Indonesia as compared with Saudi Arabia. In the latter country Islam is overwhelmingly dominant, but in Indonesia — various statistics notwithstanding — this is far from the case. According to one source, 'Today it is estimated that 90 percent or more of Indonesians are of the Islamic faith';[28] and similar figures have been picked up and widely circulated by journalists and others. Such figures, although plausible in a sense, are highly misleading and fail to take account of the complexity of Indonesia's cultural traditions.

According to James L. Peacock, who has written extensively and sympathetically about Islam in Indonesia, 'only a minority of Indonesians are fully practicing Muslims. . .'.[29] Mintaredja, in his *Islam and State in Indonesia*, refers to 'the empty slogans declaring the Islamic community to make up 90 percent of Indonesia's population'.[30] Allan A. Samson has compactly summarized the historical evolution as follows:

> The Islamic experience in Indonesia produced a diversity of political perceptions as it has developed over the past three centuries. Central to such diversity has been the division of Indonesian society along religious-cultural-political lines ranging from the strongly Islamic to the nominally or even non-Islamic. The strongly Islamic-nominally Islamic dichotomy is especially pronounced in Java, where Islamic culture, after its introduction in the sixteenth century, interacted with a highly eclectic Javanese culture comprised of animist, Hindu, and Buddhist elements. What resulted was a checkered pattern of exclusivity and syncretism, in which the Islamic and Indic-influenced civilizations warily interacted with each other — neither being able fully to subjugate or absorb the other. Many Islamic practices were incorporated into Hindu-Javanese ceremonies and rituals, while much that was syncretically Javanese found its way into Islamic practice.[31]

It is vitally important to grasp the power and vitality of the Indonesian spiritual and religious synthesis. As one report has expressed it, 'The strongest effect on the traditional thoughts and attitudes of Indonesians still comes from the religious base';[32] and that religious base is rich in its diversity and beauty. Moreover, references to occasional religious fanaticism must never blind one to the fact that the overwhelming majority of Indonesian students, and Indonesians generally, are moderate both religiously and politically. Extremism of the right, while potentially highly dangerous, is a phenomenon manifested by a statistically minute proportion of the population.

It is much to the credit of Sukarno and Soeharto that they have both greatly contributed to fostering the spirit of religious toleration. But if religious fanaticism in Indonesia is to be contained and curtailed, much more must be done. It is the government's policy — no doubt a correct one — to isolate the fanatics. But this of course requires far more than dealing with them as individuals or groups of individuals. One must pay close attention to the wider environment in which the fanatics thrive or shrivel up. If our analysis, in Chapter 9, of the Iranian crisis makes sense, it shows that the failure to contain religious fanaticism in that country stemmed very largely from such seemingly non-religious matters as mistaken policies on national development and on the role of the youth.

From the earliest days of the faith, Islam has claimed jurisdiction over secular as well as spiritual affairs. What is commonly referred to in the West as the principle of separation of church and state has no counterpart in Islamic doctrine. In the words of Charles J. Adams, 'For Muslims, the religious dimension of existence extends to encompass the whole of life and not only that small segment of activity concerned with specific acts of worship or the fulfilment of religious duties. For this reason all issues of social policy in Muslim countries are also religious questions requiring to be examined in the light of tradition and religious teaching.'[33]

From the religious point of view, as Abdulgani has indicated, the phraseology of Pancasila represented a compromise.[34] Islamic groups had wanted any such ideological statement to make specific mention of Islam; but Sukarno, emphasizing as always the importance of national unity and seeking to satisfy all religious groups, opted for a broad reference to the one supreme God. Islamic spokesmen likewise tried unsuccessfully to have Islam referred to in the preamble to the 1945 Constitution. Under the New Order as well, Islamic leaders have repeatedly attempted to have their doctrine given a special place either in the Constitution or in legislation or in both.[35]

It should be stressed that most such leaders could in no way be called fanatics. They have simply been trying to do justice to their faith. Yet the dilemma faced by Sukarno has remained. In 1960 he felt obliged to dissolve the Masjumi party, which had become the most politically assertive major Islamic group; and in 1973 the New Order government compulsorily consolidated the then four Islamic parties into a single one.[36] Both Sukarno and Soeharto have been known as devout followers of Islam (along with the strong Javanese mystical streak in each case), and both the Old Order and New Order governments have welcomed and encouraged the faith as such; but both have sought to subordinate its political role in the cause of national unity.

In the assessment of Peacock, 'While at one time, some Indonesian Muslims aspired toward an Islamic state that would subsume all ethnicities, override such political divisions as the nationalist and the Communist, and guide all affairs in life, few seriously entertain such a vision today'. Culturally, he continues, 'the Indonesian scene has long been a mixture only partially blended. The animistic base, richly varied among the several thousand islands, has never been completely absorbed by any of the world religions — Hinduism, Confucianism, Buddhism, Islam, or Christianity — which have penetrated this . . . cross-roads of culture. . . .'[37] In my discussions with many Indonesians in diverse walks of life, I have found that most of them demonstrate remarkable detachment and objectivity about the role of religion in Indonesia. They recognize their country's astonishing religious and cultural diversity, and in general they want to keep it that way.

A further reason for their attitude may arise from their keen awareness of events abroad. They recognize that Islam, in spite of its great strengths, contains no specific blueprint for a viable state; by way of example, they need only to recall the widely divergent programmes of such devoutly Islamic leaders as the Shah of Iran, Nasser, Sadat, Gadafi, and Khomeini. Moreover, in the light of their own bitter experience with both the extreme

Faces of Indonesia

Ceremonial gifts and decorations prepared for a Balinese wedding

The officiating priest at the wedding (the bride is on the extreme left)

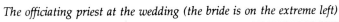

left and the extreme right, Indonesians naturally view with both fascination and alarm the strange combinations of these two extremes which have appeared in some parts of the world. As Sayyed Hossein Nasr points out, some Arab leaders, for example, 'combine leftist political tendencies with very strong Islamic convictions. One observes in the Arab world today not only traditional rulers who are devout Muslims or at least espouse the cause of Islam publicly, but also the most revolutionary governments which combine an extreme "leftist" policy with a degree of adherence to the . . . Islamic tradition.'[38]

Loyal Indonesians will wish to avoid the extremes of left or right or any unholy alliance between them. Pancasila should — provided it can be properly systematized and implemented — commend itself as a more attractive political and ideological alternative and one firmly rooted in Indonesia's culture. Among Pancasila's virtues is that it allows for full religious freedom — for all religious groups — in harmony with the principles of the Universal Declaration of Human Rights. And Indonesia's Pancasila philosophy illustrates how, in manifold ways, she can provide cultural inspiration to the world at large.

Ideology and Development

In Indonesia, as Allen M. Sievers points out, 'The term *technocrat* is now an honorific for the economists, administrators, and other professional men who have come into the government in alliance with the military. . .'.[1] But whether the terms 'technocrat' and 'technocracy' are used in Indonesia or elsewhere, many people who employ them have no idea of their origins or dubious lineage.[2] As one standard source expresses it, the technocracy concept

> was introduced to the public by the Technocracy Movement, which burst upon the American scene in the early 1930s. Although technocracy is offered as the only rational form of government for an increasingly industralized world, the concept has been criticized for its materialistic approach to human society and for its offering of managerial solutions to political problems.
>
> The Technocracy Movement began in New York City . . . as a study group centred on Howard Scott . . ., a charismatic figure. . . . Scott proclaimed the invalidation, by technologically produced abundance, of all prior economic concepts based on scarcity; he predicted the imminent collapse of the price system and its replacement by a bountiful technocracy. In the fall of 1932 a depression-weary nation seized on this optimistic theory, and countless technocratic organizations sprang up across the country. Just as fast as the movement had grown, however, it shrank; by . . . 1933 technocracy had largely disappeared from the news. . . .[3]

The movement, by then thoroughly discredited, lingered on for a few more years, but by the early 1940s it had become virtually extinct. The terminology has, however, persisted. According to an authoritative dictionary definition, 'technocracy' means 'government by technicians . . . management of society by technical experts' and 'technocrat' means 'an adherent of technocracy'.[4]

In earlier usage, the term 'technocrat' referred chiefly to engineers and technologists. Then it became generalized to refer to technicians in general. In practice, the term has come to be associated especially with technicians in the shape of economic planners — such as, in the Indonesian case, the so-called 'Berkeley gang' or 'Berkeley Mafia' composed of economic planners who were trained at the University of California. The staff of

Becaks in Medan, northern Sumatra

A covered bullock cart near Yogyakarta, Java

Opposite, *an elegant young dancer from Palembang, southern Sumatra*

Batak girls from Lingga in the Karo highlands, northern Sumatra

Indonesia's National Development Planning Agency — best known as Bappenas — includes a number of such planners who, by international standards, are probably among the most capable whom one could find anywhere.

The same was the case with Iran's Plan and Budget Organization in the days of the Shah. That central planning agency in fact bore a remarkable resemblance to Indonesia's Bappenas. The Shah and his government had gathered together in the agency many of Iran's most brilliant economic technocrats; and they were largely responsible for the country's astonishing pace of economic growth, and her spectacular general development, in the years leading up to the overturn in 1979. Robert Graham has well described the Plan and Budget Organization's failure to come to grips with the real situation.[5] The PBO indeed shared with the Shah much of the responsibility for the two cardinal errors described in Chapter 9.

Let there be no misunderstanding. Indonesia's Bappenas — together with the ministries and agencies with which it works in close liaison — deserve much of the credit for the country's manifold achievements under Repelita I and Repelita II as well as for her initial performance under Repelita III. But just as in any country where technocratic planners play a prominent role, serious shortcomings must be guarded against. One scarcely exaggerates by saying that the more brilliant the technocrats, the greater is the potential hazard which their viewpoint entails. For the technocratic mentality is almost invariably compartmentalized, and this all too easily lays it open to errors such as were committed in Iran. One finds 'accident-prone' technocrats in many countries — including Communist ones, whose bureaucracies are again commonly staffed largely by technocrats.

In the Indonesian context, and apart from the persistent problem of corruption, no less than *five* major developmental dangers particularly stand out. The first can well be termed the *Fallacy of Ideological Irrelevance*. Reference has already been made in Chapter 11 to Brian May's caustic critique of Pancasila and to his own evident ideological naiveté. But May merely reflects a cultural syndrome which was all too prevalent in the West in the 1960s and early 1970s. That intellectual episode was symbolized by Daniel Bell's book *The End of Ideology*, as published first in 1960 and in a revised edition in 1962.[6] To a remarkable degree the book managed to forecast and capture and magnify the spirit of those years; even the book's very title struck an instant responsive chord with many people who had never read it or even seen it. For it seemed to suggest an end to old dogmas and outworn creeds and a refreshing new reliance upon practical pragmatic experience.

Ideology, declared Bell in his book, 'which once was a road to action, has come to be a dead end'. A social movement, he went on to explain, 'can rouse people when it can do three things: simplify ideas, establish a claim to truth, and, in the union of the two, demand a commitment to action. Thus, not only does ideology transform ideas, it transforms people as well.'

'Ideology', explained Bell, 'is the conversion of ideas into social levers.' But today, Bell assured his readers, such ideologies — including Marxism — 'are exhausted'.[7] Bell was to show a broader awareness in a much more satisfactory book which was not, however, published until nearly fifteen years later; and meanwhile the end-of-ideology infection had spread far and wide in the West, particularly on Western campuses. Budding technocrats, including those who had come from the East for studies in the West, were especially susceptible to the infection, which left many of them marked for life.

In general, and regardless of country, technocrats tend to view philosophy and ideology with indifference if not outright suspicion. Paradoxically, this reduces their efficiency even in purely technocratic terms. As technicians they tend to perceive problems in terms of means and options isolated from ideological objectives. In pursuing what are thought to be good practical, pragmatic approaches, they too easily fell victim to opportunism. As Geoffrey D. Straussman puts it in his book *The Limits of Technocratic Politics*, 'Expertise will be in more, not less, demand in the future. But the basic questions remain. Who is served? What are the values behind the analysis? What goals are being pronounced? Whose goals are they. . . ?'[8] Where a technocrat bypasses such philosophical and ideological questions as these, he does so at his and his country's peril.

This truth is well exemplified by the second fallacy among our five. The *Fallacy of Beneficent Growth* must be viewed in its proper perspective. As H.W. Arndt has suggested,

> The public men, politicians, economists and others, who in western countries in the years after the Second World War proclaimed the importance of attaining a high rate of economic growth were neither ignorant nor stupid nor evil. They did not ignore, or dismiss as unimportant, problems of poverty and an equitable distribution of income, problems of conservation of natural resources and protection of the environment, improvement in standards of education, health, and other public services, or of conditions of work and living in industrial cities. They believed that all these problems could be solved or alleviated more easily if the capacity to provide goods and services for all these purposes was increased year by year through economic growth. . . .
>
> It is therefore a mistake to imagine that anyone wanted economic growth 'for its own sake'. . . .[9]

The same principle applied in the emerging countries as well. The leaders of such countries hoped that rapid growth would bring widespread benefits — not least in the rural sector. They and their technocrats prepared elaborate development plans pointing the way to the rapid growth which — so they believed — could bring the other benefits to which Arndt refers. But as he points out,

> In the less developed countries. . ., the pursuit of economic growth was frequently causing inequality, without any automatic assurance that the benefits of modernization which accrued in the first instance to privileged groups would 'trickle down' to the rest, that even high rates of growth would bring 'development'.
>
> . . . Economic growth, it has become increasingly apparent, is not enough. Deliberate policies are needed to modify the pattern of growth so as to reduce the costs of economic growth and ensure a more equitable distribution of its benefits.[10]

But the growth quest has brought even more serious complications than the foregoing suggests. In country after country economic growth has been

Karonese tribal people at Lake Toba, northern Sumatra

accompanied by grave social and cultural tensions and dislocations. Iran provides a pre-eminent example, but Indonesia is by no means immune. According to one comment on May's book, 'For the author, Indonesia's "tragedy" lies in the military rulers' blind attempt to enforce a Western economic model on a backward and superstitious people, whose culture and psychology are unsuited to it'.[11] Whether or not this is a fair characterization of the book, it does seem true that the work suffers, as it were, from a split personality. While on the one hand May regales his readers with a series of often intemperate personal attacks on members of the New Order government, on the other hand his main message appears to be quite otherwise; using Indonesia as his prime example, he is attempting to deal with cultural side-effects of growth such as have been noted in many emerging countries.

May is entirely correct in suggesting that such side-effects should receive the most serious consideration from Indonesia's leadership. One can indeed go further and say that Indonesia's whole economic as well as cultural strategy needs to be re-examined. We shall in fact find that a fundamental change in economic strategy will be required in order to minimize the adverse cultural repercussions arising from the process of growth. As a journalist, May is perhaps ill-equipped to deal with these matters; but on the other hand the international brotherhood of technocrats has been both indolent and slipshod in the way it has tackled them or failed to tackle them in the Third World in recent years.

This brings us naturally to what can be termed the *Fallacy of Keynesian Applicability*. John Maynard Keynes (1883-1946), who spent most of his working life at the University of Cambridge, has been called a man of such stature that he 'may in the end rival Adam Smith in his influence on the economic thinking and government policy of his time and age'.[12] John Kenneth Galbraith has correctly characterized Keynes's *The General Theory of Employment, Interest and Money* (as first published in 1936) as 'the most influential book on economic and social policy so far in this century. . .'.[13] As Harlan L. McCracken points out in his *Keynesian Economics in the Stream of Economic Thought*, 'Keynes observed that practically all of the modern depressions in advanced countries were due to a failure in demand — "goods without a buyer" — "poverty in the midst of plenty". . .';[14] and he was prepared to challenge the established orthodoxy in order to propose remedial measures.

As noted by Eric Roll in his *A History of Economic Thought*, 'The implied assumption of the classical system . . . is that the economic system spontaneously tends to produce full employment of given resources'. Keynes built his theory 'upon a rejection of this assumption'.[15] In the words of Alvin H. Hansen, 'It is the analysis of the problem of *aggregate demand*, together with the implications of this analysis for practical policy, which challenges the old orthodoxy'.[16] As Paul A. Samuelson puts it, 'I . . . believe the broad significance of the *General Theory* to be in the fact that it provides a relatively realistic, complete system for analyzing the level of effective demand and its fluctuations'.[17]

In his *General Theory*, Keynes himself points out that 'if effective demand is deficient, . . . the public scandal of wasted resources' becomes intolerable.[18] This awareness led him to develop, more than any economist before him, a system of *demand management* involving fiscal and other measures including 'pump-priming' through government deficit spending. Particularly in the decades immediately after the Second World War, such measures achieved spectacular success in fostering rapid economic growth and high levels of employment, notably in industrialized Western countries.

But as economists have belatedly realized, the emerging countries present a different picture. In the words of Michael P. Todaro in his *Economic Development in the Third World*, 'What may have appeared to be a "general theory" of employment . . . has now been recognized . . . as a "special" theory of unemployment for the developed countries. . .'.[19] According to Subrata Ghatak in his *Development Economics*, 'It is . . . difficult to see the application of Keynesian theory to the special features of an underdeveloped country'.[20] Charles P. Kindleberger and Bruce Herrick refer, in their *Economic Development*, to the phenomenon called *cultural lead*,

> which occurs when economic institutions are borrowed from a more developed country and grafted onto a society which they do not fit. This is a well-known phenomenon in the political sphere, where constitutions, parliaments, cabinets and elections abound in countries which are far from being democracies. But it is not missing in economics. . . . One of the basic and devastatingly expensive examples of cultural lead today is the application to underdeveloped countries of Keynesian economic analysis needed for developed countries in periods of unemployment.[21]

Todaro has, in the following passage, compactly summarized one of the chief shortcomings of the Keynesian model as applied to the less developed countries:

> . . . Since the model is derived from advanced country economies, it is implicitly based on the institutional and structural assumption of well functioning product, factor and money markets that characterize these countries. Specifically, it is based on the assumption, correct for developed nations but not for LDCs, that firms and farms can respond quickly and effectively to increases in the demand for their products by rapidly expanding output and employment. But in most Third World countries, the major bottleneck to higher output and employment levels typically is not insufficient demand but *structural constraints on the supply side*. Shortages of capital, raw materials, intermediate products, skilled and managerial human resources, combined with poorly functioning and inefficiently organized commodity and loan markets, poor transport and communications, shortages of foreign exchange and import-dominated consumption patterns among the rich — all of these, and many other structural and institutional factors, militate against the simple notion that expanded government and private demand will be effective measures to solve unemployment (and poverty) problems in most Third World countries. In fact, under conditions of severe *constraints on the supply side* (i.e. where the aggregate supply curve of national output is price 'inelastic'), expanding aggregate demand through deficit-financed government expenditure may merely result in higher prices and chronic inflation. . . .[22]

Development economists have for many years sought to accelerate output and growth in the emerging countries. According to Pan A. Yotopoulos and Jeffrey B. Nugent, however, the 'respectable rates of growth' achieved in the 1950s and 1960s by many developing countries 'have apparently had little or no effect on the large numbers of people who live in abject poverty';[23] and unfortunately this has remained largely the case through the 1970s as well. Indonesia registered higher growth rates throughout the 1970s than did many other emerging countries, yet she nevertheless failed to deal adequately with unemployment, underemployment, poverty, and inequity. Steadily accumulating evidence indicated that economists in Indonesia and other developing countries lacked sufficiently powerful instruments to do the job.

But a similar deficiency had also become apparent in the industrialized West. In the words of Geoffrey Barraclough, 'What Keynes contributed above all else to the Keynesian armoury was the fearsome weapon of aggregate demand management'.[24] But that weapon, plus the rest of the Keynesian armoury, were no longer adequate in the West. As Roll has remarked, 'we are faced with a turning away . . . from the new orthodoxy into which Keynesianism had developed'; and this turning away arises primarily from 'dissatisfaction aroused by the system's declining ability to cope with practical economic problems'.[25] As Michael Shanks points out, 'For the first time, . . . governments are going to have to consider full employment as an objective apart from overall Keynesian demand management'.[26]

It is of course in the context of the mixed economy that the Keynesian apparatus has characteristically been employed; and anybody who was tired of the mixed economy could theoretically opt for one of the various available socialist models. Indonesia, having in the 1960s almost succumbed to the imported Western Marxist socialist ideology, has no wish to repeat that experience. Moreover, one of the prime lessons of the 1970s has been that Marxist states, notably those in Eastern Europe, are by no means immune to inflation or stagnation or the combination of the two which has come to be called stagflation. There are, on the other hand, various countries which are governed by so-called democratic socialist parties or regimes. In reality, however, such countries in virtually every case in practice operate mixed economies which are subject to the very sorts of economic problems that plague the other countries comprising the modern global order. The search for fresh post-Keynesian approaches must accordingly continue.

From now on, according to W. W. Rostow, 'We shall have to think and act on problems of supply as sedulously as the Keynesian revolution taught us to think and act on problems of demand'.[27] Elsewhere, I had earlier proposed the use of the term *supply management*, and I had suggested that the concept which it represents should be emphasized in the context of both national and global supply systems.[28] This newer approach diverges sharply from those that dealt with growth in conventional economic terms. It stresses the role and importance of structural factors such as those mentioned by Todaro, and it views these in their cultural setting. *Supply management is therefore by definition an interdisciplinary pursuit.*

There is no necessary inconsistency whatever between fiscal and monetary measures — including tight monetary controls — and the supply management approach. Any such appropriate measures can be pursued concurrently with supply management.

As an approach which is pre-eminently interdisciplinary in character, supply management among other things takes account of evolving technology in its social and cultural context. A cardinal reason why Keynesianism has now come unstuck in both developing and industrialized countries is indeed that it has failed to deal dynamically with technology. This points the way to what we may term the *Fallacy of Postulated Technology*.

With his usual clarity Keynes expressed his fundamental assumptions as follows:

> We take as given the existing skill and quantity of available labour, the existing quality and quantity of available equipment, the existing technique, the degree of competition, the tastes and habits of the consumer, the disutility of different intensities of labour and of the activities of supervision and organization, as well as the social structure. . . .[29]

In making such static assumptions, Keynes fell into a serious intellectual trap. By taking as given the existing skill, the existing equipment, the existing technique, he in a very real sense begged the entire question. Curiously, enough, Keynes's assumptions are, in this particular context, remarkably parallel to those of Marx;[30] and the error in his overall reasoning is likewise remarkably parallel. In each case the error is a crucial one which can lead to fundamental distortions of policy.

With regard to the technological factor in particular, the supply management approach adopts a *diametrically opposite* position from that of Keynes — and from that of Marx as well. For obvious and compelling reasons it views technology as one of the core factors in the developmental process. Far from treating it as a 'given', the supply management approach regards technology as one of the most creatively dynamic factors of all. It considers innovative technology, when properly developed with social and cultural considerations in mind, to offer a highly effective means for dealing with many of the structural impediments to development to which reference has already been made.

Keynes was a man of very broad outlook; for example, it was he who, in 1936, founded the Cambridge Arts Theatre, which remains to this day the crowning jewel of the ancient university city.[31] But Keynes was all too ignorant about technology; and unhappily this has been even more the case with many of his more recent disciples, who have given the impression of knowing nothing and caring less about technology in its creative role. They — and their Marxist counterparts as well — have typically perpetuated the static assumptions made by Keynes on the one hand and by Marx on the other. The inescapable need for truly interdisciplinary approaches — encompassing the several natural sciences and technology as well as the several social sciences and philosophy — has eluded them. The message has not got through. They have failed to fathom the supply side, and poverty-stricken people in many countries have been suffering for it.

This leads directly to what we may call the *Fallacy of Technocratic Ascendency*. Serious semantic confusion surrounds the relationship between the terms 'technocrat' and 'technology', which sound as though they are closely akin to each other. Indeed, as already indicated, in earlier usage they *were* akin; up until about the time of the Second World War, 'technocrat' was in fact associated mainly with engineers and technologists. But subsequently, as we have seen, the term came to refer chiefly to planners and administrators; and in practice such men were usually Keynesian-oriented. Latter-day technocrats do not necessarily know anything worth mentioning about technology — often quite the reverse. Even more to the point, technocrats, including those in emerging countries who were trained in the West, not infrequently possess no more than the foggiest notion about the real strategy and tactics of scientific and technological innovation.

To express the matter more broadly, the shortcomings of non-Marxist technocrats trace back very largely to the defects in the Keynesian intellectual system. (In the same way, the shortcomings of the technocrats found in the big Communist bureaucracies trace back very largely to the defects in the Marxist intellectual system.) As Fred Hirsch has suggested in his *Social Limits to Growth*, 'Keynes opposed extreme laissez-faire by an essentially technocratic, pragmatic, empirical, apolitical, and counterphilosophical approach. . .'.[32] Initially, in his attack on outmoded classical doctrines, this gave him strength, but eventually it proved his undoing.

I know from personal experience of the brilliance of many of Indonesia's technocrats. The country requires not fewer, but many more, such men. But they must be trained as true interdisciplinarians. They must become accustomed to working in interdisciplinary teams. They must acquire a keen sense of the strategy and tactics of creative technology. They must equip and motivate themselves to pursue post-Keynesian supply management and other approaches to Indonesia's particular problems. The nation's technocrats (along with their counterparts in other developing countries) have had all too little relevant and reliable development theory to go on, and they must remedy this deficiency. They must be prepared to pioneer.

There is the durable precept that experts should be on tap and not on top, and this needs to be translated into Indonesian terms. The country's top leaders are by definition generalists; and they are generalists who have benefited from Indonesia's unique tradition, as referred to in Chapters 2 and 5, of the dual role of the military. For expert advice, the top leaders rely upon upper-level and lower-level technocrats. Both the top leaders and the technocrats should recognize that expert advice can at best provide only partial answers to major problems of statecraft. Technocrats, as has already been intimated, commonly leave important philosophical and ideological questions unanswered — if indeed they even think to ask them. In addition, as has likewise been noted, the technocrats have been starved of adequate developmental doctrines. Accordingly, the top leaders must at all times guard against succumbing to the fifth fallacy.

In an allegorical sense the five fallacies remind one of the five principles of Pancasila, and indeed they need to be intellectually linked to Pancasila. As we saw in Chapter 11, an official syllabus on Indonesia's ideology has frankly stated that 'so far we have not yet substantiated and also not yet implemented Pancasila properly'. Certainly much more needs to be done to broaden and deepen the formulation of Pancasila, with particular reference to making it more attractive to the youth. Notwithstanding its fundamental defects such as noted in Chapter 8, Marxism is essentially a system, and one with its own systematic body of literature. Pancasila stands very much in need of a parallel body of codified literature.

EMERGING INDONESIA

The Pancasila principles, crucially relevant though they are, provide only a partial basis for such a literature. Just as with any other philosophy, Pancasila's fundamental principles must be spelled out and illustrated in concrete terms. The concrete expressions of the philosophy must obviously harmonize with its fundamental principles, but they must be pitched especially in terms of relevant social issues — notably those concerned with national development. This must be done in a way that will appeal to students and other thoughtful people throughout the land.

Indonesia has no shortage of such relevant social issues, and the four described in Chapter 6 — population, food, jobs, and exports — can provide an excellent beginning. Likewise one can readily think of further issues related to the foregoing five fallacies. But it is not enough merely to describe these issues as such; one must elucidate a body of principles and techniques that can serve as effective tools for tackling the issues in ways which harmonize with Indonesian traditions — including those enshrined in Pancasila. As we shall find in the next chapter, science and technology, when appropriately adapted to serve Indonesia's needs, can provide some of the most powerful of such tools.

13

Investment Dynamics

Developing countries commonly exhibit a love–hate attitude toward foreign business enterprises. Such companies are referred to as exploitative neo-colonialist appendages, yet they are sought after for the technological and managerial expertise which they can provide. Marxists take special pleasure in castigating the so-called multinational corporations, which they identify as among the most hated symbols of capitalism and imperialism. The Marxists weep crocodile tears about the alleged depredations of such corporations; meanwhile, through an amalgam of ignorance and hypocrisy they conveniently overlook the close relationships which have developed between the enterprises and leading Marxist governments themselves.

We shall see more of this in a moment, but first it is important to define what have variously been called global, planetary, multinational or transnational corporations, companies or enterprises. Numerous alternative names and definitions are employed by various writers, and before settling upon any it is well to note two relevant cautions given by Michael Clapham. The first is that strictly speaking a multinational or equivalent corporation or company could exist only within a framework of international law; and so far the appropriate body of law has never been established. Hence the term 'enterprise' clearly seems the appropriate one.[1]

The second caution relates to the size of multinational enterprises. As Clapham puts it, 'In popular demonology they are a small group of enormous enterprises. . . . In fact they are immensely numerous and they are based in a great number of countries. . . .' Although accurate figures are exceedingly hard to come by, he estimates the world total of multinational enterprises 'as being in the area of 12,000-15,000. These would be the parent companies only. The total number of companies in multinational groups is enormously larger. . . . My guess is that the figure lies nearer 200,000 than 100,000.'[2]

Estimates of the aggregate number of multinational enterprises obviously depend in part upon the definition employed; and some definitions are unnecessarily complicated or restrictive. In framing a definition it must be remembered that it has now become common for multinational enterprises to have foreign affiliates in which they maintain little or no equity holding and in which the control itself may be shared with others such as partners in a joint venture. Likewise a definition should not be so restrictive as to exclude distribution and service organizations to the extent to which these may be allowed by the host country.

With these realistic considerations in mind, I adopt the definition that a multinational enterprise is one which exercises or participates in the ownership or control of activities in more than one country.

Multinational enterprises play an ever more important role in the emerging world economy, and the Marxist states have been unable to resist their attractions. As Michael Ellman points out in his *Socialist Planning*,

> During the 1970s, . . . East-West economic contacts widened and deepened. The state socialist countries made a major effort to close the technology gap by the import of technology from the capitalist countries. A classic example was Poland in the early 1970s. There an investment boom took place, largely financed by Western credits. This was intended to lead to the creation of a substantial internationally competitive sector of the economy that would earn sufficient foreign exchange to at least repay the credits. . . . In the 1970s the East European countries moved beyond the import of licenses, machines and entire plants to more intimate collaboration with the multinationals. . . . This collaboration took a number of forms.
>
> The USSR organized direct R & D cooperation between big capitalist firms and the State Committee on Science and Technology. . . .
>
> Another approach to the import of technology is firm-to-firm industrial cooperation. This goes beyond the mere one-off purchase of machines and licenses to long-term technological, production and marketing cooperation. . . .
>
> A third approach to technology transfer is the creation, on the territories of the state socialist countries, of joint venture enterprises with investment and management participation by Western firms. . . .[3]

As Alec Nove explains in *The Soviet Economic System*,

> Factories have been erected in the Soviet Union by Western firms and consortia. 'Compensation agreements' are negotiated involving long-term Western credits to be repaid by part of the output which these credits are used to expand. The smaller countries of Eastern Europe have concluded a variety of agreements with Western firms, ranging from the production of components to joint projects to which Western firms contribute capital (e.g. such hotels as the Intercontinental in Budapest and the Forum in Warsaw). Rumania has adopted laws making possible direct investment by Western firms.[4]

Perhaps even more striking has been the change in policy on foreign multinational enterprises adopted by the People's Republic of China. As one Western financial journal has expressed it,

> Foreign companies are to be allowed to return to China as owners or part-owners of industrial enterprises. The law on joint capital ventures . . . represents a remarkable change of attitude on the part of the Chinese authorities towards foreign capitalists, who have been the target of contempt and ridicule for most of the past 30 years. China is not about to set out on the capitalist road, but the present rulers seem convinced that if the

country's serious economic problems are to be solved they will need to make full use of the capital, technology and managerial skills available in foreign countries; joint ventures are seen as one way of tapping that resource.[5]

Indonesia's attitudes and policies relating to foreign multinational enterprises have, during the years since 1945, likewise shown considerable variation. In the period following the Declaration of Independence, as Franklin B. Weinstein points out, both President Sukarno and Vice-President Hatta emphasized Indonesia's need for Western capital investment as well as aid.[6] In the 1950s, however, increasing friction with the Dutch, alleged American complicity in the rebellion (already referred to in Chapter 3) which broke out in Sumatra and Sulawesi, and the growing strength of the PKI, all helped to sour relations with the West including the Western business community. As Howard Palfrey Jones cryptically expresses it, 'Nationalism and xenophobia were so intense and widespread, partly owing to continuing Communist influence, that foreign investment was not welcome'.[7]

Following the economic chaos of the later Sukarno years and the coming of the New Order, however, attitudes and policies rapidly changed. The Soeharto regime in effect embraced the concept of the mixed economy. Programmes for encouraging selective foreign investment became an integral part of the government's developmental planning and were duly reflected in Repelita I and its successor five-year plans. The government established an Investment Co-ordinating Board to encourage foreign investment in Indonesia, to receive applications for such, and to process them in co-operation with the appropriate ministries. Valuable investment incentives have been offered including tax holidays for priority projects, exemption from import duties on machinery and equipment needed for such projects, and liberal provisions for transferring funds abroad.[8] Of the projects thus processed, many have gone through to the production stage, and collectively they have significantly boosted Indonesia's national output.

Yet in Indonesia, just as in various other developing countries, the attitudes of many government officials, opinion-makers, and students toward foreign investment remain ambivalent. On the one hand, they recognize the need for such investment and for the managerial and technical expertise that commonly comes with it. But on the other hand they remain suspicious of it. Weinstein has referred to 'an inferiority complex spawned by the trauma of colonialism';[9] but, as we shall see, the trouble goes much deeper than that.

Paradoxically, the non-Communist emerging countries would do well to borrow from Marxist states in their dealings with foreign multinational enterprises. It is on the basis of cool calculations of likely benefits that Marxist regimes enter into agreements with the multinationals, and it is likewise on the basis of the undisputed sovereignty of the host country. Executives of leading multinationals have themselves embraced these points, and this has helped them to win business in all parts of the world including countries ruled by the most doctrinaire of Communists. For example, one of the largest American banks, which operates in more than 100 countries, has issued the following code of conduct as applicable to its worldwide activities:

1. We must never lose sight of the fact that we are guests in foreign countries. We must conduct ourselves accordingly. We recognize the right of governments to pass local legislation and our obligation to conform.
2. Under these circumstances, we also recognize that we can survive only if we are successful in demonstrating to the local authorities that our presence is beneficial.
3. We believe that every country must find its own way politically and economically. Sometimes we feel that local policies are wise; sometimes we do not. However, irrespective of our own views, we try to function as best we can under prevailing conditions.
4. We have always felt free to discuss with local governments matters directly affecting our interests, but we recognize that they have final regulatory authority.[10]

As part of the love–hate attitude mentioned at the beginning of this chapter, much confusion persists as to where to pin the blame for ill-advised projects sometimes undertaken by multinational enterprises in developing countries. It is perfectly true that some such companies are less reliable than others, that companies may mount high-pressure sales drives, and that occasionally they may resort to bribes or favours or enticements of one kind or another. But none of this absolves the host country of the principal responsibility. When ill-advised projects have been undertaken, the fault may have lain in part with multinational enterprises where they have proposed them, but even more with host countries where they have approved them.

In justice to its own citizens, no country — and especially no large and powerful sovereign state like Indonesia — can abdicate its responsibility for unilaterally deciding whether proposed projects should or should not go forward. In all too many cases, developing countries have opted for projects which later became white elephants; Ghana, under the leadership of its flamboyant former President Nkrumah, provides an excellent example. Happily, Indonesia has thus far been much freer from such white elephants than have a number of her sister emerging countries, but ominous danger signals have lately appeared. As we shall see later in this chapter, the government has yet to readjust its project priorities sufficiently to cope with such imperatives as the overriding need for more jobs.

According to Richard Ensor, Indonesia's 'wealth of resources and surplus of labor are matched by a shortage of capital. That's why Indonesia welcomes foreign investors, especially in those areas where capital, advanced technology and management skills are not internally available.'[11] Certainly my discussions with Indonesian leaders bear this out. They have made it abundantly clear that they both need and want much more foreign investment — especially when it is accompanied by technological and managerial expertise and particularly when it comes from the West or Australasia. In recent years around a third of all foreign investment in Indonesia has come from Japan, and another big chunk has come from Hong Kong, which in this regard serves largely as a conduit for Chinese and Japanese funds.[12] Indonesia wants a much better balance in terms of the sources of foreign investment.

It should nevertheless be emphasized that an important and impressive Western and Australasian business presence already exists in Indonesia. Many reputable British, American, Dutch, French, West German, and other Western business enterprises are active there, as well as their counterparts from Australia and New Zealand; and typically they are in joint-venture partnership with Indonesian interests. India, the Philippines, and other developing Asian countries also maintain a business presence in Indonesia, and this is particularly significant from the point of view of the economical use of capital. As Louis T. Wells, Jr. and V'Ella Warren point out, 'Foreign investors from developing countries in Indonesia are in important ways quite different from the investors from the advanced countries. Their projects seem to be smaller and their technologies are certainly considerably more labour-intensive. . . .'[13]

The British, American, French, Australian and other embassies in Jakarta have lists of businessmen from their respective countries who are resident in Indonesia, and they can likewise offer other valuable information and advice. The Australian example is particularly interesting because of the embassy's explicit linkage of practical business guidance with Australian national policy. As its comprehensive *Notes on the Market for Potential Australian Investors* suggests at the outset,

> Prospective Australian investors should be aware of the Australian Prime Minister's statement . . . that the Australian Government is concerned to encourage private Australian investment in developing countries on a joint-venture basis in accordance with the country's social and economic development plans, and that the Australian Government is conscious of the wishes of the developing countries in the Asian and Pacific region to attract private Australian investment, which, apart from the flow of funds, will encourage technical know-how and advance local management skills.
> . . . It is important, therefore, that Australian companies investing overseas realise the aspirations of host countries, seek to operate properly within their laws, and generate a good corporate citizen image. Such efforts will greatly assist in the total relationship between Australia and its neighbours in the Asian and Pacific region, such as Indonesia.[14]

The report follows with sections on Indonesian investment law, the mechanics of obtaining approval for foreign investment in Indonesia, representative offices and service companies, domestic investments, investment opportunities for foreign companies, advisory organizations for prospective investors, business entities and company incorporation, capital structure and voting rights, local partners, and so forth. The Americans, among others, publish parallel information; for example, one American report, entitled *Indonesia: A Survey of US Business Opportunities*,[15] runs to 320 pages of useful information. Western as well as Indonesian bankers in Jakarta and other parts of the country can provide information and valuable contacts; and the same applies to the Indonesian Chamber of Commerce and Industry and its numerous affiliated functional groups.[16]

The British, American, Australian, and various other nationality groups have their own quasi-chambers of commerce in Indonesia, and through these one can discuss common problems and make further useful contacts.

There are likewise numerous Western-affiliated and other consulting firms, and these can undertake relevant preliminary or detailed studies. One can meanwhile establish good contacts at the Investment Co-ordinating Board and at the appropriate ministries.

Yet in spite of all this, Western businessmen who want to investigate investment possibilities in Indonesia all too often go at it in exactly the wrong way. Surprising though it may seem, they sometimes take a hotel room in Singapore, fly over to Jakarta for the day, and attempt to form an impression of Indonesia's investment climate. Or they may stay for a few days in Jakarta at one of the numerous so-called international hotels, talk to people who have no intimate contact with the indigenous cultural scene even inside that very large metropolis, see little or nothing of the country's rich diversity outside of the capital city, and again attempt to assess the investment climate. I know a Western businessman, now a long-standing resident of Indonesia, who described to me how thoroughly misled he had been by his initial impressions when he first visited Indonesia. For example, having heard tales of rampant corruption, he concluded that the whole economy must soon grind to a halt. Subsequent experience taught him, however, that the economy was not grinding to a halt; to the contrary, it was growing at around double the current growth rates of America or Britain. In no way did he condone such corruption, but he had learned to place that perennial Indonesian problem in its larger historical and cultural perspective.

The investment climate naturally depends upon a number of factors, not least the political. For example, the 1974 student demonstrations, as mentioned in Chapter 9, had a profound effect on the then investment climate and proved again the crucial role played in Indonesian affairs by the youth. Likewise, the outcome of the government's efforts to contain inflation or promote exports in turn reacts back on the investment climate. But the only possible way to make an adequate assessment is to pay an extended visit or visits to the country and to immerse oneself in its culture to the full. And this principle applies not only to conducting investigations but also to consummating agreements. Cultural illiteracy can readily undo any negotiations, and cultural awareness can on the other hand work wonders. It is essential to acquire some real grasp of the country's fascinating cultural complexities and subleties, including those that relate directly to the conduct of business. Moreover, Westerners should learn from their Japanese competitors, who are prepared to stay put in Indonesia for as long as may be required for negotiations to mature; as they know, a sound investment of funds requires a generous and spacious investment of time. The Western 'Time Is Money' business precept translates in an entirely different way when it is applied to Indonesia.

In spite of the striking differences between Indonesia's culture and those of Western countries, there is one outstanding common denominator. As Bernard E. Meland has written, 'However valid it may have been a generation or more ago to set the West apart from the East in its encounter with science and technology, the notion that these disciplines and technical processes are alien to Asian thinking and life is no longer tenable. . .'.[17] Japan of course provides the pre-eminent example. For many years, and especially since the Second World War, Japan has been famous for copying

American and other Western technology and often improving upon it. Indeed, when Indonesian students and others criticize the 'Western' impact on their country, they often forget that that impact largely emanates straight from a sister Asian country in the shape of Japan. It is Japan which, for better or worse, serves as the great transmission belt into Asia for Western technology and for other fruits of Western culture as well. Whether those Western cultural components arrive by way of Japan or by other means, the sad fact remains that they are not necessarily what Indonesia wants or needs.

Much of the difficulty traces back to the Industrial Revolution. In the words of a standard source, that revolution was 'the sudden acceleration of technical development which occurred in Europe from the late 18th century. . .'.[18] Historians often like to distinguish between the First Industrial Revolution, symbolized by the steam engine and the widespread installation of powered machinery, beginning in Britain; and the Second Industrial Revolution, which from around the 1870s onward brought the application of electricity, many new industrial techniques including those arising from chemistry, and the inauguration of the nuclear age. The term Industrial Revolution is likewise widely used in the composite sense as encompassing both the original phase and the subsequent one.

Britain was of course the pioneer industrial nation and the original home of the Industrial Revolution,[19] and this tradition has never entirely deserted her. It used to be said that the sun never set on the British Empire; and now one can say that the sun never sets on British engineers and technologists who are at work in emerging and other countries all over the world. Their American, French, German, Scandinavian, and other Western colleagues are likewise active in many countries; and, along with their British counterparts, they carry with them certain basic assumptions.

For more than 150 years, British engineers have been trying to *save labour*.[20] From the beginning of the Industrial Revolution, their objective — which they have thought to be entirely laudable— has been to produce more goods of equal or better quality with less man-hours. That their achievements were regarded with great pride is well illustrated by the following description, as published in 1835, of a British steam-powered cotton mill:

> . . . The various machines . . . all derive their motion from the mighty engine, which . . . toils through the day with the strength of perhaps a hundred horses. Men in the mean while, have merely to attend on this wonderful series of mechanism, to supply it with work, to oil its joints, and to check its slight and infrequent irregularities; each workman performing, or rather superintending, as much work as could have been done by *two or three hundred men* sixty years ago. At the approach of darkness the building is illuminated with jets of flame, whose brilliance mimics the light of day. . . . When it is remembered that all these inventions have been made within the last seventy years, it must be acknowledged that the cotton mill presents the most striking example of the dominion obtained by human science over the powers of nature, of which modern times can boast.[21]

The Industrial Revolution multiplied the availability of goods and thus brought many benefits, but its social costs were high. For example, the large new mechanized textile mills meant unemployment and privation for many people who had previously produced textiles by cottage industry methods; ironically, the same sort of thing has been happening in Indonesia in very recent years, and the students understandably complain about it. Yet Western engineers for the most part continue to pursue, in developing countries as well as elsewhere, the same labour-saving objective which motivated their predecessors of 100 or 150 years ago. And the same point largely applies to Eastern engineers and technologists trained in the Western curricular tradition. Again it must be said that the engineers and technologists are not so much to blame as the policy-makers of the sovereign host countries concerned.

A similar comment applies to what has become the flourishing international technology transfer industry. Not only the US and other governments, but also a number of multinational enterprises, have built up large computerized data banks from which they make available — at a price — technological information which is eagerly sought after by emerging countries. At international conferences and otherwise, certain representatives of such countries have argued that technological information should be made freely available to all, but this misses the main point. As Mark Casson remarks with commendable understatement, 'It would seem that in the immediate future the world-wide socialization of information is not politically feasible. . . . The major issue facing host nations is, therefore, . . . how proprietary information can be used to greatest advantage.'[22]

One American group, which engages in large-scale technology transfer to many countries of the world, has established a special category of labour-intensive and other technology well adapted to the needs of emerging countries. This was in fact done on the recommendation of the company's resident representative in Indonesia. The company also holds, both in Southeast Asia and elsewhere, periodic technology fairs to facilitate transfers of what it is hoped will be appropriate technologies.[23] But commendable though such activities may be, they in no way relieve emerging countries of the duty to create their own appropriate technology from their own resources.

The challenge can be restated in Indonesian terms. From the early days of the Industrial Revolution onward, Western engineers — and Indonesian engineers who have more recently emulated them — have for the most part stood for generous, even profligate, inputs of capital and of energy in order to save labour. Clearly this tradition must now be reversed. To reverse it will require highly selective imports of suitable technology and the careful adaptation of it to Indonesia's particular needs; but even more importantly it will require the generation of much new appropriate technology within the country — far more than anything hitherto envisaged.

As Charles Cooper points out, 'Labour-intensive techniques, by definition, have lower physical labour productivity than capital-intensive ones. To make up for this, labour-intensive alternatives must have a higher level of output per unit of investment.'[24] In the quest for efficient labour-intensive techniques, *both traditional techniques and modern ones are largely irrelevant* — the former because they are not productive enough for today's world, the latter because they are too expensive in terms of capital or energy requirements or both.[25]

This brings us to the field — new in terms of modern history — of what I choose to call *capital conservation*. In one sense engineers have long sought to keep capital costs within bounds, but they have given a higher priority to saving labour. To achieve this saving of labour, they have designed for large inputs of capital and of energy as well. Now, in the interests both of employment and of cultural sanity, the priorities must be reversed. At the same time the engineer's habitual emphasis upon productivity must be retained.

In terms of this new field, the industrialized countries must in effect be *reclassified as underdeveloped*. Their massive research and development establishments are for the most part eminently ill-fitted to deal with the task at hand. It is true that they have great strength in basic science, and that this can be mobilized in support of innovation in the new field; but this will take much budgetary and other readjustment. Indonesia, along with her sister emerging countries, must meanwhile seize the initiative.

The capital conservation challenge therefore becomes a global one, and one offering immense possibilities for creative activity. As we shall see in the next chapter, the role of technology, crucial as it is in fostering development and employment, in turn depends heavily upon political and administrative and entrepreneurial factors. A resource-rich country such as Indonesia provides plenty of potential scope for growth, investment, and legitimate profits, but only if one is guided by the realities of the 1980s.

Transcending Anti-Communism

When, in a meeting with Indonesia's Vice President Adam Malik, I asked if he approved of importing Western technology, he replied that he was against it. After a whimsical smile and a suitable pause, he went on to explain what he meant. He was against it, he said, unless the imported technology had first been properly selected in the light of the nation's needs and then carefully adapted to serve those needs.

When Indonesia earlier imported certain ideologies as distinguished from technologies, these same plausible requirements were unfortunately not met. It was, as we have seen, a foreigner who imported the Marxist creed into Indonesia. No proper assessment was made as to whether it fitted the nation's needs, and subsequent efforts to adapt it and apply it ended in disaster. Even before the Marxist debacle, Western liberal democracy had foundered in the Indonesian milieu. It, too, had been imported without proper assessment, and attempts to adapt it and apply it had proved ill-fated. Some people blame its demise on Sukarno, but the real causes would seem to lie much more deeply embedded in the culture.

After the collapse of Communism in the mid-1960s, followed by the exit of Sukarno, the New Order government sought to consolidate and activate a viable governmental structure and administrative system. As we saw in Chapter 11, the new leadership took over the fundamental Pancasila philosophy from Sukarno, and it likewise embraced the Constitution of 1945 which Sukarno had reinstated. The Constitution vests the highest authority in the People's Consultative Assembly (the *Assembly*) and provides for four supposedly independent branches of government under the Assembly: the President, the House of People's Representatives (the *House*), the Supreme Audit Board, and the Supreme Court. The Constitution also provides for a Supreme Advisory Council to advise the President.[1]

Under the Constitution the Republic of Indonesia is structured as a unitary state. Sovereignty is vested in the people as a whole and is exercised by the Assembly, which formally speaking is the highest authority of the state. It elects the President and Vice President and determines (or in practice largely ratifies) the broad outlines of state policy to be implemented by the President.

The Constitution prescribes that the Assembly shall meet at least once in every five years and that its membership shall include all members of the

Vice President Adam Malik, shown with his mother

House *plus* delegates representing both geographical regions and also *functional groups*, including farmers, youth, veterans, co-operatives, businessmen, women, and labour. The 1969 General Election Law, which has remained in effect, provides that the Assembly shall comprise 460 members *appointed by the government*. The appointed members consist of the regional and functional representatives plus those nominated by the political parties in proportion to the results of the general elections held to elect members to the House. Assembly members are elected for a term of five years.

The President is responsible only to the Assembly. He has authority and responsibility for conducting the administration of the state, and he is supreme commander of the armed forces. He has the right, with the approval of the House, to declare war, make peace, conclude treaties with other states, and make statutes.

The Constitution provides that the House, which must meet at least once a year, will serve as the legislative body. Of the above-mentioned 460 members of the House, 360 are elected by the people from among the political associations approved by the government, and the remaining 100 are directly chosen by the government.

The government in effect decides which political parties or associations shall exist and which shall not. The government-sponsored party is an association of functional groups known as Golkar. In addition, two other political associations function with the approval of the government: the PPP, an association of four Islamic parties; and the PDI, an association of the Nationalist, Christian (i.e. Protestant), Catholic, Independence Upholders', and People's parties. The government-sponsored Golkar group normally wins elections with a handsome margin; with this electoral ascendency together with its appointive powers, the New Order government finds itself

A founding father: Indonesia's first Vice President Mohammad Hatta, 1902–1980

in an excellent position to retain control of the state apparatus. And since Army officers occupy prominent positions in the New Order hierarchy, the Army can readily help to reinforce such control.

In a semi-mystical way the structure and functioning of government in Indonesia reflect the people's traditional reliance — particularly in the rural setting — upon discussion and consensus. As Allen M. Sievers notes with reference to two venerable Indonesian concepts, '*Musjawarah* refers to settlement of problems and disputes by mutual discussion and conferences, chaired by a peacemaker. *Mufakat* is the consensus or unanimous agreement, which emerges from *musjawarah*.' These and other associated principles 'constitute the village "democracy" which Sukarno attempted to translate to the national level'.[2]

Many Indonesian traditionalists — apart from those in Islamic circles who may feel that their voices are not sufficiently heard in affairs of state — consider the structure and workings of government in Indonesia as eminently in keeping with the country's cultural heritage. Western liberals, and some Indonesian students conforming to the Western liberal mould, may take a diametrically opposite position. They may be shocked and dismayed at what they regard as a farce and a caricature of democratic government.

A balanced view would seem to lie somewhere between the two. In framing a considered attitude, one should constantly bear in mind that the present structure and system were very largely bequeathed by Sukarno and others of Indonesia's founding fathers. Moreover, the present arrangements by no means preclude dissent; and in spite of occasional government crackdowns the Indonesian press remains freer than one finds in most African countries, for example, not to mention in Eastern Europe. Anybody who follows the newspapers in Indonesia is aware that members of the

146

House of People's Representatives and others frequently make decidedly forthright statements and get them reported in the press; they are at liberty, for instance, to assert that the national development programme requires drastic change.[3]

As a summary assessment, one could say that Indonesia's governmental structure and administrative system are not unrelated to her traditions and that they are reasonably well suited to her present state of development. But this assessment immediately leads to these two crucial questions which are very much in the minds of the country's rising generation: (A) Given the existing constitutional and governmental infrastructure — which seems unlikely to undergo any major change in the immediate future — can the New Order regime operate it in such a way as to meet Indonesia's development challenges in the 1980s? (B) Can this be done decisively enough to demonstrate, to Indonesia's young people and others, the superiority of her model to others such as found in Marxist countries or in Iran? It is important to study and evaluate various views on this general subject.

According to Harold Crouch, writing in the light of his observation of Indonesia,

> The decline of the political parties and the absence of other civilian organizations able to countervail the army's power meant that the system grew less capable of responding to popular discontent. When the emasculated political parties ceased to serve as channels to carry nonelite aspirations upward, popular resentments were deprived of institutional means of expression. . . . The failure of the government's program of economic development to bring about improvements for the mass of the people meant that popular frustration and discontent continued to spread, while the government showed no signs of being capable of tackling the basic long-term problems of growing unemployment, overpopulation, and poverty. Despite the government's achievement of 'political stability', it had no program to cope with the inevitable growth of popular discontent which it faced except to rely on the instruments of repression.[4]

Crouch's conclusions, although containing important elements of truth, clearly require amendments; and so too do those of Karl D. Jackson. According to him,

> . . . The Indonesian political system is best understood as a bureaucratic polity with political power and participation monopolized by the highest levels of the civil and military bureaucracies. Political life revolves around a small number of key decision-makers responding primarily . . . to the values and interests of the small, capital-city elite. . . . Interest groups, political parties, and horizontal groupings of all kinds remain weak and incapable of consistently influencing the basic political decisions determining Indonesian domestic and foreign policies.[5]

Jackson then attempts to forecast the likely trend of events with such statements as the following:

> Although bureaucratic polity is the most probable form of government in Indonesia for the next several decades, with bureaucratic polities nothing fails like success. . . . To the extent that education, mass media, and

modern organizational forms involve an increasing proportion of the population, . . . the desire for political participation will increase. . . . The choices taken by the Indonesian political elite over the next decade will affect long-term economic and political stability. . . . The available alternatives fall into three categories: (1) movement toward a more open, competitive democratic system, expanding the power of the government by sharing control more widely; (2) foundation of an ideologically based, single-party mobilization regime (of Right or Left), extending government organization and political mobilization into every town and village in the society; and (3) the continuation of bureaucratic polity under conditions of increasing challenge from social elements generated by economic expansion. Although all three alternatives are within the purview of the current elite, the third choice remains the most probable. . . . The bureaucratic and military elites probably will continue to limit participation, and increased coercion will be the most likely response to participatory energies released by the modernization process. The most likely outcome in Indonesia over the next several decades is a hardening of the bureaucratic polity, a harsher use of power, and increasingly authoritarian practices. . . .[6]

The validity of any seemingly-plausible forecast depends upon whether or not indicated corrective action is meanwhile undertaken. (Jackson, in the extract above, in effect suggests that it will *not* be undertaken.) If a ship's lookout signals the commanding officer that dangerous rocks lie not far ahead, orders may be given to alter course in time to prevent a calamity. So too it is with the ship of state. Forecasts are in a real sense *made to be proved wrong*; by calling attention to the need for corrective action, they can motivate intelligent leaders to alter course. Less perceptive leaders will simply deny that the forecasts possess any validity: and indeed, in the manner of certain medieval kings, they may wish only to penalize the bearers of disturbing tidings.

We are in this book, and particularly in Chapters 6 to 15, examining a range of Indonesia's key problems of balanced national development and making constructive comments and suggestions concerning them. The present chapter especially considers one particular developmental problem which underlies virtually all the others — that of administrative improvement. My own observations in a number of emerging countries have led to the conclusion, which is also shared by many people in the international aid field, that in such countries the most important practical obstacles to effective development are commonly administrative in nature.

In more than a few of the emerging countries, plausible policies are formulated and promulgated, but then not much seems to happen. Policies tend to become empty slogans. Programmes habitually fall short of targets. The people, hearing much fine talk but seeing few results of benefit to them, become disillusioned.

Among such developing countries, Indonesia fares better than most. As we saw in Chapter 6, impressive results have been achieved under Indonesia's successive five-year development plans. Moreover, Indonesia, far more than many of her sister emerging countries, has emphasized extra-economic as well as economic development; and as we have found, this has extended across the board even into the realm of culture and ideology. Yet in terms of effective administration, serious anomalies remain.

A good example concerns the relative failure to delegate. Many people, including expatriates and Indonesians both in the government and outside of it, have remarked on the inability or unwillingness of not a few senior civil servants to delegate responsibilities and decision-making to their subordinates. This, it is pointed out, can and often does reduce administrative action to a snail's pace. Some cynics suggest that officials decline to delegate because to do so would reduce their opportunities to benefit from corruption; but a more relevant factor may lie in the grossly inadequate number of Indonesians who received professional training in the days of Dutch control. Yet much water has passed under the bridge since then, and thousands of young Indonesians have attained professional competence. Relatively few, however, have been trained in the theory and practice of public administration as such.

Another example concerns administrative overemphasis on large capital-intensive projects. In this matter cynics sometimes suggest that big projects are favoured because they offer bigger opportunities for corruption than do small ones. Yet the fact must be faced that tardiness in embracing job-creating labour-intensive projects has by no means been confined to Indonesia; indeed, the World Bank and other international agencies have, through a sort of intellectual lag, likewise been notoriously slow in emphasizing such projects. A general conceptual reorientation is required.

A third example concerns the administrative handling of the country's export programme — a matter with plenty of paradoxes. On the face of it one might think that since Indonesia has lots of low-cost labour and ample raw materials, nothing stands in the way of a vast increase in her exports. But this would be living in a dream world. The Indonesian economy in fact has certain rigidities which have in recent years consistently impaired efforts to expand exports, and of these two particularly stand out. They relate to shipping and to what are euphemistically called 'leakages'.

Container rates between Jakarta and Western European ports, for instance, are strikingly higher than those between Singapore or Bangkok or Hong Kong and those same Western European ports. This situation has continued mainly because the government has failed to disturb a comfortable quasi-monopolistic hold which certain shipping interests have on the trade. If the government seriously wants to expand exports — as indeed it does — then one of its first prescriptions should be vigorous administrative action to make Indonesian shipping rates fully competitive, and likewise to make more ocean cargo capacity available. Moreover, the government should greatly increase the availability and efficiency of Indonesia's inter-island shipping. Making more ocean and inter-island cargo space available at more reasonable rates could — by boosting volume — in due course actually help rather than hurt the companies concerned.

Discussions with many businessmen and others confirm that leakages — or, if one must use a cruder term, corruption — seriously impair Indonesia's competitive position in exports. Here, again, one finds fascinating paradoxes. It was in 1972 that I first visited Tanjong Priok, the port of Jakarta, and I found it a shambles. Ships had to wait for weeks to discharge their cargo, the whole port was littered with goods that appeared to have no known home, and the general atmosphere was one of complete lethargy.

My next visit to the port was in 1979, and by then the transformation was truly unbelievable. Ship turnaround time had been reduced to a few days or less. The entire vast port area looked neat, clean, orderly, and dynamic. A dedicated port administrator had established a highly efficient administrative system including delegation that really works. Some of Indonesia's other ports have likewise been transformed. But on the other hand there remained the continuing problem of customs administration or maladministration; according to Indonesian and expatriate businessmen who knew the situation intimately, excessive numbers of signatures continued to be required in order to clear any given consignment, and leakages abounded during the clearance process. If you wanted quick action, you could get it — but only at a price, and one which in a cumulative sense prejudiced your competitive standing in international markets. In addition, the government continued with an archaic system of official export levies which did nothing to enhance the country's position in world trade.

Container terminal, port of Tanjung Priok, Jakarta

To be fair, Indonesia's export performance has, as we saw in Chapter 6, shown remarkable gains, and it has done so *in spite of* such deplorable constraints as these. Moreover, most members of Indonesia's indigenous and expatriate business community maintain their indispensable sense of humour; they good-naturedly look forward to the day when the government will remove certain obvious obstacles to the further growth of exports and the winning of much-needed foreign exchange. The government already has its vigorous National Agency for Export Development, with branch offices in several Western cities.[7] But the export problem is an essentially inter-ministerial one which must, to a far greater extent than hitherto, be tackled in an objective and co-ordinated manner. Only then can Indonesia's administrative system overcome the shipping and other bottlenecks which retard the needed further expansion of the country's exports.

The whole matter of the administrative system must be viewed in proper perspective. In 1978, as a prelude to the preparation of Repelita III and its launching in 1979, President Soeharto appointed the Third Development Cabinet. The new Cabinet comprised 24 ministers, including three co-ordinating ministers respectively for Defence and Political Affairs, Social Affairs, and Economic, Financial and Industrial Affairs; four ministers of state; and seventeen ministers as such. In addition the Cabinet included six vice ministers with particular portfolios.[8]

Having been privileged to have had personal meetings with eighteen ministers or vice ministers in the Development Cabinet, and having seen them in action and discussed their accomplishments with other close observers of the Indonesian scene, I have acquired a very high opinion of them and their abilities. Moreover, one of the ministers has Administrative Reform as his explicit portfolio. Yet, as the foregoing examples suggest, serious anomalies still persist; and an overriding need is for better training in the associated fields of public and business administration. Indonesian public servants, many of whom have been excessively conditioned in state bureaucratic responses, need intensive work in both of these complementary fields.

Further official encouragement should be given to Indonesia's so-called Wiraswasta Entrepreneurship movement, which helps small enterprises including those in the villages.[9] Beyond that, there must be a very large increase in the emphasis given by the universities to training in public and business administration. Many thousands of university students should receive such training; and mature civil servants and businessmen should be brought back to the campuses for the same purpose. Speaking nationally, Indonesia has been lagging badly in this area.

The government, through its anti-graft organization known as Opstib, has been waging a campaign against corruption both inside and outside the public service, and a number of convictions, carrying fines or prison sentences or both, have been secured.[10] As government officials agree, the campaign must be viewed as necessarily a long-term one, and raising the salaries of civil servants to realistic levels will form part of the process. Public opinion, and especially student opinion, would seem to favour the government's focusing much more on the 'big fish' among the corruptors and making object lessons of them. Anti-corruption progress reports should likewise be prepared in more systematic and cumulative form and made available to the press, the universities, and so forth. The government has been considering giving qualified students an active role in investigating alleged corruption, and this should be encouraged. Far from being a purely Eastern phenomenon, corruption is of course also well known in the West.[11]

An excellent test of Indonesia's administrative capacity is provided by the country's imperative need to generate far more new technology suited to her economy and culture. The Third Development Cabinet includes a Ministry of Research and Technology which is equipped with dynamic leadership and a substantial budget. Among other things the ministry has appointed national committees for recommending R & D priorities in several strategic fields: basic human needs, natural resources and energy, defence and security, and socio-economic and cultural aspects. The ministry has established a new Agency for the Development and Application of Technology, and construction of a Research, Science and Technology centre has been proceeding on a large site near Jakarta.[12].

Such steps have clearly been commendable, but time will be required for them to show practical results. There was indeed the danger that they would have a minimal developmental impact during the period of Repelita III. The urgency of the task — to meet job-creation and other needs — is such that a genuine 'crash' programme is required. When, during the Second World War, President Franklin D. Roosevelt established unprecedented production targets for planes and ships and other war material, some people thought that he had literally taken leave of his senses; but the targets were attained and surpassed. The same thing was achieved in the field of research and technology related to the war effort. In the present Indonesian situation, a similar spirit is required.

At least four further programmes seem called for — not instead of, but in addition to, those which the government has already undertaken. The first programme concerns the interdisciplinary campus centres proposed in Chapter 9. These can among other things become focal points of creative technological research and development with particular reference to job-creation and to the needs of the region where each university, institute or college is located. The second programme would comprise R & D contracting on a very big scale, with government agencies, academic institutions, and private companies both at home and abroad — and with Indonesian direction in every case. R & D contracting provides one of the best ways of achieving rapid results; and valuable advice on it can be obtained from the US aid programme's intermediate technology office in Jakarta, from the Intermediate Technology Development Group in London, and from other sources.[13]

The third programme would provide individual grants under which qualified graduate or research students or faculty members would pursue intermediate technology projects either at home or abroad. This would serve to integrate their studies with research experience on subjects of greatest need. The fourth programme would bring the Army into the picture. The Army, with its broad experience in project management, could readily give a boost in any of the three foregoing fields; and this would constitute a logical extension of Indonesia's doctrine of the dual role of the military.

As already indicated in Chapter 10, and as an inspection of the text of Repelita III confirms,[14] the country's national economic planners have not yet properly assimilated the powerful potentialities of science and technology into their thinking. Moreover, much better inter-ministerial co-ordination is needed in regard to giving an optimum role to job-creating technology; as one of many examples, businessmen have found it exceedingly difficult to get Investment Co-ordinating Board approval for the import of capital-saving, labour-intensive second-hand machinery. The Board should positively encourage the import of such machinery, and it could well follow the examples offered by some other emerging countries by contracting with a qualified group to provide a certification service for used machinery in acceptable condition.[15]

It is no exaggeration, then, to say that the problem of technological mobilization furnishes an excellent test of Indonesia's administrative capacity. The country's balanced development indeed depends in no small measure upon success in such a mobilization effort; it must not be allowed to fail or to materialize 'too little and too late'. Success in mobilizing technological resources can in turn have an important bearing on the country's performance in competition with Communism.

In working with students in a number of countries including Indonesia, I have found that they display considerable impatience with mere negative anti-Communism. It shows a sound instinct on their part, because a country's national salvation can scarcely be based upon negative doctrines alone. Transcending anti-Communism therefore becomes a highly practical matter.

If Indonesians as a whole are known for their staunch opposition to Communism, they are also known for much more besides. Pancasila, the national ideology, dates from the memorable days of Indonesia's Declaration of Independence, and so does the Constitution under which the country operates. The Indonesian dual role doctrine, which again stems from the beginning of the Republic, still serves both to broaden the outlook of military officers and men and to engage them in major developmental tasks. The country's administrative system, although linked in a more tenuous way with the Republic's early days, has more recently evolved into the relatively systematized form represented by the Third Development Cabinet with its associated ministries and agencies.

Transcending anti-Communism means taking steps to provide a better system than Communism can offer. This is exactly what the New Order government has undertaken to do. In many ways its success in the post-1965 period has been nothing short of remarkable — even if a very great deal remains to be done. Indonesia, as the world's fifth most populous country, faces a multiple challenge encompassing the ideological component plus the political, the military, the economic, the technological, the cultural — and, in full-circle fashion, back to the ideological.

A good example can be drawn from the President's 1979 Independence Day speech, in which among other things he spoke of the duty to safeguard the country from 'the latent danger from remnants and elements of the Indonesian Communist Party (PKI) and/or other extreme anti-Pancasila forces'. Referring to the release of detainees from 'the former Communist Party', he warned in particular that 'the possibility of the growth of vulnerability in the community has certainly increased'; and he emphasized 'the need to heighten vigilance over the possibility of negative activities from those former detainees'.[16]

Admiral Sudomo, as Commander-in-Chief of the Operational Command for the Restoration of Security and Order (Kopkamtib) as well as Vice Commander-in-Chief of the Armed Forces of Indonesia, has key responsibility for safeguarding not only the national interest generally but also the individual interests of all the country's citizens including the released detainees. He, along with other Indonesian leaders, realize that security and stability and individual well-being depend in the last analysis upon Indonesia's demonstrating the superiority of her evolving model over any

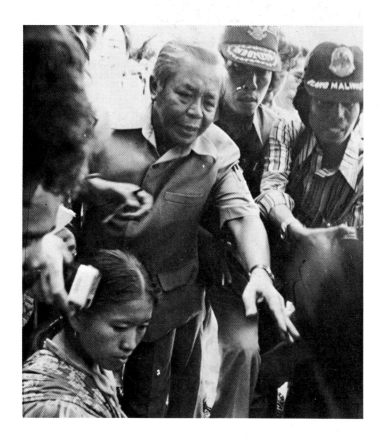

Admiral Sudomo at a public market

Communist one or any other extremist one.

And they realize that this means facing the multiple challenge already referred to — and dealing with such a range of matters as those set forth in the several chapters of this book.

The Indonesian Synthesis

When President Soeharto went on a state visit to Britain in November 1979 as a guest of Queen Elizabeth II, this was in no way inconsistent with the prevailing Indonesian attitude toward Western culture. Indonesians increasingly distinguish between on the one hand the best of the West and on the other hand what must be regarded as its seedier cultural components. From their own Eastern vantage point, Indonesians are often better able to exercise such selectivity than are Westerners themselves.

Considerable symbolic significance attaches to the fact that the state visit was to the very country which, as we have seen, was the original home of the Industrial Revolution. Further symbolic significance resides in the fact that the Queen's consort, H.R.H. Prince Philip, Duke of Edinburgh, had been among the first clearly and lucidly to point out that man must learn to exercise social discrimination in the application of technology. As he expressed the matter, we are 'beginning to realize that unless we are very careful indeed we can make serious and long-lasting mistakes in *the indiscriminate application of scientific techniques'.* We must, he suggested, learn to use the power of science and technology 'to create the sort of environment in which mankind . . . can thrive and prosper'.[1]

More recently I have had the privilege of discussing this matter with Prince Philip in its Indonesian context. He and Queen Elizabeth had been entranced by Indonesia's exotic and unique culture in the course of a state visit there in 1974, and he was thoroughly aware of the problem of technological and other cultural intrusions.

As a country which is so justly proud of its indigenous culture, Indonesia faces the ever-present problem of guarding against such intrusions; and the impact of tourism provides an excellent example. I have seen the looks of wide-eyed amazement on the faces of graceful Indonesian girls as they behold certain Western female tourists; such apparitions, they are led to believe, are supposed to symbolize the progressive, affluent West.

In principle Indonesia, along with many other countries, welcomes tourists and the revenue which tourism brings. But the potentials for cultural contamination are enormous and should be carefully heeded by discerning leaders. A number of countries have rued the day when they decided to welcome large numbers of tourists, who may end up by largely destroying the very cultural riches at which they come to gape. Fiji is one such country,

Left, Queen Elizabeth II and President Soeharto during the President's state visit to Britain in November 1979. Below, the President and Madame Soeharto with Prince Charles, Queen Elizabeth, Prince Philip, Princess Alexandra and her husband, Angus Ogilvy

and she has pioneered in requesting the United Nations to do a survey not on how to promote tourism but on how to be more selective about it. Indonesia could well emulate this example.

The problem of cultural pollution of course extends far beyond tourism. As James L. Peacock, an experienced observer of Indonesia, has expressed it,

Initially filtered by Dutch education, Western culture in Indonesia now includes asphalt-jungle-style hoodlums, rock 'n' roll singing and dancing, and the seamier sides of capitalistic hedonism (such as X-rated movies). Major Western-based movements — nationalism, socialism, Communism — have also been grafted onto . . . the indigenous tradition.[2]

Around the hotels and discotheques of Jakarta and other large Indonesian cities, one finds plenty of examples of young men and girls who seem to be under no parental control and who make a pathetic spectacle of aping the trendy ways of the West.[3] Some among the worst offenders are sons and daughters of senior civil servants or military officers, and they tend to set a pattern for other teenagers whose parents are in less exalted positions. The Jakarta police chief has more than once threatened to close various of the discotheques if they continue to lead so many young girls astray.

Some Indonesians, concerned though they are about such phenomena, nevertheless point out that they relate only to the major metropolises and not to the 'real' Indonesia of the smaller towns and villages. But one can find no comfort here, for the major centres largely set the national cultural tone; and this effect has been compounded by the import of Western communications technology. In terms of the country's cultural integrity, such technology offers a serious threat as well as a promise.

By 1977 Indonesia had attained the distinction of being the fourth country in the world — after the United States, Canada, and the Soviet Union — to own and operate its own domestic communications satellite system. The satellites were produced in America, launched at Cape Canaveral, Florida, and placed in stationary orbits above the Indonesian archipelago. The satellites and their associated ground equipment have helped to bring about a vast improvement in Indonesia's internal and international communications by telephone and telex; and in addition they have brought the capability of extending television and radio broadcasts to all 27 of Indonesia's provinces.[4] Thus, through the wonders of modern technology, the entire vast country — even including small settlements with their village television sets — is more and more being blanketed by the electronic media.

And what is the nature of the television output? Much of it is excellent, reflecting as it does Indonesia's great heritage in music and the arts. Some of the imported programmes are likewise well selected and in general harmony with the indigenous culture. A few of the domestically-produced and imported programmes are, however, to say the least ill-considered; and the worst offenders seem to be the commercials. Some of these are in singularly poor taste, out of joint with the country's culture, and calculated to cause social tension by raising false expectations especially among the great majority of citizens who live in rural areas. What a contrast with the basic needs approach to human problems!

The role of all the media indeed needs to receive much more careful attention from the point of view of maintaining the nation's cultural integrity. For example, Indonesians on the whole smoke vastly excessive numbers of cigarettes; and the media, far from being harnessed to promote their use, should be employed to warn how they can undermine the nation's health. Some people have suggested that the government could not afford to do without its excise revenue from cigarettes; but as experience in other countries has shown, the social cost of cigarette-related disease and premature death outweighs the excise revenue received. Moreover, Indonesians tend to prefer cigarettes which incorporate cloves along with the tobacco; and so great has become the consumption of cloves for this purpose that Indonesia, traditionally a supplier of cloves in world markets, has become a substantial net importer. A curtailment of cigarette smoking can therefore boost the country's export earnings as well as the health of her people.

Likewise, if the government were to ban all television commercials, the value of the resulting social benefits would probably far outweigh the loss of advertising revenue. It must be remembered that Indonesia's populace, and especially her youth, have hitherto been largely shielded from such disruptive cultural influences. But now what has come to be known as the world science-based culture is increasingly intruding into the nation's daily life, and television and radio are greatly accelerating the process. The experience of other countries suggests that a weakening of religion, and of the general cultural fabric, is likely — in the absence of strong counteracting measures — to be the sorry outcome.

In 1979, during his historic visits to Ireland and the United States — when an estimated one billion people throughout the world saw him on television — Pope John Paul II had a special word for young people. Do not, he exhorted them,

> close your eyes to the moral sickness that stalks your society today, and from which your youth alone will not protect you. How many young people have already warped their consciences and have substituted the true joy of life with drugs, sex, alcohol, vandalism and the empty pursuit of mere material possessions.

It is important to recall that the Nazis had overrun the Pope's native Poland when he was a young man, that by 1947 the Communists had seized full control of his beloved homeland, and that he had continued to live under atheistic Communism until his election as Pope in 1978. In his warning of the moral sickness which stalks society and which particularly threatens the welfare of the youth, clearly the Pope was speaking in broad international terms; indeed he confirmed this in his reference to the moral dilemmas 'which spare no society in our age'.[5] And his warning is one that is echoed and re-emphasized by leaders of *all* the great world religions.

Moreover, it becomes ever more clear that the global science-based culture in many ways collides with traditional moral and cultural values. Science and technology, ruthlessly impinging upon cherished traditions, commonly undermine or even destroy them. This is particularly the case in rapidly-changing societies such as one finds in Indonesia. People, especially devoutly religious people, understandably become alarmed, and a violent backlash may ensue.

This is exactly what happened in Iran. The Shah, in his zeal to modernize the country as rapidly as possible, gave an unstinting welcome to Western technology and to all the paraphernalia of the world science-based culture. People with religious sensibilities — mainstream moderates as well as the more fanatical elements — watched with horror as the country's ancient culture became increasingly inundated with Western films and television programmes, pop music carried by cheap transistor radios to the remotest corners of the land, and Western curricular concepts. They were aghast to see girl students reduced to promiscuity on the country's fine new university campuses and to witness the dissolution of family traditions and the rapid rise of divorce. Thus the Shah unwittingly played into the hands of the extremists, who soon unleashed a revolution.

The lesson is clear. Moderates must *pre-empt the field* of safeguarding moral and cultural values. This is essential *for national stability and security*. National planning in this field must command equal priority with national economic planning. Firm action must follow, and it must be in the spirit not of extremism but of mainstream moderation in the Indonesian tradition.

In the rapidly-changing societies which are most threatened with moral and cultural disintegration, national policies on these matters have too often been superficial to say the least. Reliance has commonly been placed upon incessant platitudinous sloganeering which can give a totally false sense of security. In spite of much good work in Indonesia in the fields of religion and culture and education, the country has yet to face squarely the threat posed by the impact of science-based culture.

Moreover, it makes no sense merely to engage in negative criticisms of so-called Westernization. The problem now goes far beyond the West — as witness the cultural complexities of technology-immersed Japan. In Indonesia as in other countries, the cultural vacuum will be filled — with the right thing or the wrong thing. Moreover, culture is not something dead which is confined to museums; especially in the minds of the youth, it is active and ever-changing. Platitudes about preserving the nation's culture simply will not suffice.

The danger of platitudes applies equally to the realm of creating appropriate technologies. As one thoughtful study points out, 'The advocacy of self-reliance does not often go beyond waxing eloquent about the inappropriateness of Western technologies and the need to develop labour-intensive techniques. . . . Examples of such successful innovation are few and far

Temple restoration at Borobudur, near Yogyakarta

between.'[6] Much the same point applies to oft-repeated statements about Indonesia's need for more and better-trained indigenous entrepreneurs.

It is vital to realize that innovation, whether in the technological or the entrepreneurial sphere, *is a cultural thing*. It is chiefly for cultural reasons that some societies are more innovative than others, and the innovation process takes place in a particular cultural context. R.H. Tawney, in his famous *Religion and the Rise of Capitalism*, first published in 1926,[7] was among the pioneers in bringing a proper awareness of this principle. More recently, James L. Peacock, in his *Muslim Puritans*,[8] has developed an analogous line of reasoning with respect to Islam in Southeast Asia.

Innovation requires intellectual creativity, and that in turn demands imagination. 'The initiative for the kind of action that is distinctively scientific', as the Nobel laureate P.B. Medawar points out, arises 'not from the apprehension of "facts", but from an imaginative preconception of what might be true'. In his experience, 'an imaginative or inspirational process enters into *all* scientific reasoning at every level. . .'. Moreover,

> The analysis of creativity in all its forms is beyond the competence of any one accepted discipline. It requires a consortium of the talents: psychologists, biologists, philosophers, computer scientists, artists and poets will all expect to have their say. That 'creativity' is beyond analysis is a romantic illusion we must now outgrow. It cannot be learned, perhaps, but it can certainly be encouraged and abetted. . . .[9]

The cultural conditions — in Indonesian homes, schools, wherever the youth are nurtured and conditioned — must become such as to foster their scientific imagination.

In her drive to acquire or create new technology attuned to her cultural needs as well as to her production requirements, Indonesia has a variety of options. For example, according to one study, 'Over the years, the cumulative cost to Japan of technology purchases from abroad — more than 25,000 contracts covering essentially all the technology the West had to offer, most of it from the United States — has been about six billion dollars. . .'.[10] Typically the Japanese have acquired such technology either through licences or outright purchase, and it has provided a basis not only for production for domestic and world markets but also for their own vigorous R & D programmes which have in turn led to further improvements. Such acquired and improved technology — together with Japan's abundant supply of managerial expertise — has likewise largely furnished the basis of her bold programmes of foreign investment.[11]

According to one of her ministers, Singapore's industries

> are living on borrowed technology. They are quite content to be left to themselves so long as profit margins can be obtained from cheap labour. South Korea and Taiwan on the contrary have been pursuing long range policies by actively engaging in R & D on behalf of their national companies. The pay-off came when both countries surpassed Singapore in achieving a higher growth rate . . . in recent years. The strategy of living off borrowed technology has served us well for the past 10 years but unless we promote the technological level of our own industries we will be like the proverbial hare overtaken by the tortoise. . . .[12]

It should be added that Singapore has latterly begun to take steps to upgrade the level of her domestically-available technology.

Clearly Indonesia must mobilize science and technology in aid of balanced national development and with full regard to cultural consequences. Acquiring and adapting technology is difficult enough, and assessing its social and cultural implications is if anything even more difficult.[13] But this is no reason for defeatism. According to Adrian Moyes, 'When technology is transferred from one society to another, the principles and techniques remain the same, but they can be rearranged and combined with a different set of social and economic activities — to make a technology that has been "transformed".' As he sees it,

> Technology that is not transformed almost always fails. . . . Appropriate technology (which may be simple, intermediate or high) can be developed by outsiders (i.e., people who are not going to use it); but it can only be transformed by insiders — by the people who are going to use it and benefit from it. Failure to appreciate this is a major reason why the very poor do not use more technology.[14]

The United States, and latterly Japan, have become world leaders in the production of the cheap and durable silicon chips or microprocessors that lie at the heart of the powerful new miniature computers which in effect play the role of robots.[15] These robots will have profound social and cultural effects all over the world,[16] and Indonesia will by no means be immune. On the other hand, as Brian May[17] and others have pointed out, Indonesia is by no means immune to the effects of even so simple a technological change as that from the *ani-ani* to the ordinary sickle. The *ani-ani*, a small knife used especially by Javanese village women to cut the rice stalk by stalk, has for centuries formed part of an established social ritual; and where the more efficient sickle— let alone a power-driven harvester— displaces it, the social and cultural consequences are profound.

Christopher Evans, in his authoritative book *The Mighty Micro*, forecasts that, in the late 1980s, 'a vast array of tasks which could previously only be performed by highly-trained human beings, including the majority of those involving the control of factory machinery, will . . . fall to the robot'. Evans is, moreover, clearly correct when he states that the 'coming of inexpensive robots will allow much deeper penetration of labour-intensive industries'.[18] Meanwhile, at the other end of the scale, the displacement of the *ani-ani* has similarly disrupted labour-intensive patterns.

All of this shows the need for social and cultural sensitivity of a very high order. It shows the danger and futility of simplistic economic growth approaches. It shows the dire necessity for multidisciplinary methods. It shows the inescapable need for *combined operations* including all of the natural and social sciences together with the arts and with philosophy as the queen of the disciplines.

Indonesia, suspended as she is between the old and the new, must learn to create her own technology in response to her own needs. Just as she has, through painful experience, learned to shun alien ideologies and to rely upon her own ideological resources, so likewise should she so far as possible rely upon indigenous technology. Obviously she must, in the immediate future, borrow a great deal of technology from abroad; but increasingly, in the realm of technology as distinguished from that of essentially inter-nationalized basic science, she should be able to stand on her own feet.

Thomas Alva Edison (1847-1931), the famous researcher and inventor, amassed over 1,000 inventions to his credit.[19] He was the first man to undertake inventions to order on a regular commercial basis, and in a real sense he fathered what has since become the vast research contracting industry in the United States and other countries which lead in research and development. Edison was an intensely practical man, and he set a model for making inventions that would find their way into viable industrial and commercial practice. One can well borrow from his example.

Indonesia, as intimated in Chapter 14, needs a large-scale and com-prehensive network of research and development contracts with univer-sities, research institutes, and private enterprises both at home and — during the interim period when she is building up her own R & D resources — abroad. The R & D projects should provide *tailored technology* — tailored to the country's cultural and social as well as economic needs. Combined operations teams should plan appropriate projects, watch their progress, and decide on how best to apply the results. The aim should be to achieve the maximum constructive impact during the period of Repelita III and on into that of Repelita IV.

As E.F. Schumacher suggests in his posthumously-published book *Good Work*,

> Today we have enough technological and scientific knowledge to make things small again. . . . It may not be true in every field: I don't suppose that one could produce Boeing aircraft on a small scale. But let's begin with basic human requirements. And there I can't see anything that man really *needs* that cannot be produced very simply, very efficiently, very viably on a small scale with radically simplified technology, with very little initial capital, so that even little people can get at it.[20]

Clearly the best small-scale answers may involve various levels of technol-ogy; for example, inexpensive miniature microprocessors can bring added efficiency to diesel engines such as are often used to power small factories. For those willing to rid themselves of outmoded assumptions, the prospects are clear. As Schumacher adds, 'things that were not possible to do very easily in the nineteenth century we *can* do on a small scale now . . . I'm not saying in every instance, but as regards all basic human requirements'.[21]

As already affirmed in Chapter 10, in this book I do *not* contend that economic growth, or economic planning, or capital-intensive projects are irrelevant. Likewise, I do *not* for a moment maintain that sophisticated high technology has no place in the less developed countries; quite the contrary is the case, for example, with their national, not to mention international, communications systems. But the big question concerns where the real priorities lie and where the main developmental emphasis should be placed. This book calls for a major, even drastic, shift of emphasis toward capital conservation, energy conservation, culture consciousness, and develop-ment projects which more directly reach the ordinary people.

Where there is a will there is a way, particularly if the will is that of the nation's youth. I have already mentioned my meetings with numerous groups of Indonesian students in various parts of the country, and referred

Traditional hand weaving

to my meetings with no less than eighteen of the government's ministers and vice ministers. As a result of all these discussions, a remarkable phenomenon has indeed become apparent: a *convergence tendency* between students on the one hand and many (even if not all) ministers on the other. On the whole *both* the students and the ministers show a keen awareness of the tragedies which can stem from ignoring the cultural side-effects of economic growth; and *both* want far more emphasis to be placed upon meeting basic human needs through culturally acceptable technologies.

In 1979, in keeping with the dual role concept already discussed, the Army's Command and General Staff College mounted, at its headquarters at Bandung, a large seminar focused on the economic and social development of the historic city of Yogyakarta. A striking feature of the seminar was that civilian as well as military students were invited, and I was able to join them. The seminar particularly dramatized two points: first, that Indonesia's students want to play a much larger role both in planning the nation's development and in helping to implement the plans; and secondly, that the Army is perfectly capable of tackling multidisciplinary research in the civilian sector.

Academic institutions in any country commonly tend toward bureaucracy and sluggishness as well as compartmentalization in disciplinary terms, and those in Indonesia are no exception. The Army, which is both highly motivated and spans many disciplines, could perfectly well collaborate in sponsoring the sort of interdisciplinary campus centres recommended in Chapter 9. The Army can, without ruffling too many academic feathers, thus bring some dynamic movement to the situation. The students, if they are to eschew negative activities, must have the chance to join in positive ones — those directly related to overall national development. Beyond a certain point, they will not wait.

The rising generation will, needless to say, likewise largely determine the course of Indonesia's future relations with the rest of the world. Her present policy — a plausible enough one — is that she does not want Communism or any other form of extremism within her own shores but that she is not trying to tell other countries what sort of system they should embrace. At the same time she realizes that the ideological complexions of other countries' regimes inevitably influence the international political and social climate and, at least indirectly, even that within her own domain.

Indonesia was a leader in the establishment, in 1967, of the Association of Southeast Asian Nations, or ASEAN, whose members include Indonesia, Malaysia, the Philippines, Singapore, and Thailand. The organization has, in the words of Donald W. Fryer, 'achieved a modest success' in promoting co-operation in such fields as postal services, telecommunications, transport, fisheries, agricultural technology, and scientific and technical education.[22] Earlier it had been hoped that ASEAN might develop its own common market, and this may yet come to pass. Although ASEAN is in no sense a military alliance, one hopes that in the future it may foster joint action in dealing with ideological or guerrilla dangers facing any of its members.

General Jusuf with friends

Although Indonesia of course maintains diplomatic and trade relations with many countries, she has particularly close links with her sister members of the Inter-Governmental Group on Indonesia, or IGGI, composed of Australia, Austria, Belgium, Canada, France, Italy, Japan, the Netherlands, New Zealand, Switzerland, the United Kingdom, the United States, and West Germany as well as Indonesia. The major international aid agencies participate in IGGI meetings, and various other representatives sit in as observers.[23] Knowledgeable Indonesians are indeed grateful for the large amounts of aid which have in recent years been supplied both by IGGI as such and by individual IGGI country members and participating international aid agencies. Substantial further aid likewise comes from additional individual countries and from a large number of non-governmental organizations, mostly located in the West.[24] Indonesia maintains correct diplomatic relations with the Soviet Union but— in the light of the events surrounding the attempted coup of 1965 — does not as yet exchange ambassadors with the People's Republic of China. As for another key part of the world, Indonesia's Co-ordinating Team for the Middle East is actively fostering close trading and cultural relations with the more moderate of the countries in that region.

Moderation indeed characterizes the attitude of Indonesia's present leadership toward both domestic and overseas affairs; and the same attitude — mixed, however, with understandable impatience — prevails among the vast majority of her students from whom will come her leaders of tomorrow. In this connection it is vitally important to repudiate any temptation to fall into what I shall term 'backlash thinking'. Sukarno justly ranks as independent Indonesia's foremost founding father; yet he made a complete shambles of the country's economy, and his policies caused vast hardship and misery among ordinary people. He and his regime must therefore not be over-romanticized.

The policies of the New Order government, by contrast, have in many ways brought remarkable, even astonishing, economic progress; nevertheless, they now require decisive reorientation. In this essential process the generation gap can be bridged and the youth can be welcomed into comprehensive collaboration with their elders. Indonesians are avid sportsmen and have won many international trophies. Now they can engage in a different sort of international competition in which the prize goes to those who best achieve a social order that is both viable and humane. Let the youth, in concert with their elders, show what they can do!

The analysis in this book, and especially that in Chapters numbered 6 to 15, carries many major policy implications. Moreover, it is a rolling analysis which lends itself to revisions with the passage of time. The suggestions and recommendations can readily be amended and supplemented as events unfold. The book can in this way continue to furnish useful guidelines which can aid in fostering the country's stability and continued progress.

This book is dedicated to the proposition that Indonesia can chart a constructive course through all of the difficulties which undoubtedly lie ahead. She can do this first and foremost by mobilizing the dedicated skills of her young people. She can safeguard and uphold her national cultural integrity in the process. She can create a new Indonesian synthesis which can furnish inspiration both at home and abroad. May Indonesia's youth, and her people as a whole, receive the blessings which they so richly deserve!

Appendix

The Third Development Cabinet

As of 1st April 1980

CO–ORDINATING MINISTRIES	MINISTER
Defence and Political Affairs	Gen. Maraden Panggabean
Social Welfare	Surono Reksodimejo
Economic, Financial and Industrial Affairs	Prof. Dr. Widjojo Nitisastro

STATE MINISTRIES	
Administrative Reform	Dr. Johannes B. Sumarlin
Development Supervision and the Environment	Prof. Dr. Emil Salim
Research and Technology	Prof. Dr. Burhanuddin Jusuf Habibie
State Minister/State Secretary	Sudharmono

MINISTRIES	
Home affairs	Armirmachmud
Foreign Affairs	Prof. Dr. Mochtar Kusumaatmadja
Defence, concurrently Armed Forces Commander	Gen. Andi Muhammad Jusuf
Justice	Moedjono
Information	Ali Moertopo
Finance	Prof. Dr. Ali Wardhana
Trade and Co-operatives	Drs. Radius Prawiro
Agriculture	Prof. Soedarsono Hadisaputro
Industry	Abdoel Raoef Soehoed
Mines and Energy	Prof. Dr. Subroto
Public Works	Dr. Purnomosidi Hadjisaroso
Communications	Roesmin Nurjadin
Education and Culture	Dr. Daoed Joesoef
Manpower and Transmigration	Prof. Dr. Harun Alrasyid Zain
Health	Dr. Soewardjono Surjaningrat
Religious Affairs	Alamsjah Ratu Prawiranegara
Social Affairs	Sapardjo

VICE–MINISTRIES	VICE–MINISTER
Public Housing	Drs. Cosmas Batubara
Youth Affairs	Dr. Abdul Gafur Tengku Idris
Transmigration	Martono
Food Crops	Achmad Affandi
Co-operatives	Bustanil Arifin
Women's Role	Mrs. Lasiyah Soetanto

166

Notes

CHAPTER 1 THE ROAD TO INDEPENDENCE

1 Malcolm Caldwell, *Indonesia* (London: Oxford University Press, 1968), p. 33.
2 Article on Raffles in *Encyclopædia Britannica* (Chicago: Encyclopædia Britannica, 1973), Vol. 18, p. 1102. See also the biographies by J. Bastin, D.C. Boulger, Maurice Collis, R. Coupland, Emily Hahn, and C.E. Wurtzburg.
3 Referring to the record of the Dutch in the East Indies, the historian John D. Legge, in his *Indonesia* (2nd ed., Sydney: Prentice-Hall of Australia, 1977), p. 121, suggests that 'if one were to try to draw up a moral balance sheet of their imperialism, its credit side would compare very favourably with that of other European colonial powers'.
4 Alexander Solzhenitsyn, *Letter to Soviet Leaders* (London: Index on Censorship and Collins, 1974), p. 21.
5 Conversation with the author, July 1978, Jakarta.

CHAPTER 2 STRIVING FOR NATIONHOOD

1 Sukarno, *Sukarno: An Autobiography*, as told to Cindy Adams (Jakarta: Gunung Agung, 1966), p. 308.
2 *Ibid.*, p. 20.
3 *Ibid.*, pp. 61-62, 209.
4 *Ibid.*, p. 217.
5 Anthony J.S. Reid, *The Indonesian National Revolution, 1945-1950* (Victoria: Longman Australia, 1974), p. 42.
6 Sukarno, *op. cit.*, pp. 232-233.
7 *Ibid*, p. 230.
8 *Ibid.*, p. 261.
9 Ulf Sundhaussen, 'Social Policy Aspects in Defense and Security Planning in Indonesia, 1947-1977' (paper submitted to the IXth World Congress of Sociology, Research Committee on Armed Forces and Society, Uppsala, August 1978), pp. 23-24.
10 Sukarno, *op. cit.*, p. 264.

CHAPTER 3   THE LATER SUKARNO PHASE

1   Sukarno, *Sukarno: An Autobiography*, as told to Cindy Adams (Jakarta: Gunung Agung, 1966), p. 231.
2   Jean Blondel, *Political Parties: A Genuine Case for Discontent?* (London: Wildwood House, 1978), p. 45.
3   *Ibid.*, pp. 8-9.
4   Different authorities give varying figures for the number of parties; e.g., Donald W. Fryer and James C. Jackson, in *Indonesia* (London: Ernest Benn; Boulder, Colo.: Westview Press, 1977), p. 71, suggest that the total number of parties rose to 'more than fifty'.
5   Roger K. Paget (ed.), *Indonesia Accuses!: Soekarno's Defense Oration in the Political Trial of 1930* (Kuala Lumpur: Oxford University Press, 1975), pp. 80-81, 82.
6   Quoted by Bernhard Dahm, *Sukarno and the Struggle for Indonesian Independence* (Ithaca and London: Cornell University Press, 1969), p. 200.
7   Sukarno, *Autobiography*, *op. cit.*, p. 278.
8   John D. Legge, *Indonesia* (2nd ed., Sydney: Prentice-Hall of Australia, 1977), p. 151.
9   Sukarno, *Autobiography*, *op. cit.*, p. 312.
10   Printed in Herbert Feith and Lance Castles (eds.), *Indonesian Political Thinking, 1945-1965* (Ithaca and London: Cornell University Press, 1970), pp. 81-82.
11   Printed *ibid.*, pp. 82-83.
12   Printed *ibid.*, pp. 84-85.
13   Sukarno, *Autobiography*, *op. cit.*, p. 278.
14   Printed in Feith and Castles, *op. cit.*, pp. 85, 87.
15   Charles A. Fisher, *South-East Asia* (London: Methuen & Co., 1971), p. 360.
16   C.L.M. Penders, *The Life and Times of Sukarno* (Kuala Lumpur: Oxford University Press, 1975), p. 159.
17   Sukarno, *Autobiography*, *op. cit.*, pp. 269-271.
18   Howard Palfrey Jones, *Indonesia: The Possible Dream* (Singapore: Mas Aju, 1973), pp. 78-79, 153-154.
19   Printed in Feith and Castles, *op. cit.*, pp. 99-100.
20   J.D. Legge, *Sukarno: A Political Biography* (Harmondsworth, Middlesex: Penguin Books, 1973), pp. 305-306.
21.   Fryer and Jackson, *op. cit.*, p. 85.
22   Penders, *op. cit.*, p. 163.
23   Quoted by Penders, *op. cit.*, pp. 175-176.
24   J.A.C. Mackie, *Konfrontasi: The Indonesia-Malaysia Dispute of 1963-1964* (Kuala Lumpur: Oxford University Press, 1974), p. 335.

CHAPTER 4   THE GRAND CONSPIRACY

1   Guy J. Pauker, *The Rise and Fall of the Communist Party of Indonesia* (Santa Monica, Calif.: The Rand Corporation, 1969), pp. 10-11.

2   Arnold C. Brackman, *Indonesian Communism: A History* (Westport, Conn.: Greenwood Press, 1976), pp. 3-4; Ruth T. McVey, *The Rise of Indonesian Communism* (Ithaca: Cornell University Press, 1968), pp. 14ff.

3   Brackman, *op. cit.*, pp. 18-19.

4   McVey, *op. cit.*, p. 353; cf. also Donald Hindley, *The Communist Party of Indonesia: 1951-1963* (Berkeley and Los Angeles: University of California Press, 1964), pp. 18-19.

5   Bruce Grant, *Indonesia* (2nd ed., Melbourne: Melbourne University Press, 1966), p. 63.

6   Brackman, *op. cit.*, p. 31.

7   Pauker, *op. cit.*, p. 6.

8   *Ibid.*, pp. 9-10.

9   Nena Vreeland *et al.*, *Area Handbook for Indonesia* (3rd ed., Washington, D.C.: US Government Printing Office, 1975), pp. 269-270.

10   Antonie C.A. Dake, *In the Spirit of the Red Banteng: Indonesian Communists between Moscow and Peking* (The Hague: Mouton, 1973), p. 461. (Italics deleted.)

11   Pauker, *op. cit.*, p. 39.

12   Nugroho Notosusanto and Ismail Saleh, *The Coup Attempt of the 'September 30 Movement' in Indonesia* (Jakarta: P.T. Pembimbing Masa, 1968), pp. 36-37; S. Tas, *Indonesia: The Underdeveloped Freedom* (Indianapolis: Bobbs-Merrill, 1974), p. 317. Some writers occasionally use the term 'coup' as a shorthand for the 1965 attempted coup; but the context always makes clear that they are referring to an attempt which was unsuccessful.

13   Pauker, *op. cit.*, pp. 43-44.

14.   J.D. Legge, *Indonesia* (2nd ed., Sydney: Prentice-Hall of Australia, 1977), p. 162.

15   Notosusanto and Saleh, *op. cit.*, p. 7.

16   Wilfred T. Neill, *Twentieth Century Indonesia* (New York: Columbia University Press, 1973), p. 350.

17   Notosusanto and Saleh, *op. cit.*, p. 10.

18   *Ibid.*, pp. 14-18.

19   *Ibid.*, pp. 20-29; O.G. Roeder, *The Smiling General: President Soeharto of Indonesia* (Jakarta: Gunung Agung, 1969), p. 16.

20   *Ibid.*, pp. 11-14. For additional interpretations, see Arnold C. Brackman, *The Communist Collapse in Indonesia* (New York: Norton, 1969), Ch. 7; and John Hughes, *The End of Sukarno* (London: Angus and Robertson, 1968), Chs. 5 and 6.

21   Notosusanto and Saleh, *op. cit.*, pp. 66ff.

22   For the test of 'Decree No. 1', see Roeder, *op. cit.*, pp. 201-203.

23   For the text of the Soeharto Statement, see *ibid.*, p. 205.

24   Notosusanto and Saleh, *op. cit.*, p. 70.

25   Roeder, *op. cit.*, pp. 25-26.

26   Tas, *op. cit.*, p. 319.

27   Notosusanto and Saleh, *op. cit.*, p. 78.

CHAPTER 5   LEADERSHIP AND NECESSITY

1 Donald W. Fryer and James C. Jackson, *Indonesia* (London: Ernest Benn; Boulder, Colo.: Westview Press, 1977), p. 98.
2 O.G. Roeder, *The Smiling General: President Soeharto of Indonesia* (Jakarta: Gunung Agung, 1969), pp. 26-27.
3 According to Roeder (*idem*), however, Sukarno in a subsequent cabinet meeting took to task a Communist minister for being involved in 'creating this cursed affair'.
4 Rex Mortimer, *Indonesian Communism under Sukarno: Ideology and Politics, 1959-1965* (Ithaca and London: Cornell University Press, 1974), p. 418. Regarding the term 'coup' as against 'attempted coup', see above Chapter 4, note 12.
5 Benedict R. Anderson and Ruth T. McVey (with the assistance of Frederick P. Bunnell), *A Preliminary Analysis of the October 1, 1965 Coup in Indonesia* (Ithaca: Cornell University Southeast Asia Program, 1971), p. viii.
6 Nugroho Notosusanto and Ismail Saleh, *The Coup Attempt of the 'September 30 Movement' in Indonesia* (Jakarta: P.T. Pembimbing Masa, 1968), Part II.
7 J.D. Legge, *Sukarno: A Political Biography* (Harmondsworth, Middlesex: Penguin Books, 1973), p. 391. At pp. 390-391 Legge includes a useful list of citations on varying interpretations of the attempted coup.
8 J.D. Legge, *Indonesia* (2nd ed., Sydney: Prentice-Hall of Australia, 1977), p. 163.
9 Howard Palfrey Jones, *Indonesia: The Possible Dream* (Singapore: Mas Aju, 1973), p. 372.
10 For a summary of the Warren Commission Report and other relevant documents and citations, see Peter Dale Scott *et al.*(eds.), *The Assassinations: Dallas and Beyond* (Harmondsworth, Middlesex: Penguin Books, 1978).
11 Jones, *op. cit.*, p. 438.
12 This account of Soeharto's early years is based chiefly on Roeder, *op. cit.*, pp. 77ff. Cf. also Nugroho Notosusanto, *The Peta Army During the Japanese Occupation of Indonesia* (Tokyo: Waseda University Press, 1979).
13 Roeder, *op. cit.*, pp. 99ff.
14 *Ibid.*, p. 129
15 Arnold C. Brackman, *Indonesia: The Critical Years 1976-78* (London: The Institute for the Study of Conflict, 1974), p. 8.
16 Roeder, *op. cit.*, pp. 25, 39, 41, 56.
17 Fryer and Jackson, *op. cit.*, p. 104.
18 Ulf Sundhaussen, 'Social Policy Aspects in Defense and Security Planning in Indonesia, 1947-1977' (paper submitted to the IXth World Congress of Sociology, Research Committee on Armed Forces and Society, Uppsala, August 1978), pp. 27-28.
19 Nugroho Notosusanto, *The National Struggle and the Armed Forces in Indonesia* (Jakarta: Republic of Indonesia, Department of Defence and Security, Centre for Armed Forces History, 1975), p. 70.
20 H. Roeslan Abdulgani, 'The Role and Function of the Indonesian Army

as Agent of Social Change' (unpublished paper, n.d.), p. 1.

21 *Ibid.*, p. 7.
22 Soeharto, *The Military in Indonesia* (Jakarta: Republic of Indonesia, Department of Information, 1970), pp. 6-7.
23 *Ibid.*, pp. 11-12.
24 M.S.H. Panggabean, *The Function and Role of the Indonesian Armed Forces in the Period of Consolidation and Integration* (Jakarta: Republic of Indonesia, Department of Defence and Security, 1970), p. 14.
25 *Ibid.*, p. 15.
26 *Ibid.*, pp. 16-17.
27 Staff for the Operasi Bhakti, *Visual Momentum of the Indonesian Armed Forces' . . . Civic Mission . . .* (Republic of Indonesia, Department of Defence and Security, Staff for the Operasi Bhakti, 1972), pp. 44-45.
28 Legge, *Sukarno, op. cit.*, p. 6.
29 Sundhaussen, *op. cit.*, p. 34.
30 Fryer and Jackson, *op. cit.*, p. 101.
31 Legge, *Sukarno, op. cit.*, p. 320.
32 Roeder, *op. cit.*, p. 166.
33 Jones, *op. cit.*, p. 426.
34 *Ibid.*, p. 431.

CHAPTER 6   THE INDONESIAN TIGHT–ROPE

1 *The Encyclopedia Americana* (New York: Americana Corporation, 1977), Vol. 15, pp. 81-82.
2 Donald W. Fryer and James C. Jackson, *Indonesia* (London: Ernest Benn; Boulder, Colo.: Westview Press, 1977), p. 4.
3 Nena Vreeland *et al.*, *Area Handbook for Indonesia* (3rd ed., Washington, D.C.: US Government Printing Office, 1975), p. 1.
4 The World Bank, *World Development Report: 1978* (Washington, D.C.: The World Bank, 1978), p. 45.
5 Terence H. Hull *et al.*, 'Indonesia's Family Planning Story: Success and Challenge', *Population Bulletin*, Vol. 32, No. 6 (Washington, D.C.: Population Reference Bureau, 1977), pp. 4-7.
6 C. Chandrasekaran and Sam Soeharto, 'Indonesia's Population in the Year 2000,' *Bulletin of Indonesian Economic Studies*, Vol. XIV, No. 3 (November 1978), p. 93.
7 Hull *et al.*, *op. cit.*, p. 1.
8 Bank Indonesia, *Indonesia: Selected Economic Data* (Jakarta: Bank Indonesia, 1979), Table 1.
9 Raphael Pura, 'Births of a Nation', *The Asian Wall Street Journal*, 15 July 1978, p. 1; American Embassy, USAID, Jakarta, *Indonesia Family Planning Program* (Jakarta: American Embassy, 1978), p. 28.
10 National Family Planning Co-ordinating Board, *National Family Planning Program: 1969-1978* (Jakarta: National Family Planning Coordinating Board, 1978), p. 3.
11 National Family Planning Coordinating Board, *The Indonesia Family*

Planning Program: Basic Strategies (Jakarta: National Family Planning Coordinating Board, 1978), pp. 13-15.

12 Remarks of Haryono Suyono, Ph.D., before The House Select Committee on Population, United States House of Representatives, 27 April 1978 (mimeographed), p. 10.

13 Robert S. McNamara, *Address to the Massachusetts Institute of Technology* (Cambridge: M.I.T., 1977), p. 3.

14 US Department of State, Agency for International Development, *Annual Budget Submission, FY 1980: Indonesia, Annex A—F* (Jakarta: USAID, 1978), p. 3.

15 American Embassy, Jakarta, *Foreign Economic Trends and Their Implications for the United States: Indonesia* (Jakarta: American Embassy, 1978), p. 11.

16 American Embassy, Jakarta, *Indonesia: Agricultural Situation* (Jakarta: American Embassy, 1978), pp. 1, 11. According to a World Bank report, *Indonesia: Supply Prospects for Major Food Crops* (Washington, D.C.: The World Bank, 1979), p. 69, in the absence of 'a series of unexpected events which lead to a substantial increase in food crop production', Indonesia faced rice deficits of 'between 1.5 and 2.5 million tons in 1985' and around 3 million tons by 1990.

17 National Development Information Office, *Indonesia Economic Profile, 1978* (Jakarta: National Development Information Office, 1979), Sec. 9, p. 2.

18 American Embassy, Jakarta, *Indonesia: Agricultural Situation, op. cit.*, p. 8.

19 National Development Information Office, *Fact File* (Jakarta: National Development Information Office, 1978), Sec. 9, p. 1.

20 Colin Norman, 'The Staggering Challenge of Global Unemployment', *The Futurist*, Vol. 12. No. 4 (August 1978), p. 233.

21 American Embassy, Jakarta, *Annual Labor Report* (Jakarta: American Embassy, 1978), pp. 4-5, and *Annual Labor Report* (Jakarta: American Embassy, 1979), pp. 6-8.

22 World Bank, *World Development Report, 1978, op. cit.*, p. 44. (Italics added.)

23 American Embassy, Jakarta, *Annual Labor Report, op. cit.*, pp. 2-3; The World Bank, *Employment and Income Distribution in Indonesia* (Washington, D.C.: The World Bank, 1979), p. vii.

24 Sevinc Carlson, *Indonesia's Oil* (Boulder, Colo.: Westview Press, 1977), p. 9.

25 H.W. Arndt, 'Survey of Recent Developments', *Bulletin of Indonesian Economic Studies*, Vol. XIV, No. 1 (March, 1978), p. 15.

26 National Development Information Office, *Indonesia Economic Profile, 1978, op. cit.*, Sec. 10, p. 7.

27 Carlson, *op. cit.*, p. 121.

28 *Indonesia Development News* (Jakarta), Vol. 2, No. 8 (April 1979), p. 8.

29 Bruce Glassburner, 'Survey of Recent Developments', *Bulletin of Indonesian Economic Studies*, Vol. XIV, No. 2 (July 1978), p. 13.

30 The World Bank, *Indonesia: Growth Patterns, Social Progress and Development Prospects* (Washington, D.C.: The World Bank, 1979), p. 107.

31 National Development Information Office, *Indonesia Economic Profile,*

1978, op. cit., Sec. 4, p. 2.

32 Adapted from National Development Information Office, *Indonesia 1967-1977: Decade of Development* (Jakarta: National Development Information Office, 1978), pp. 35-36.

33 Kuhn Loeb Lehman Brothers International *et al.*, *The Republic of Indonesia* (Jakarta, 1978), p. 22.

34 Adapted from National Development Information Office, *Indonesia 1967-1977: Decade of Development, op. cit.*, pp. 38-47.

35 *Standard Chartered Review* (London), December 1978, p. 20.

36 Quoted in *Indonesia Development News*, Vol. 2, No. 6 (February 1979), p. 1.

CHAPTER 7   THE HUMAN RIGHTS DILEMMA

1 Amnesty International, *Amnesty International Report, 1978* (London: Amnesty International Publications, 1979), p. 3. (Italics added.)

2 *Ibid.*, pp. 3-4.

3 Lester A. Sobel (ed.) *Political Prisoners: A World Report* (New York: Facts on File, 1978), p. 1.

4 Quoted by Sir Ivor Jennings, *The Queen's Government* (Harmondsworth, Middlesex: Penguin Books, 1954), p. 9.

5 Printed in William Miller (ed.), *Readings in American Values* (Englewood Cliffs, N.J.: Prentice-Hall, 1964), p. 55.

6 Printed in Ian Brownlie (ed.), *Basic Documents on Human Rights* (Oxford: Clarendon Press, 1971), pp. 8-10.

7 Printed *ibid.*, pp. 11-13.

8 Miller, *op. cit.*, p. 342.

9 *Universal Declaration of Human Rights: Final Authorized Text* (New York: United Nations Office of Information, 1972), pp. 3-6.

10 Brownlie, *op. cit.*, Parts Two-Ten.

11 Alexander Solzhenitsyn, *The Gulag Archipelago: 1918-1956* (London: Collins & Harvill Press, 1975).

12 Amnesty International, *Prisoners of Conscience in the USSR: Their Treatment and Conditions* (London: Amnesty International Publications, 1975). See also Valery Chalidze, *To Defend These Rights: Human Rights in the Soviet Union* (London: Collins & Harvill Press, 1975).

13 Tufton Beamish and Guy Hadley, *The Kremlin's Dilemma: The Struggle for Human Rights in Eastern Europe* (London: Collins & Harvill Press, 1979), p. 28.

14 *Ibid.*, p. 260.

15 *Ibid.*, pp. 260-261.

16 *Ibid.*, p. 215.

17 Robert Conquest, *Present Danger: Towards a Foreign Policy* (Oxford: Basil Blackwell, 1979), p. 61.

18 Egon Larsen, *A Flame in Barbed Wire: The Story of Amnesty International* (London: Frederick Muller, 1978), pp. 87-88; Victor Sparre, *The Flame in the Darkness* (London: Grosvenor Books, 1979), pp. 102-104.

19 *A Chronicle of Current Events: Journal of the Human Rights Movement in the USSR* (London: Amnesty International Publications).

20 For the full text of Charter 77, see Beamish and Hadley, *op. cit.*, Appendix II.
21 *Dissent in Poland* (London: Association of Polish Students and Graduates in Exile, 1977). See also Beamish and Hadley, *op. cit.*, especially Ch. 2.
22 Sobel (ed.), *op. cit.*, p. 137.
23 Amnesty International, *Political Imprisonment in the People's Republic of China* (London: Amnesty International, 1978).
24 *Ibid.*, p. xii.
25 *Ibid.*, pp. ix-x.
26 *Ibid.*, pp. 28-29.
27 *Ibid.*, pp. 56-57, 61-69.
28 *International Encyclopedia of the Social Sciences* (New York: The Macmillan Company & The Free Press, 1968), Vol. 5, p. 544.
29 Niall MacDermot, Introduction to International Commission of Jurists, *Human Rights in a One-Party State* (London: Search Press, 1978), p. 9.
30 *Amnesty International Report, 1978, op. cit.*, p. 1.
31 *Idem.*
32 *Universal Declaration of Human Rights: Final Authorized Text, op. cit.*, Article 30, p. 8. The full text of the Universal Declaration is also conveniently available in Brownlie (ed.), *op. cit.*, pp. 106-112.
33 Amnesty International, *Indonesia* (London: Amnesty International Publications, 1977), p. 9.
34 US Department of State, Agency for International Development, *Annual Budget Submission, FY 1980: Indonesia, Annex A–F* (Jakarta: USAID, 1978), p. 25.
35 US Department of State, *Report on Human Rights Practices in Countries Receiving US Aid, Submitted to the Committee on Foreign Relations, US Senate, and Committee on Foreign Affairs, US House of Representatives* (Washington, D.C.: US Government Printing Office, 1979), p. 361. This statement refers not only to the figures given in the 1977 Amnesty International report but also to those given in a four-page supplement issued by Amnesty International in October 1978.

CHAPTER 8 'GOING STRAIGHT'

1 Harold Crouch, *The Army and Politics in Indonesia* (Ithaca, N.Y. and London: Cornell University Press, 1978), pp. 224-225.
2 Department of Foreign Affairs, Republic of Indonesia, *Indonesian Government Policy in Dealing with the G-30-S/PKI (The 30th September Movement of the Indonesian Communist Party) Detainees* (Jakarta: Department of Foreign Affairs, 1978), p. 43.
3 Crouch, *op. cit.*, p. 227.
4 Department of Information, Republic of Indonesia, *Indonesia Handbook, 1977* (Jakarta: Department of Information, 1977), p. 51.
5 Department of Foreign Affairs, *op. cit.*, p. 43.
6 Obtained from the Operational Command for the Restoration of Security and Order, Jakarta, 1979.

7   Donald Wilhelm, *Creative Alternatives to Communism: Guidelines for Tomorrow's World* (London: The Macmillan Press, 1978); published in the Indonesian language edition (with the title and sub-title transposed) as *Menuju Dunia Mendatang: Alternatif-Alternatif Terhadap Kommunisme* (Jakarta: Penerbit Universitas Indonesia, 1979).

8   Crouch, *op. cit.*, p. 224.

9   Department of Foreign Affairs, *op. cit.*, pp. 17-18.

10 Henri Coursier, *The International Red Cross* (Geneva: International Committee of the Red Cross, 1961), pp. 20ff.

11 Obtained from confidential non-ICRC sources, 1979.

12 Amnesty International, *Indonesia* (London: Amnesty International Publications, 1977), October 1978 supplement, p. 1.

13 Howard Palfrey Jones, *Indonesia: The Possible Dream* (Singapore: Mas Aju, 1973), p. 80.

14 *Ibid.*, p. 126; Sukarno, *Sukarno: An Autobiography*, as told to Cindy Adams (Jakarta: Gunung Agung, 1966), pp. 272-274.

15 Donald W. Fryer and James C. Jackson, *Indonesia* (London: Ernest Benn; Boulder, Colo.: Westview Press, 1977), p. 73; Karl D. Jackson and Lucian W. Pye (eds.), *Political Power and Communications in Indonesia* (Berkeley and London: University of California Press, 1978), p. 209.

16 *The Indonesia Times* (Jakarta), 19 January 1979, p. 1; *Indonesian Observer* (Jakarta), 19 March 1979, p. 4.

17 *Idem.*

18 Satrio, *The Role of the Indonesian Red Cross in East Timor, 1975-1977* (Jakarta: Indonesian Red Cross, 1977), pp. 10-11. For an alternative but already-dated interpretation, see Oey Hong Lee, *Indonesia: Facing the 1980s* (Hull, England: Europress, 1979), pp. 164-180, 352.

19 *Marxism, Communism and Western Society: A Comparative Encyclopedia* (New York: Herder, 1973, eight volumes), Vol. VII, pp. 36-37; Karl Marx, *Capital: A Critical Analysis of Capitalist Production* (Moscow: Progress Publishers, 1974), Vol. II, pp. 36-37; Karl Marx, *The Poverty of Philosophy* (Moscow: Progress Publishers, 1973), p. 95.

20 Paul A. Samuelson, *Economics* (8th ed., New York: McGraw-Hill, 1970), p. 818. The 10th edition (1976) carries a modified and perhaps less satisfactory version.

21 Karl Marx and Friedrich Engels, *The Communist Manifesto* (Harmondsworth, Middlesex: Penguin Books, 1975), p. 79.

22 Andrei Sakharov, *Sakharov Speaks* (London: Collins & Harvill Press, 1974), pp. 124ff.

23 Alexander Solzhenitsyn, *Letter to Soviet Leaders* (London: Index on Censorship and Collins, 1974), pp. 21f.

24 Andrei D. Sakharov, *My Country and the World* (London: Collins & Harvill Press, 1975), pp. 12-13.

25 *Ibid.*, p. 18.

CHAPTER 9   THE YOUTH CHALLENGE

1   Interview with Dr. Slamet Santosa, Jakarta, 30 December 1978.

2 Howard Palfrey Jones, *Indonesia: The Possible Dream* (Singapore: Mas Aju, 1973), p. 55.

3 Stephen A. Douglas, *Political Socialization and Student Activism in Indonesia* (Urbana, Ill.: University of Illinois Press, 1970), p. 3.

4 *Ibid.*, pp. 154-155.

5 *Ibid.*, p. 156; Allen M. Sievers, *The Mystical World of Indonesia: Culture and Economic Development in Conflict* (Baltimore and London: The Johns Hopkins University Press, 1974), pp. 181-183.

6 Off-the-record interview, Jakarta, 27 December 1978.

7 Harold Crouch, *The Army and Politics in Indonesia* (Ithaca and London: Cornell University Press, 1978), p. 166; Douglas, *op. cit.*, p. 157.

8 Crouch, *op. cit.*, pp. 173-174.

9 *Ibid.*, pp. 181-183.

10 *Ibid.*, pp. 294-195.

11 *Ibid.*, p. 299.

12 R. William Liddle, in Karl D. Jackson and Lucian W. Pye (eds.), *Political Power and Communications in Indonesia* (Berkeley and London: University of California Press, 1978), p. 185.

13 *Idem.*

14 *Ibid.*, p. 187.

15 Heri Akhmadi *et al.*, *White Book of the 1978 Students' Struggle*, English translation printed in *Indonesia* (Ithaca, N.Y.), No. 25 (April 1978).

16 *Ibid.*, p. 164.

17 *Ibid.*, p. 166.

18 Amnesty International, *Amnesty International Report, 1978* (London: Amnesty International Publications, 1979), p. 257.

19 Robert Graham, *Iran: The Illusion of Power* (London: Croom Helm, 1978), pp. 77-91.

20 *Ibid.*, p. 212.

21 *Idem.*

22 Fred Halliday, *Iran: Dictatorship and Development* (Harmondsworth, Middlesex: Penguin Books, 1979), p. 227.

23 *Idem.*

24 The Economist Intelligence Unit, *Quarterly Economic Review of Iran: 2nd Quarter 1979* (London: The Economist Intelligence Unit, 1979), pp. 7-8.

25 Crouch, *op. cit.*, p. 351.

26 Soedjatmoko, 'Some Thoughts on Higher Education', *Prisma: Indonesian Journal of Social and Economic Affairs* (Jakarta), Vol. I, No. 2 (November 1975), p. 47.

CHAPTER 10   TRANSMIGRATION AND TRANSFORMATION

1 Vannevar Bush, *Science, the Endless Frontier* (Washington, D.C.: US Government Printing Office, 1945).

2 Donald W. Fryer and James C. Jackson, *Indonesia* (London: Ernest Benn; Boulder, Colo.: Westview Press, 1977), pp. 59, 146.

3   Cf. J.M. Hardjono, *Transmigration In Indonesia* (Kuala Lumpur: Oxford University Press, 1977), pp. xiv-xv.

4   *Ibid.*, Ch. III.

5   Projected from Martono, *Transmigration As an Integrated System of Development* (Jakarta: Ministry of Manpower and Transmigration, 1978), p. 75.

6   *Ibid.*, pp. 84, 121.

7   *Indonesian News* (London), Vol. 6, No. 6 (June 1979), p. 10.

8   M.J. Gauchon, *Watershed Rehabilitation and Development, The Most Critical Problem Facing Indonesia: Past Performance and Future Guidelines* (Solo, Indonesia: Upper Solo Watershed Management and Development Project, 1977), p. 1.

9   Transmigration Training and Research Centre, *Transmigration in the Context of Area Development* (Jakarta: Department of Manpower, Transmigration and Co-operatives, 1974), p. 25.

10 Hardjono, *op. cit.*, pp. 11-14.

11 Alan M. Strout, 'Aspects of Agricultural Productivity on Java and the Outer Islands, and Second Thoughts About the Demise of Agricultural Involution' (unpublished paper, 1978), p. 5. See also his 'Agricultural Growth, Employment and Income Distribution: Dilemmas for Indonesia's Next Five Year Plan', *Prisma: Indonesian Journal of Social and Economic Affairs*, No. 7 (September 1977), pp. 3-14.

12 See International Rice Research Institute, *Major Research in Upland Rice* (Los Banos, Philippines: International Rice Research Institute, 1975).

13 Ministry of Public Works, *Five Year Programme of Transmigration, 1979/80-1983/84* (Jakarta: Ministry of Public Works, 1978), Appendix III.

14 Leslie S. Cobley, *An Introduction to the Botany of Tropical Crops* (2nd ed., London and New York: Longman, 1976), pp. 301-302, 318, 320.

15 For further comments on unsponsored transmigration, see Martono, *op. cit.*, pp. 4, 7, 84; Suratman and Patrick Guiness, 'The Changing Focus of Transmigration', *Bulletin of Indonesian Economic Studies* (Canberra), Vol. XIII, No. 2 (July 1977), especially pp. 99-101; H.W. Arndt and R.M. Sundrum, 'Transmigration: Land Settlement or Regional Development?', *Bulletin of Indonesian Economic Studies*, Vol. XIII, No. 3 (November 1977), pp. 72ff.; J.M. Hardjono, 'Transmigration: A New Concept?', *ibid.*, Vol. XIV, No. 1 (March 1978), pp. 107ff.

16 Martono, *op. cit.*, p. 74.

17 Directorate General of Transmigration, Ministry of Manpower, Transmigration and Co-operatives, *Estimated Requirements for Transmigrating 50,000 Families Each Year* (Jakarta: Ministry of Manpower, Transmigration and Co-operatives, n.d.), pp. 3-7.

18 Strout, 'Aspects of Agricultural Productivity on Java. . .,' *op. cit.*, p. 25.

19 E.F. Schumacher, *Small Is Beautiful: a Study of Economics as if People Mattered* (London: Sphere Books, 1975).

20 *Ibid.*, p. 16

21 *Ibid.*, pp. 122-123.

22 *Ibid.*, p. 126.

23 *Ibid.*, pp. 158-159.

24 *Ibid.*, p. 246. For Schumacher's comparison of the intermediate and appropriate technology concepts, see Daniel Dhakidae and J.D. Wick-

ert, 'People Really Matter: Two Exclusive Interviews. . .', *Prisma: Indonesian Journal of Social and Economic Affairs*, No. 7 (September 1977), pp. 55-56.

25 The Intermediate Technology Development Group Ltd. is a non-profit company and registered charity. Its address is 9 King Street, London WC2E 8HN, England.

26 Based on ITDG reports.

27 E.F. Schumacher and George McRobie, 'Intermediate Technology in Action' (Jakarta: Indonesian Institute of Sciences, 1977).

28 *Ibid.*, pp. 16-25; Hans Singer, *Technologies for Basic Needs* (Geneva: International Labour Office, 1979), pp. 143-158.

29 Schumacher and McRobie, *op. cit.*, p. 17.

30 Soedjatmoko, 'National Policy Implications of the Basic Needs Model', *Prisma: Indonesian Journal of Social and Economic Affairs*, No. 9 (March 1978), p. 16.

31 *Ibid.*, p. 18.

32 *Ibid.*, p. 14.

33 Singer, *op. cit.*, p. 3.

34 *Idem.*

CHAPTER 11   THE NATIONAL PHILOSOPHY

1 Both of these documents are of course available in a variety of places, e.g., the Declaration of Independence can be found in William Miller (ed.), *Readings in American Values* (Englewood Cliffs, N.J.: Prentice-Hall, 1964), pp. 55f., and one translation of the Communist Manifesto is found in Karl Marx and Friedrich Engels, *The Communist Manifesto* (Harmondsworth, Middlesex: Penguin Books, 1975).

2 Quoted by Roeslan Abdulgani, *Pantjasila: The Prime Mover of the Indonesian Revolution* (Jakarta: Prapantja, 1965), pp. 308-309. 'Pantjasila' represents one of the earlier spellings which have since given way to 'Pancasila' as the officially preferred spelling.

3 Roeslan Abdulgani, 'Nationalism, Pancasila, Soekarno', in Haryati Soebadio and Carine A. du Marchie (eds.), *Dynamics of Indonesian History* (Amsterdam: North-Holland Publishing Company, 1978), pp. 268, 270.

4 Sukarno, *The Birth of 'Pantjasila': The Five Principles of the Indonesian State* (Jakarta: Ministry of Information, n.d.), p. 34. For alternative interpretations, see, e.g., Mohammad Hatta, *Pengertian Pancasila* (Jakarta: Idayu Press, 1978); Mohommad Hatta *et al.*, *Uraian Pancasila* (Jakarta: Penerbit Mutiara, 1977); Nugroho Notosusanto, *Naskah Proklamasi Yang Otentik dan Ramusan Pancasila Yang Otentik* (Jakarta: PN Balai Pustika, 1978); A.G. Pringgodigdo, *Sekitar Pantjasila* (Jakarta: Departemen Pertahanan Keamanan, Pusat Sejarah Abri, 1978); and H. Muhammad Yamin, 'Tindjanan Pantjasila Terhadap Revolusi Fungsional', in Moch. Said (ed.), *Pedoman Untuk Melaksanakan Amanat Penderitaan Rakjat* (Surabaya: Penerbit Permata, 1961), pp. 2491-2492.

5 *The 1945 Constitution of the Republic of Indonesia* (Jakarta: Department of Information, 1968), pp. 5-6.

6 Abdulgani, 'Nationalism, Pancasila, Soekarno', *op. cit.*, pp. 270-271.

7 *The Guide to the Living and the Practice of Pancasila and the Broad Outlines of the State Policy* (Jakarta: Centre for Strategic and International Studies, 1978), pp. 11-15. The phraseology shows some slight variations from that given in the official source cited in Chapter 8 above.

8 Sukarno, *op. cit.*, p. 28.

9 *Idem*.

10 Abdulgani, *Pantjasila, op. cit.*, pp. 57, 143, 153, 156, 158, 171, 217, 223, 247, 254, 286, 287, 288, 298, 318, 319, 328, 329, 337, 338, 339. Sukarno often used the term 'Indonesian Socialism', but it was never adequately defined.

11 Brian May, *The Indonesian Tragedy* (London: Routledge & Kegan Paul, 1978), pp. 401-402.

12 Donald Wilhelm, *Creative Alternatives to Communism: Guidelines for Tomorrow's World* (London: The Macmillan Press, 1978), pp. 22-23 and other references under 'ideology'.

13 *Guide to the Living and Practice of Pancasila, op. cit.*, pp. 27, 37.

14 *Ibid.*, p. 38.

15 *Ibid.*, pp. 44, 47.

16 *Ibid.*, pp. 59, 70.

17 Team for Fostering Upgraders and Upgrading Materials for Civil Servants of the Republic of Indonesia, *Material for Upgrading Course on Guidelines for Substantiating and Implementing Pancasila* (Jakarta: Department of Information, 1978), pp. 59, 70.

18 *Ibid.*, Foreword, p. 1.

19 *Ibid.*, Foreword, p. 2.

20 *Ibid.*, Sec. I, p. 1.

21 *Ibid.*, Sec. I, pp. 2, 3.

22 *Ibid.*, Sec. II, p. 2.

23 *Ibid.*, Sec. II, p. 4. (Italics added.)

24 *Ibid.*, Foreword, p. 3.

25 Abdulgani, *Pantjasila, op. cit.*, p. 12.

26 Ernst Utrecht, 'The Communist Party of Indonesia (PKI) Since 1966', in Malcolm Caldwell (ed.), *Ten Years' Military Terror in Indonesia* (Nottingham: Bertrand Russell Peace Foundation, 1975), p. 281.

27 Ministry of Information, Kingdom of Saudi Arabia, *Saudi Arabia Today* (Riyadh: Ministry of Information, 1977), p. 5. Cf. also Geoffrey Parrinder, *Jesus in the Quar'an* (London: Sheldon Press, 1977).

28 National Development Information Office, *Indonesia Economic Profile, 1978* (Jakarta: National Development Information Office, 1979), Sec. 2, p. 5.

29 James L. Peacock, *Purifying the Faith: The Muhammadijah Movement in Indonesian Islam* (Menlo Park, Calif.: The Benjamin/Cummings Publishing Company, 1978), p. 106.

30 Mintaredja, *Islam and Politics, Islam and State in Indonesia* (Jakarta: Siliwangi, 1974), p. 38.

31 Allan A. Samson, 'Conceptions of Politics, Power, and Ideology in Contemporary Indonesian Islam', in Karl D. Jackson and Lucian W. Pye (eds.), *Political Power and Communications in Indonesia* (Berkeley and London: University of California Press, 1978), pp. 197-198.

32 Nena Vreeland *et al.*, *Area Handbook for Indonesia* (3rd ed., Washington, D.C.: US Government Printing Office, 1975), p. 5.
33 Charles J. Adams, 'Islamic Faith', in *Introduction to Islamic Civilization* (Cambridge, England: Cambridge University Press, 1977), p. 35.
34 Abdulgani, *Pantjasila, op. cit.*, p. 106.
35 Samson, *op. cit.*, pp. 217ff.
36 *Ibid.*, pp. 198, 225.
37 Peacock, *op. cit.*, pp. 106, 109.
38 Sayyed Hossein Nasr, *Islam and the Plight of Modern Man* (London and New York: Longman, 1975). p. 94. Cf. Maxime Rodinson, *Marxism and the Muslim World* (London: Zed Press, 1979).

CHAPTER 12   IDEOLOGY AND DEVELOPMENT

1 Allen M. Sievers, *The Mystical World of Indonesia: Culture and Economic Development in Conflict* (Baltimore and London: The Johns Hopkins University Press, 1974), p. 184.
2 For a description of forerunners of the Technocracy Movement, see Jean Meynaud, *Technocracy* (London: Faber and Faber, 1968), Ch. 4.
3 *The New Encyclopædia Britannica: Micropædia* (Chicago: Encyclopædia Britannica, 1974), Vol. IX, p. 859.
4 *Webster's Third New International Dictionary* (Chicago: Encyclopædia Britannica, 1971), Vol. III, p. 2348. These are the usages relevant to the present discussion.
5 Robert Graham, *Iran: The Illusion of Power* (London: Croom Helm, 1978), especially Chs. 5 and 11.
6 Daniel Bell, *The End of Ideology* (New York: The Free Press; London: Collier-Macmillan, 1962).
7 *Ibid.*, p. 393. The sequel referred to was his *The Coming of Post-Industrial Society: A Venture in Social Forecasting* (London: Heinemann Educational Books, 1974). See also his *The Cultural Contradictions of Capitalism* (2nd ed., London: Heinemann Educational Books, 1979).
8 Jeffrey D. Straussman, *The Limits of Technocratic Politics* (New Brunswick, N.J.: Transaction Books, 1978), p. 145.
9 H.W. Arndt, *The Rise and Fall of Economic Growth: A Study in Contemporary Thought* (Melbourne: Longman, Cheshire, 1978), pp. 151-152.
10 *Ibid.*, pp. 152-153.
11 Publisher's announcement in *Economy and Society* (London), Vol. 8, No. 2 (May 1979), p. 124.
12 Alvin H. Hansen, 'The General Theory (2)', in Seymour E. Harris (ed.), *The New Economics: Keynes' Influence on Theory and Public Policy* (London: Dennis Dobson, 1968), p. 144.
13 John Kenneth Galbraith, 'How Keynes Came to America', in Milo Keynes (ed.), *Essays on John Maynard Keynes* (Cambridge, England: Cambridge University Press, 1975), p. 132.
14 Harlan L. McCracken, *Keynesian Economics in the Stream of Economic Thought* (Baton Rouge: Louisiana State University Press, 1968), p. 171.
15 Eric Roll, *A History of Economic Thought* (London: Faber and Faber, 1973), p. 550.

16 Hansen, *op. cit.*, pp. 134-135.
17 Paul A. Samuelson, 'The General Theory (3)', in Harris (ed.), *op. cit.*, pp. 150-151.
18 John Maynard Keynes, *The General Theory of Employment, Interest and Money* (London: Macmillan, 1974), p. 245.
19 Michael P. Todaro, *Economic Development in the Third World* (London and New York: Longman, 1978), p. 176.
20 Subrata Ghatak, *Development Economics* (London and New York: Longman, 1978), p. 20.
21 Charles P. Kindleberger and Bruce Herrick, *Economic Development* (3rd ed., McGraw-Hill Kogakusha, 1977), p. 35.
22 Todaro, *op. cit.*, pp. 177-178. (Italics added.)
23 Pan A. Yotopoulos and Jeffrey B. Nugent, *Economics of Development: Empirical Investigations* (New York and London: Harper & Row, 1976), p. 430.
24 Geoffrey Barraclough, 'The Keynesian Era in Perspective', in Robert Skidelsky (ed.), *The End of the Keynesian Era: Essays on the Disintegration of the Keynesian Political Economy* (London: The Macmillan Press, 1978), p. 104.
25 Roll, *op. cit.*, p. 550.
26 Michael Shanks, *What's Wrong with the Modern World? Agenda for a New Society* (London, Sydney, and Toronto: The Bodley Head, 1978), p. 64.
27 W.W. Rostow, *Getting from Here to There: A Policy for the Post-Keynesian Age* (London: The Macmillan Press, 1979), p. 53.
28 Donald Wilhelm, *Creative Alternatives to Communism: Guidelines for Tomorrow's World* (London: The Macmillan Press, 1978), pp. 118, 142.
29 Keynes, *op. cit.*, p. 245.
30 For elucidation, see Wilhelm, *op. cit.*, Ch. 7.
31 See, e.g., Norman Higgins, 'The Cambridge Arts Theatre', in Milo Keynes (ed.), *op. cit.*, pp. 272ff.
32 Fred Hirsch, *Social Limits to Growth* (London: Routledge & Kegan Paul, 1978), p. 125.

CHAPTER 13   INVESTMENT DYNAMICS

1 Sir Michael Clapham, *Multinational Enterprises and Nation States* (London: The Athlone Press, 1975), p. 6.
2 *Ibid.*, pp. 13-14.
3 Michael Ellman, *Socialist Planning* (Cambridge, England: Cambridge University Press, 1979), pp. 60-61.
4 Alec Nove, *The Soviet Economic System* (London, Boston, and Sydney: George Allen & Unwin, 1978), p. 286.
5 Geoffrey Owen, 'China: Risks and Rewards for Foreign Ventures', *Financial Times* (London), 10 July 1979, p. 22.
6 Franklin B. Weinstein, *Indonesian Foreign Policy and the Dilemma of Dependence: From Sukarno to Soeharto* (Ithaca and London: Cornell University Press, 1976), pp. 207-208.
7 Howard Palfrey Jones, *Indonesia: The Possible Dream* (Singapore: Ayu Mas, 1973), p. 84.

8   Investment Co-ordinating Board, *Incentives for Investors; Investment Priorities; New Investment Procedures; Investment Opportunities; List of Priority Scales for Fields of Domestic Investment and Foreign Investment* (Jakarta: Investment Co-ordinating Board, 1978).

9   Weinstein, *op. cit.*, p. 356.

10   William I. Spencer, 'Who Controls MNCs?', *Harvard Business Review*, Vol. 53, No. 6 (November-December 1975), p. 99.

11   Richard Ensor, *Indonesia: The Awakening Giant* (London: Euromoney Publications, 1979), p. 30.

12   *Ibid.*, p. 31.

13   Louis T. Wells, Jr. and V'Ella Warren, 'Developing Country Investors in Indonesia', *Bulletin of Indonesian Economic Studies* (Canberra), Vol. XV, No. 1 (March 1979), p. 82.

14   The Office of the Minister (Commercial) and Senior Trade Commissioner, *Notes on the Market for Potential Australian Investors* (Jakarta: Australian Embassy, 1978), p. 1.

15   Bureau of International Commerce, US Department of Commerce, *Indonesia: A Survey of US Business Opportunities* (Washington, D.C.: US Government Printing Office, 1977).

16   Indonesian Chamber of Commerce and Industry, *Indonesian Chamber of Commerce and Industry (Kadin Indonesia)* (Jakarta: Kreasi Dinamika, 1979).

17   Bernard E. Meland, *The Secularization of Modern Culture* (New York: Oxford University Press, 1966), p. 61.

18   E.M. Horsley (ed.), *The New Hutchinson 20th Century Encyclopedia* (London: Hutchinson, 1977), p. 657.

19   See, e.g., Peter Mathias, *The First Industrial Nation: An Economic History of Britain, 1700-1914* (London: Methuen, 1975).

20   For valuable insights on this matter I am indebted to Mr George McRobie, Chairman of the Intermediate Technology Development Group, London.

21   Quoted in Anthony Burton, *Remains of a Revolution* (London: André Deutsch, 1975), pp. 214-215.

22   Mark Casson, *Alternatives to the Multinational Enterprise* (London: The Macmillan Press, 1979), p. 101.

23   For information of these matters I am indebted to Mr. Jacques Prindiville of Dr. Dvorkovitz & Associates.

24   Charles Cooper in Austin Robinson (ed.), *Appropriate Technologies for Third World Development* (London: The Macmillan Press, 1979), p. 404.

25   For valuable insights on this matter I am indebted to Professor Sir Austin Robinson of Cambridge University.

CHAPTER 14   TRANSCENDING ANTI–COMMUNISM

1   Adapted from National Development Information Office, *Indonesian Economic Profile, 1978* (Jakarta: National Development Information Office, 1979), Sec. 3, pp. 1-2, 5.

2   Allen M. Sievers, *The Mystical World of Indonesia: Culture and Economic Development in Conflict* (Baltimore and London: The Johns Hopkins

University Press, 1974), p. 8.

3 See, e.g., *The Indonesia Times* (Jakarta), 7 August 1979, p. 7.

4 Harold Crouch, *The Army and Politics in Indonesia* (Ithaca and London: Cornell University Press, 1978), pp. 350-351.

5 Karl D. Jackson in Karl D. Jackson and Lucian W. Pye (eds), *Political Power and Communications in Indonesia* (Berkeley and London: University of California Press, 1978), p. 395.

6 *Ibid.*, pp. 396-397.

7 See, e.g., *Indonesia Exports* (Jakarta: National Agency for Export Development), Vol. 1, No. 1 (1978).

8 National Development Information Office, *op. cit.*, Sec. 3, pp. 2-3. See also Department of Information, *Explanation and Announcement on the Establishment of the Third Development Cabinet. . .* (Jakarta: Department of Information, 1978); and see the Appendix to the present book.

9 Suparman Sumahamijaya, *Wiraswasta Entrepreneurship: The Key to Development and Progress* (Jakarta, 1979).

10 For interesting examples of cases involving the uncovering of corruption in both the public and private sectors, see *The Indonesia Times*, 21 July 1979, p. 1; 11 August 1979, p. 1; and 13 September 1979, p. 1.

11 See, e.g., Hurd Baruch, 'The Foreign Corrupt Practices Act', *Harvard Business Review* (Boston, Mass.), Vol. 57, No. 1 (January-February 1979), pp. 32ff.

12 B.J. Habibie *et al.*, in 'The Jakarta Report' *SRI International* (Menlo Park, Calif.), No. 38 (1978), p. 42.

13 See Chapter 10, Note 25.

14 Department of Information, *The Third Five-Year Development Plan (Repelita III), 1979/80-1983/84* (Jakarta: Department of Information, 1979).

15 The Intermediate Technology Group already provides such a service to various emerging countries.

16 *Address of State by His Excellency the President of the Republic of Indonesia Soeharto before the House of the People's Representatives on the Occasion of the 34th Independence Day, August 17th* (Jakarta: Department of Information, 1979), p. 20.

CHAPTER 15   THE INDONESIAN SYNTHESIS

1 H.R.H. Prince Philip, Duke of Edinburgh, 'The Impact of Science on the Human Community', *The Advancement of Science* (London), November 1963, p. 288.

2 James L. Peacock, *Purifying the Faith: The Muhammadijah Movement in Indonesian Islam* (Menlo Park, Calif.: The Benjamin/Cummings Publishing Company, 1978), p. 109.

3 Erwin Ramedhan, 'The Disco Way of Life in Jakarta: From Subculture to Cultural Void', *Prisma: Indonesian Journal of Social and Economic Affairs* (Jakarta), Vol. 6 (June 1977), pp. 16f.

4 National Development Information Office, *Indonesia Economic Profile, 1978* (Jakarta: National Development Information Office, 1979), Sec. 11, p. 5.

5   Printed in *Briefing* (Abbots Langley, Hertfordshire, England), Vol. 9, No. 37 (12 October 1979), pp. 20, 21.

6   Alastair I. MacBean and V.N. Balasubramanyam, *Meeting the Third World Challenge* (2nd ed., London: The Macmillan Press, 1978), p. 124.

7   R.H. Tawney, *Religion and the Rise of Capitalism: A Historical Study* (Harmondsworth, Middlesex, England: Penguin Books, 1977).

8   James L. Peacock, *Muslim Puritans: Reformist Psychology in Southeast Asian Islam* (Berkeley and London: University of California Press, 1978).

9   P.B. Medawar, *Induction and Intuition in Scientific Thought* (London: Methuen, 1969), pp. 51, 55, 57.

10 James C. Abegglen and Thomas M. Hout, 'Facing Up to the Trade Gap with Japan', *Foreign Affairs*, Vol. 57, No. 1 (Fall 1978), p. 160.

11 Sueo Sekiguchi, *Japanese Direct Foreign Investment* (London: The Macmillan Press, 1979), pp. vi, 135.

12 Toh Chin Chye, 'The Case for Government Support for R & D', *Singapore Economic Bulletin* (Singapore), August, 1979, p. 8.

13 David Elliott and Ruth Elliott, 'Limitations of Technology Assessment', in Godfrey Boyle, David Elliott and Robin Roy (eds.), *The Politics of Technology* (London: Longman, 1977), pp. 130ff.

14 Adrian Moyes, *The Poor Man's Wisdom: Technology and the Very Poor* (Oxford, England: Oxfam, 1979), pp. 13, 15.

15 Christopher Evans, *The Mighty Micro: The Impact of the Computer Revolution* (London: Gollancz, 1979), pp. 89ff.

16 *Ibid.*, Chs. 6, 16; Iann Barron *et al.*, *The Future with Microelectronics* (London: Frances Pinter, New York: Nicholas, 1979), pp. 18-20, 199-205.

17 Brian May, *The Indonesian Tragedy* (London: Routledge & Kegan Paul, 1978), pp. 356-360.

18 Evans, *op. cit.*, p. 148.

19 E.M. Horsley (ed.), *The New Hutchinson 20th Century Encyclopedia* (London: Hutchinson, 1977), p. 433. See also Ronald W. Clark, *Edison: The Man Who Made the Future* (London: Macdonald and Jane's, 1977).

20 E.F. Schumacher, *Good Work* (London: Jonathan Cape, 1979), p. 21.

21 *Ibid.*, p. 55.

22 Donald W. Fryer, *Emerging Southeast Asia: A Study in Growth and Stagnation* (2nd ed., London: George Philip & Son, 1979), pp. 28, 494. See also Association of Southeast Asian Nations, *10 Years ASEAN* (Jakarta: ASEAN Secretariat, 1978).

23 National Development Information Office, *op. cit.*, Sec. 4, p. 30.

24 For a comprehensive listing, see United Nations Development Programme, Indonesia, *Report on Development Assistance to Indonesia in 1977* (Jakarta: UNDP, 1978).

Picture credits

Black-and-white illustrations

Associated Press: pages 22, 29.
Camera Press: pages 41, 43, 48 (right), 49, 51 (both), 159.
Douglas Dickins: pages 14, 61.
Hill & Knowlton: pages 55, 57, 59, 60, 62, 63 (both), 92, 99, 102, 107, 150.
'Idaya Foto': page 16.
Indonesian Times: page 154.
'Ipphos': pages 32, 33, 35, 37, 39 45.
Mary Evans Picture Library: pages 11, 12, 13.
Nicholas Nugent: page 163.
Popperfoto: pages 19, 26, 48 (left).

Colour plates

James Cudney: pages 72 (centre), 73 (right, top and bottom), 76 (top), 77 (bottom), 120 (top, left and right).
Douglas Dickins: pages 65, 68 (both), 69 (top), 76 (bottom), 77 (top), 80, 121 (both), 125 (all), 128.
Garuda Indonesian Airways: page 69 (bottom), 72 (bottom), 113, 116 (both), 117 (both).
Hill & Knowlton: page 120 (bottom).
Nicholas Nugent: pages 72 (top), 73 (left), 124.

Index

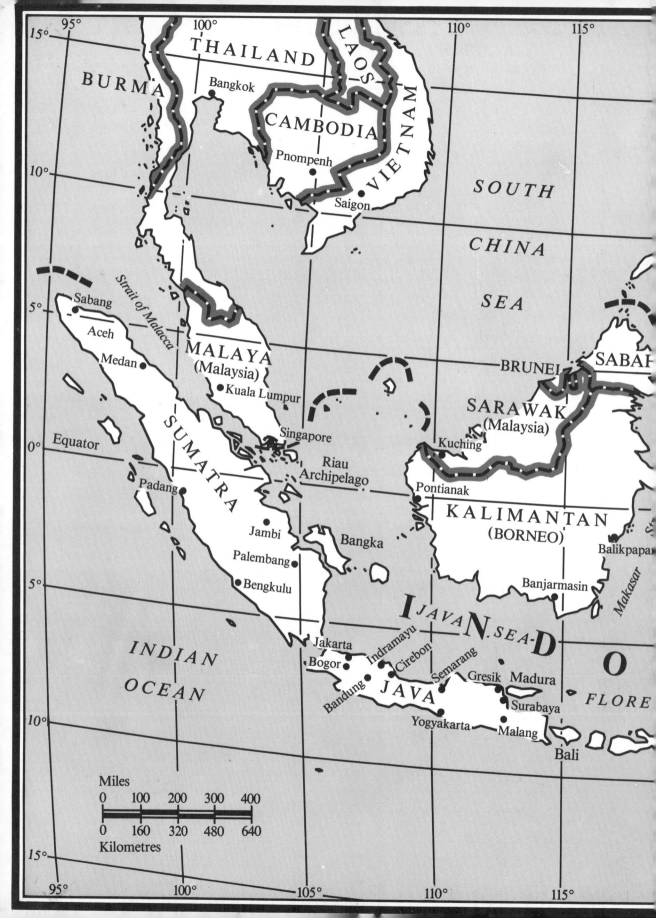